STUDIES IN AMERICAN LITERATURE
Volume VIII

☆☆☆☆☆☆☆☆☆☆☆☆☆☆☆☆☆☆☆☆☆☆☆☆☆☆☆☆☆☆☆☆☆

THE ROLE OF NEMESIS
IN THE
STRUCTURE OF SELECTED PLAYS
BY
EUGENE O'NEILL

by

CHESTER CLAYTON LONG

University of Washington

1968

MOUTON

THE HAGUE · PARIS

LIBRARY OF CONGRESS CATALOG CARD NUMBER 68-15526

Printed in The Netherlands by Mouton & Co., Printers, The Hague.

To Professor George Frederick Dell of Capital University, who first initiated me into the study of literature in informal but intense conversation.

PREFACE

Nemesis is the personification of an idea, the idea of justice. This personification permits a conception of justice in action, rather than in stasis. It may also contain within itself significance in relation to distributive, retributive, divine, and tragic justice.[1] Poetic justice is not included here, for poetic justice is largely static, and is limited primarily to distributive functions, rather than retributive and tragic functions. Nemesis, on the other hand, can be distributive, retributive, divine, or tragic, separately or simultaneously.

The problem is one of function. How does one describe the function of Nemesis in a text? Does the idea have an appreciable function in the text being studied? In what does that function consist? How may it be established? What is the significance of the function? Is the function qualitative, quantitative, or both? Obviously these should be "questions of fact",[2] and cannot be fully answered until the study is completed.

The study of *form* is a study of the *relationships* that exist between *all* the individual elements in any single piece of literature. It is not primarily a study of the specific nature of any particular element in literature, such as imagery, meaning, structure, action, language, or style. The study of form treats the piece of literature as a unique and whole object. It does this first through observing

---

[1] Henry Alonzo Myers, *Tragedy: A View of Life* (Ithaca, New York, Cornell University Press, 1956), pp. 23-27.
[2] R. S. Crane, *The Languages of Criticism and the Structure of Poetry* (Toronto, University of Toronto Press, 1957), p. 146. This implies an empirical approach, and in Crane's words "this means that the first principle of our analysis must be an induction of which the only warrant is the evidence of the poem itself".

particular relationships between elements in the piece. And finally formal analysis attempts to induct and synthesize a general description of how the piece relates all of its structures of elements into a unique whole.

In this way, formal analysis provides an organic picture of the unique wholeness of the piece. And in doing this it provides a context of perception in which (1) any specific element can be perceived in its relationship within the piece to any other specific element; and (2) it provides a context of perception in which one or more specific elements may be perceived in the light of their relationship to the whole.

Formal analysis, then, provides a clear image of the overall *means* through which individual elements in a piece of literature relate themselves into larger structures; and it provides a clear image of the *manner* in which the larger structural elements relate themselves into a concrete whole. This end product of inductive formal analysis, the *formal description*, provides, in effect, an image of the unifying, or formal power of the piece, which can be referred to technically as its *dynamis*, or central controlling principle: its *form*.

Practical criticism, the study of factors intrinsic to the literary text, will be the method employed here in dealing with the focal point of this study which is Nemesis. The three questions then, of the function of an idea in a dramatic text, of the nature of Nemesis, and of the nature of dramatic structure, are actually designed to get at the individual nature of each play studied in relation to its use of Nemesis. The interest here will be primarily in the function of Nemesis in the structure of the individual play, and not in these problems divorced from the context of the play.

However, ideas and concepts are not usually devoid of present modifications in regard to their essential being. Therefore, the first chapter of the study will consist of a definition of the terms, of their present significance, and a brief outline of how they will be utilized in the study.

The subsequent chapters of the study will devote themselves to an application of the method developed in the first chapter. Chapter two will examine the early plays *Abortion, Thirst, The*

Moon of the Caribbees; chapter three, *The Hairy Ape*; chapter four, *Desire Under the Elms*; chapter five, *Mourning Becomes Electra*; chapter six, *The Iceman Cometh*; chapter seven, *Long Day's Journey into Night*. Chapter eight, the concluding chapter, will consist of a survey of the findings.

No significant and comprehensive study of Nemesis in the structure of O'Neill's early work has ever been published to my knowledge. *Thirst* and *Moon of the Caribbees* were chosen for consideration because they are the title plays in the collections in which they appear; *Abortion* was selected because it is one of the earliest plays in its group. It is a one-act and representative of the one-acts appearing with it.

The Hairy Ape was selected from the group of expressionistic plays as being the most structurally successful of that group. *Desire Under the Elms* was selected from the more conventional group of naturalistic plays as being typical of them, and the most successful.

Mourning Becomes Electra was selected from the group of longer experimental plays because it is the most structurally successful of that group.

The Iceman Cometh and *Long Day's Journey into Night* were selected as the best plays published in what is generally referred to as the group of later plays. *Iceman* was chosen as the finest structurally of the later experimental plays; and *Journey*, because it is the best, structurally, of the group of more conventional plays published in the later period.

The published editions of the plays referred to are indicated in the bibliography appearing at the end of the study, along with all secondary sources utilized in regard to the plays and the critical ideas herein enunciated.

Forty-six O'Neill plays have thus far been published. The amount of O'Neill criticism so far published is huge. There is a special bibliography of O'Neill which contains "approximately 4,000 entries of all sorts".[3] The writer's own bibliography, which

---

[3] Jordan Yale Miller, "A Critical Bibliography of Eugene O'Neill", unpublished Ph.D. dissertation, Dept. of Philosophy, Columbia University, Ann Arbor, Michigan University Microfilms, 1957, p. 127.

is highly selective, contains references not included in the special bibliography mentioned.

No one involved in the transmission of culture through teaching and research stands free of indebtedness. These debts are complex and unique. I wish to acknowledge here the most recent of my own debts, and also those of longest standing.

To Professor Anthony Trisolini of Ohio University who first introduced me to the analysis of literature through performance I extend my thanks. I must also thank my former colleagues and teachers in the Department of Oral Interpretation at Northwestern University: Dr. Wallace A. Bacon, whose guidance and constant example were responsible for initiating this study; Dr. Robert S. Breen, whose lively and stimulating grasp of literature contributed much to the shaping of this study; and Dr. Charlotte I. Lee, whose encouragement and careful criticism made the completion of this research possible.

More recently, during final preparation of the manuscript at the University of Washington, I have received much aid and counsel. Completion and publication of the manuscript has been generously supported by the Graduate School Research Fund Committee through a grant from the Agnes H. Anderson Memorial Fund. Special thanks in this instance must be extended to Joseph L. McCarthy, Dean of the Graduate School. Professor Gregory Falls read and critiqued parts of the manuscript, and Professor Delmond Bennett's suggestions concerning analogues of empirical method for the Humanities have been invaluable. Finally, I would like to extend my thanks to Professor Barnet Baskerville, Chairman of the Department of Speech, for many considerations during the completion of this project.

University of Washington　　　　　　　　CHESTER CLAYTON LONG
Department of Speech
Seattle, Washington

March 18, 1966

TABLE OF CONTENTS

I

INTRODUCTION:
DEFINITIONS AND LIMITATIONS

NEMESIS

Nemesis, primarily the eventual punishment of the guilty, begins as a process inter-related with the acts of individuals. Fate, on the other hand, depends strictly on factors supposed to be beyond the control or foreknowledge of the individual. Nemesis is a concept of a process of checks and balances involving the inertia of circumstances, plus the individual's choices (which are taken in this concept generally to be of *importance*), and the outcome of the choices exercised in the individual's life experiences. In this view of man's experience, *two* of the factors are in his control: choice, and the resultant circumstances following on the choice.

In Aeschylus' *Oresteia* can be observed the first dramatic manipulation of all three factors mentioned above. The evil the characters confront in the first play is inherited (things beyond their control). Their choices directly increase the evil in the first play, though they do work punishment for the past evils. In the second play, the choices, through the direction of the gods, are wiser, and the punishment is not in the interest of the *lex talionis,* personal vengeance, but in the interest of social justice. But Electra and Orestes have to break the old law in order to fulfill the new. The third play reinterprets the old law (the law of blood vengeance), into the new idea of social justice rather than personal justice, through the application of divine law to the dilemma.

Agamemnon is hewn down by the demands of the *lex talionis* in the first play (his Nemesis being an ignominious death). Aegisthus and Clytemnestra are slain by the demands of the social code in the second play. In the third play the slayers of Aegisthus and Clytemnestra are not visited with the Nemesis of death, but with the Nemesis of purification and atonement; in other words, salvation, effected through the support by the gods of their reason for slaying, the maintenance of the social code.

Nemesis (justice in its final aspect), then, has four main sources: breaking of the *lex talionis* (an eye for an eye); breaking of the social code (objective judgments of particular circumstances and motivations); divine law (wherein the goodness of the gods, mercy, is the prime factor); and the individual human character "whose capacity for experiencing good is exactly equal to his capacity for experiencing evil".[1] This fourth source of Nemesis may be called "tragic", for such a balance can actually only be clearly established in an imitation of human character. As Myers says:

This conception of justice is not consonant with the notion of justice at the level of *lex talionis*, the law of the claw, for, as we have seen, tragedy recognizes the impossibility of exacting an eye for an eye. . . . Indeed, its conception is not in agreement with any of the traditional notions of either distributive or retributive justice. Because it is artistically self-sufficient, never carrying the spectator beyond the action, and because its climax is always retrospective, it cannot admit the eternal justice of rewards and punishments represented in Dante.[2]

The *lex talionis* (essentially distributive), social law (essentially retributive), and divine law (essentially ultimate), form, generally, three of the sources of Nemesis imitated in tragedy; while the fourth, tragic justice (essentially individual), is a purely aesthetic phenomenon, resulting from and totally dependent upon the imitation itself. But it is clear that Nemesis can take the form of positive or rewarding circumstances, as well as punitive, if the divine enters the picture.

The first existing dramatic record we have which deals with all four aspects of this problem, in addition to reinterpreting the source of human justice, is, as I have said, *The Oresteia*. The following speeches from that play illustrate the problem nicely.

---

[1]   Myers, p. 27.
[2]   *Ibid.*, p. 25.

Leader: Yet is such office ours, imposed by fate.
Apollo: What office? vaunt the thing ye deem so fair.
Leader: From home to home we chase the matricide.
Apollo: What? to avenge a wife who slays her lord?
Leader: That is not blood outpoured by kindred hands.
Apollo: How darkly ye dishonor and annul
　　　　The troth to which the high accomplishers,
　　　　Hera and Zeus, do honour. Yea, and thus
　　　　Is Aphrodite to dishonour cast,
　　　　The queen of rapture unto mortal men.
　　　　Know, that above the marriage-bed ordained
　　　　For man and woman standeth Right as guard,
　　　　Enhancing sanctity of trothplight sworn;
　　　　Therefore, if thou art placable to those
　　　　Who have their consort slain, nor will'st to turn
　　　　On them the eye of wrath, unjust art thou
　　　　In hounding to his doom the man who slew
　　　　His mother. Lo, I know thee full of wrath
　　　　Against one deed, but all too placable
　　　　Unto the other, minishing the crime
　　　　But in this cause shall Pallas guard the right.[3]

Apollo makes it quite clear to the "female" furies that their law, based on the blood accident of birth (blood relation, the law of blood justice, the *lex talionis,* an eye for an eye, and a tooth for a tooth), will not be *exacted* in this case, for though Orestes has broken the law of blood ties, he has done so in the service of a higher principle, the principle that embraces social justice, reasoned and ordered before the eyes of men, holding them not to blood ties, but to "ordained" and publicly "sworn" agreements. *The Oresteia* eschews the "cult of blood" and announces the triumph of the higher, objective justice, that is no respecter of blood, subjectivity, nor persons. From now on, Aeschylus' action spells out for us, in part, the root origin of justice will be in social contracts, reasoned and ordered before society; a law higher than what men "feel" in their passionate natures; and a law upheld and enforced not only by human, or quasi-divine men, but by the fully elevated and separated pantheon of gods, by the

---

[3] Aeschylus, *The Eumenides,* 11, 208-224, trans. E. D. A. Morshead, *The Complete Greek Drama,* eds. Whitney J. Oates and Eugene O'Neill, Jr., 2 vols. (New York, Random House, 1938), I, 278.

king of those gods, Zeus, and by his daughter, Pallas Athena, goddess of wisdom.

Death will still be demanded for death, but guilt will no longer be based on the spilling of kindred blood alone, but, additionally, on any breach of the social contract.

But Clytaemnestra, too, must be avenged; hence the pursuit of Orestes by the Erinyes, in the *Eumenides*, till at last the vicious circle of blood-vengeance is broken by the appearance of a new moral order.[4]

So, the family, the union of opposite blood-lines (the union of opposites, the union of the terrible law of natural justice with the transcendent divine law, Zeus), becomes symbolic of a new justice, a cosmic justice, mirrored in the earthly marriage of the nourisher of the seed of life, the wife, and its active disseminator, the husband. The concept of marriage now moves toward a more just relation between man and wife, perhaps an attempt at harmonizing the age old battle of the sexes for superiority one over the other. It is true that Apollo's later argument overdoes it a bit and makes the woman's role seemingly less important than the man's:

Apollo: This too I answer; mark a soothfast word.
  Not the true parent is the woman's womb
  That bears the child; she doth but nurse the seed
  New-sown: the male is parent; she for him,
  As stranger for a stranger, hoards the germ
  Of life, unless the god its promise blight.[5]

The emphasis here seems to be on "trust" between "strangers" rather than on "blood" ties.

We turn now from the significance of Nemesis in relation to this particular study to a brief consideration of its contemporary, and comparatively limited meaning, which is simply retributive justice stemming from righteous indignation:

But in the vast majority of cases she is nothing but retribution or righteous indignation, particularly that of the gods at human presumption, personified. ... Nemesis of Rhamnus may have been ori-

---

[4] William Chase Green, *Moira: Fate, Good, and Evil in Greek Thought* (Cambridge, Massachusetts, Harvard University Press, 1944), p. 125.
[5] Aeschylus, *The Eumenides*, 11, 657-662. *Complete Greek Drama*, p. 294.

ginally the goddess who deals or distributes, . . . appropriate gifts to her worshippers, and afterwards made abstract, a process like that which Fors Fortuna . . . seems to have undergone.[6]

The classicists, Smyth and Leach, are, however, much more exact and much more inclusive in their exposition of "Nemesis", and how it is quite different from (or how it includes), the external and imponderable force generally referred to as "fate".

But neither *moira* nor *tyche* was conceived to be derived from the conception of Fate as an all-powerful force behind all gods and men and ruthlessly predetermining the life of god and man.

. . . .

To us moderns Fate has come to signify, at least in great part, an omnipotent power indifferent to the happiness or the misery of mankind, the blind working of an external force impeding man's judgment, the force that makes man in his futility do the thing he would not and should not do. Through Fate the trifling accidents of life seem to set in motion a ruthless power that determines the issues of our own and others' lives. Through Fate, man becomes the plaything of a stern Necessity, the inner meaning of whose causal relations baffles his understanding.

. . . .

. . . character is destiny. Eteocles, for all that he rests under the shadow of the ancestral curse, proves the truth of Heraclitus' saying, not far removed from which is that of Plato: 'Your daimon is not apportioned you by lot; you choose your own daimon'. We say that lust for revenge on the part of both brothers was the instrument of Fate. Fate has no objective reality, yet its call exercises a magnetic force upon its victim. The voice of his destiny seems to call to Eteocles: 'The hour has at last come for the fulfillment of thy father's curse. Fulfill it! Kill thy brother and be slain by him'. He translates that subconscious bidding into well-nigh instant act. But he does not, like the hero in Ford's play (*Tis Pity*), juggle his conscience by deliberately setting up Fate as his divinity and thus argue himself to be swayed by its irresistible compulsion.

Unquestionably consciousness of 'fatal destiny' is but one moment in the chain of causation. It predisposes to a decision, when man finds himself confronted by the untowardness of circumstance. But the 'fateful' act is directed by man's self; predetermined as he may be, nevertheless he is himself the captain of his soul. Behind the veil of Fate, as Greek tragedy envisages it, there emerges something rooted in personality, in will.

[6]   H. J. Rose, "Nemesis", *Oxford Classical Dictionary* (1953), p. 601.

. . . .
Heaven, he says, has abandoned him – Heaven had helped him had
he helped himself. Eteocles' fate is his very self recoiling upon him
to his undoing – not Fate, but Nemesis.[7]

Miss Leach's analysis seems to agree, in many respects, with
Smyth's:

No fatalism is this, surely.

. . . .
Character interpreted by action and in action – this is the Greek
drama; and out of the far-reaching consequences of acts that are the
logical outcome of character, its structure is formed. And so, 'the
fate that overtakes the hero is no alien thing, but his own self recoiling upon him for good or evil'.

. . . .
In the seventh Olympian ode of Pindar one finds the Greek conception of life clearly expressed; Nemesis is the thing dwelt upon, not
fate.

I do not for a moment deny that fate and fortune play a part in
Greek literature and life; but that is quite different from saying that
the Greeks were fatalists.

Miss Leach then quotes from F. M. Cornford's *From Religion
to Philosophy,* pages 13-14:

We may even say that the two notions of Destiny and Right are
hardly distinguished. This comes out in the phrase "beyond what is
ordained", "beyond fate" . . . which in Homer halts between the two
meanings: "beyond what is destined, and so *must* be", and "beyond
what is right, and so *ought* to be". . . . The offenders went beyond,
not their fate, but the bounds of morality. Hence in such cases the
balance is redressed by swiftly following vengeance, which itself is
"beyond what is ordained" in the sense that the sinners brought it
upon themselves by their own wickedness, so that they, and not fate,
are responsible.[8]

It was necessary to quote these two writers at length and exactly

---

[7]   H. W. Smyth, *Aeschylean Tragedy* (Berkeley, California, University of
California Press, 1924), pp. 144, 146, 147, 148, 150. Greene calls Smyth's
work one of the most important regarding fate and related ideas in Greek
tragedy.
[8]   A. Leach, "Fate and Free Will", in Lane Cooper's *The Greek Genius
and Its Influence* (New Haven, Yale University Press, 1917), pp. 135, 139,
146, and 152, respectively.

for the concept is difficult to abbreviate and attempts at pure paraphrasing always leave something to be desired in terms of clarity and exactitude. The apparent omissions from the quotations might have a similar effect, but distortion of the essential meanings has been avoided.

The final point here, the nature of Nemesis as it is envisaged in this study, has perhaps been partially formulated by O'Neill himself in the two quotations that follow, though he does not use the specific term:

Perhaps I can explain the nature of my feeling for the impelling, in- scrutable forces behind life which it is my ambition to at least faintly shadow at their work in my plays.[9]

A comprehensive expression is demanded here, a chance for elo- quent presentation, a new form of drama projected from a fresh in- sight into the inner forces motivating the actions and reactions of men and women (a new and truer characterization, in other words) – a drama of souls, and the adventures of 'free wills', with the masks that govern them and constitute their fates.[10]

All of which is surprisingly similar in many respects to the con- cept bodied forth in Plato's "Myth of Er".[11] The quotations sug- gest that O'Neill had a deeper view of fate, and justice-in-action (Nemesis), than any of the writers on O'Neill this writer has consulted. This writer does not propose to make the mistake of insisting that a poet's own statements about the intention of his work are the final statements to be made, nor that there is necessarily a one to one relation between what happens in a poet's work and what he says he intended to happen. The writer accepts O'Neill's own statements as valuable and partial evidence that may point to aspects of O'Neill's work. Such statements are part of the evidence, albeit a small part. O'Neill refers to his materials, but these materials in themselves do not make a play

[9]   Eugene O'Neill, in letter to Barrett H. Clark, quoted in Clark's *Eugene O'Neill: the Man and His Plays* (New York, Robert H. McBride & Co., 1929), p. 43. O'Neill refers to *The Moon of the Caribbees.*
[10]   Eugene O'Neill, "Memoranda on Masks", *The American Spectator*, I (November, 1932), p. 3.
[11]   Plato, "The Republic", *Five Great Dialogues,* trans. B. Jowett, ed. Louise Ropes Loomis (New York, Walter J. Black, 1942), p. 491.

– it is what is *done* with the materials that makes a play. The greatest source of evidence, and the most objective source, even the most dependable source, must always be, in this writer's opinion, in the text.

All four aspects of Nemesis (justice-in-action), the *lex talionis*, social or reasoned justice, divine justice, and tragic justice will be examined as they are evident in O'Neill's plays. As Greene says of *The Oresteia* (see page 16, this study), Aeschylus does not exclude from his action the satisfaction of the *lex talionis* and utilize only social, divine, and tragic justice. So it must be said of O'Neill that it is *quite possible* he utilizes elements of all four types. This study will certainly search for its evidence not in terms of one, but of all four.

STRUCTURE

"Structure" in this study will mean that assemblage of constituent parts, each individual of which submits itself to the inescapable demands of the controlling, formal principle, that orders each part, individually and collectively, into the mode of the play's existence, which we may more simply call "form". In this view, "structure" means the parts seen as individuals assembled; and "form" means that which is seen as a "concrete whole" [12] wherein the individuals lose their identity as separate things in the simultaneity of their organic function as a form. This "form" is the mode of the play's existence and the final cause of its being.

---

[12]   Crane, p. 150. I quote from Crane for the sake of clarity here: "Now anything is a concrete whole, as I have said before, the unity of which can be adequately stated only by saying that it 'is such and such a form embodied in this or that matter, or such and such a matter with this or that form; so that its shape and structure must be included in our description' as well as that out of which it is constituted or made. And of the two natures which must join in any such whole, or in our account of it, 'the formal nature is of greater importance than the material nature' inasmuch as the 'form' of any individual object, such as a man or a couch, is the principle or cause 'by reason of which the matter is some definite thing'." Here Crane draws partly on statements of Aristotle in *On the Parts of Animals* i.1. 640^b 25-29; and *Metaphysics* vii. 17. 1041^b 5-8.

This, in other words, is what Aristotle means when he makes the much attacked statement: "In a play accordingly they do not act in order to portray the Characters; they include the Characters for the sake of the action in it, i.e., its Fable or Plot, that is the end and purpose of the tragedy; and the end is everywhere the chief thing." [13]

This writer depends primarily on Professor Crane's view of "structured form", and the basic verbal materials it orders. "It is not a question of regarding the *Poetics,* in Mr. Blackmur's phrase, as a 'sacred book' and certainly not of looking upon ourselves, in any exclusive sense, as forming an 'Aristotelian' or 'Neo-Aristotelian' school." [14] For this writer whole-heartedly agrees with Dryden, who wrote in the margin of his personal copy of Rymer: "It is not enough that Aristotle has said so, for Aristotle drew his models of tragedy from Sophocles and Euripides: and, if he had seen ours, might have changed his mind." [15] Crane asks us to "extend" Aristotle's useful theories and embrace what has happened in drama today; and, indeed, to use everything that we can use in illuminating poetic form. This is simply *one* way in which to approach "practical" criticism. It depends for its success or failure on inducted and synthesized evidence, the primary source of which must rest *in* the poem.

How may this inclusive and expansive form be embraced by a critical language which is essentially exclusive and reductive – that is to say, referential [16] by its very nature? Certainly if the analysis is going to remain inductive and attempt to avoid *a priori* notions in favor of *a posteriori* formulations, we cannot start with deductive statements about what the form "should be" to be considered drama. And if we are going to attempt to treat

---

[13]   Aristotle, *Poetics* 6. 2. 1450ª 20-24. trans. Ingram Bywater, ed. Friedrich Solmsen (New York, Random House, 1954), p. 231.
[14]   Crane, p. 149.
[15]   Allardyce Nicoll, *Theory of Drama* (London, George G. Harrap & Co., Ltd., 1937), p. 19.
[16]   René Wellek and Austin Warren, *Theory of Literature* (New York, A Harvest Book, Harcourt, Brace and Company, 1956), pp. 10-16. The pages referred to contain a complete exposition of referential language and how it differs from poetic language. Note that the writer has extended the meaning here in terms of Crane's notion of "form", rather than language.

with "factual" evidence we must avoid pre-conditioning the selection of those facts. Therefore we must begin by asking questions. The result of Aristotle's induction fulfilled itself in the concept of *mimesis*, formulated from the particulars in plays he observed. We will not insist that we must come to the same conclusions about the plays we observe; but we must agree that his principle of observation, induction from particulars to generals, will disturb the facts we discover less than a system based on deductive statements. Professor Crane provides us with four questions with which we may treat the elements of poetic form we discover as objects of factual inquiry:

1. What kind of human experience is being imitated?
2. By the use of what possibilities of the poetic medium is the experience being imitated?
3. Through what mode of representation is the experience being imitated?
4. For the sake of evoking and resolving what particular sequence of expectations and emotions relative to the successive parts of the imitated object is the experience being imitated?[17]

It is always some definite combination of these four things that defines, for the imitative writer, the necessities and possibilities of any work he may have in hand; for what he must do and can do at any point will differ widely according as he is imitating a character, a state of passion, or an action, and if an action (with character, thought, and passion inevitably involved), whether one of which the central figures are men and women morally better than we are, or like ourselves, or in some sense worse; and according as he is doing this in verse of a certain kind or in prose or in some joining of the two; and according as he is doing it in a narrative or a dramatic or a mixed manner; and according, finally, as he is shaping his incidents and characters and their thoughts and feelings, his language, and his technique of representation (whatever it may be) so as to give us, let us say, the peculiar kind of comic pleasure we get from *Tom Jones* or that we get from the *Alchemist* or, to add still another possible nuance of comic effect, from *Volpone*.[18]

This study will attempt to ask and to answer the four questions outlined by Crane above in relation to each of the plays selected

[17]   Crane, p. 158.
[18]   *Ibid.*, pp. 158-159.

for consideration. Answering these four questions should provide us with an immediate view of the essential "form" of the work with which we deal and an accurate view of how Nemesis fits into this form. In his essay "The Concept of Plot and the Plot of *Tom Jones*", Crane defines plot in the following manner: ". . . we may say that the plot of any novel or drama is the particular temporal synthesis effected by the writer of the elements of action, character, and thought that constitute the matter of his invention. It is impossible, therefore, to state adequately what any plot is unless we include in our formula all three elements or causes of which the plot is the synthesis; and it follows also that plots will differ in structure according as one or another of the three causal ingredients is employed as the synthesizing principle. There are, thus, plots of action, plots of character, and plots of thought." [19] The first involves as a synthesizing principle (formal principle), complete change, quick or slow, in the main character's situation (determined by character and thought); the second, complete alteration in moral character, brought on or controlled by action, and made apparent in itself and in thought and feeling; the third, a change in thought of the main character (and in his feelings, subsequently), controlled and formed by character and action. Such synthesis, in either of the three examples, will, because it imitates in words a sequence of human activities, *have the power to affect* our opinions and emotions in a certain way.

In this study the word "passion" will also be employed as designating a type of plot in the overall sense meant by Crane in his use of "character", "action", and "thought". Following Crane's suggestion, this kind of plot would involve, generally, a complete change, quick or slow, in the main character's passion (determined by character, thought, and action). It is possible, also, that the state of passion could be sustained rather than altered. This would also be possible with character and thought. This study

[19]   R. S. Crane, "The Concept of Plot and the Plot of *Tom Jones*", *Critics and Criticism*, ed. R. S. Crane, abridged edition (Chicago, University of Chicago Press [Phoenix Books], 1957), p. 66.

equates "type of tragedy" with "type of experience being imitated", and with "type of plot", in the first sense of plot, which sense does not refer exclusively to the arrangement of the incidents, but which refers to the *whole* structured form of a play.[20]

With regard to the arrangement of incidents (plot in the second sense), this study will utilize the terms "simple", "complex", and "episodic".[21] Where there is a single arrangement of incidents, that plot will, in addition, be described as "single". Where there is a double or multiple arrangement of incidents, that plot will be described, too, as "multiple".

For example, a plot of character involving a complete alteration in moral character, brought on or controlled by action and made apparent in itself and in thought and feeling, might also utilize a complex plot (structure of incidents) with single or double issue. If the issue were double, in terms of the arrangement of the incidents, two complex plots would have to be utilized, woven together in terms of two characters; or one structure of incidents could be complex in terms of one character and the other structure of incidents could be simple in terms of the other character. Still, in the first sense of plot (referring to the form itself in its completest actuality), the whole play could be referred to as employing a plot of character.

---

[20]   Crane, *The Languages of Criticism* . . . , pp. 67-68. "There remains plot (*mythos*), and concerning this there has been an extraordinary amount of confusion among commentators on the *Poetics*. . . . In both senses plot is clearly something the poet constructs, the difference being that, whereas in the second sense plot is conceived of as a part or substrate (though the most important one) of tragic form, in the first sense it is the tragic form itself in its completest actuality."

[21]   Aristotle, *Poetics* 9-10. 1451b-1452a. trans. Bywater, ed. Solmsen, p. 236. "I call a Plot episodic when there is neither probability nor necessity in the sequence of its episodes.
.   .   .   .

Plots are either simple or complex, since the actions they represent are naturally of this twofold description. The action, proceeding in the way defined, as one continuous whole, I call simple, when the change in the hero's fortunes takes place without Peripety or Discovery; and complex, when it involves one or the other, or both. These should each of them arise out of the structure of the Plot itself, so as to be the consequence, necessary or probable, of the antecedents. There is great difference between a thing happening *propter hoc* and *post hoc*."

Taking a further suggestion of Aristotle's, each play will be treated as an imagined performance in so far as that is possible.

At the time when he is constructing his Plots, and engaged on the Diction in which they are worked out, the poet should remember (1) to put the actual scenes so far as possible before his eyes. In this way, seeing everything with the vividness of an eye-witness as it were, he will devise what is appropriate, and be least likely to overlook incongruities. This is shown by what was censured in Caricinus, the return of Amphiaraus from the sanctuary; it would have passed unnoticed, if it had not been actually seen by the audience; but on the stage his play failed, the incongruity of the incident offending the spectators. (2) As far as may be, too, the poet should even act his story with the very gestures of his personages. Given the same natural qualifications, he who feels the emotions to be described will be the most convincing; distress and anger, for instance, are portrayed most truthfully by one who is feeling them at the moment. Hence it is that poetry demands a man with a special gift for it, or else one with a touch of madness in him; the former can easily assume the required, mood, and the latter may be actually beside himself with emotion.[22]

The above remarks, it can be clearly seen, provide us by extension with a method of formal and practical criticism.

"What happens" in each play selected for ananlysis will be presented in as brief a form as possible. Then the four "multiple working hypotheses" will be inducted from the brief presentation. This will be followed by a synthesized induction of the essential form of the play, that is to say, a description of the play's mode of existence. When this has been accomplished the role of Nemesis in the exposed structured form of each play will be inducted from that information. The brief presented at the beginning of each chapter will provide an immediate source of reference wherein the results of the study may be checked by each reader for accuracy. The briefs are intended to be more than the usual plot synopsis, and attempt to present every significant ictus of the unfolding temporal rhythm of each play text.

This instrument of analysis, involving a derivative series of multiple "working hypotheses",[23] clearly owes its existence to

---

[22]   *Ibid.*, 17. 1455b 21-37.
[23]   Crane, *The Languages of Criticism* . . . , p. 177.

Aristotle and Professor Crane. This formulation avoids two other possibilities practiced in contemporary criticism: "the method of the working hypothesis", and "the method of the ruling theory".[24]

---

[24] *Ibid.*, p. 206. Crane is quoting T. C. Chamberlin, "The Method of Multiple Working Hypotheses", *Journal of Geology*, XXXIX (1931), pp. 155-165.

II

ABORTION, THIRST, AND THE MOON OF THE CARIBBEES

INTRODUCTION

But he may also find in the cosmic system a pattern for human life and the social order. At any rate he will be disposed to recognize a justice* or a moral law* that binds human nature. So he will trace the inevitable sequence of man's error (*hamartia**); if prosperity (*olbos**) or a sense of surfeit (*koros**) leads a man to a deed of excess (*hybris**), he will suffer retribution* (*nemesis**), or ruin (*ate**). That is in fact justice (*dike*).[1]

The three plays to be studied in this chapter currently appear in more or less readily available collections. *Abortion* is available in *Lost Plays of Eugene O'Neill* (Citadel Press),[2] *Thirst* in *Thirst and Other One Act Plays* (Gorham Press),[3] and *The Moon of the Caribbees* in *The Plays of Eugene O'Neill* (Random House).[4]

---

[1] Greene, p. 6. Greene uses the asterisks to indicate key ideas.
[2] Eugene O'Neill, *Lost Plays of Eugene O'Neill* (New York, Citadel Press, ca. 1958), pp. 11-34. An earlier edition (New York, New Fathoms Press, 1950) came out during O'Neill's lifetime. O'Neill began a suit against New Fathoms but dropped it for reasons of health. He did not want these plays published, but apparently New Fathoms found their copyright expired in the Library of Congress and published them against his wishes.
[3] Eugene O'Neill, *Thirst and Other One Act Plays* (Boston, The Gorham Press, 1914), pp. 6-43. This is a "rare" item, but should be generally available in large university collections. O'Neill would not allow a reprint of this collection which he had published at his own and his father's expense.
[4] Eugene O'Neill, *The Plays of Eugene O'Neill*, 3 vols. (New York, Random House, 1955), I, 451-474. This play, first published in *The Smart Set* (August, 1918), pp. 73-86, was then published in a collection, *The Moon of the Caribbees and Six Other Plays of the Sea* (New York, Boni and Liveright, 1919). The first four plays in this volume were subsequently

The editions of *Abortion* and *Thirst* I refer to appear in collections that were generally not well received. O'Neill fought the publication of *Lost Plays* himself;[5] and *Thirst,* printed in an edition of 1000 copies in 1914, was reviewed only *once.*[6] *The Moon of the Caribbees'* collection was better received critically[7] and certainly bore O'Neill's approval, as he allowed the reprinting of it several times.

What we have before us then, are representatives of three collections: *Abortion* bearing the onus of the author's desire to destroy it; *Thirst* carrying the stigma of the author's youthful approval but his mature rejection; and *The Moon of the Caribbees,* apparently accepted by him and received by the critics with qualifications. All three collections represent, in the order given above, three stages of his earliest work; the first based on the copyright date (May 19, 1914), and the other two based on their dates of publication (August, 1914, and August, 1918, respectively). *The Moon of the Caribbees* was not published in collection until 1919. There is at this time no discoverable criticism of these early works which attempts to criticize them from the standpoint of trying to see what these plays actually are without forcing on them preconceptions about what they ought to be. Critical examination of the later work based on its intrinsic nature (rather than upon critical preconceptions), occurs comparatively infrequently in some books and some major articles; even in those books and articles, the special aspect of Nemesis as justice-in-action has not been treated. Clifford Leech has written a good

---

produced as *S. S. Glencairn* and have that subtitle in the Random House edition referred to above, while the remaining three plays are titled separately and follow in the same order as originally published.
[5]   Barrett H. Clark, "Lost Plays of Eugene O'Neill", *Theatre Arts,* XXXIV, 7 (July, 1950).
[6]   Clayton Hamilton, "A Shelf of Printed Plays", *Bookman,* XLI (April, 1915), 182.
[7]   *The Dial,* "*The Moon of the Caribbees*", LXVI (May 17, 1919), 524. The anonymous reviewer tells us: "The atmosphere that on the stage saturates these brief dramatic studies persists in the printed plays and carries them successfully through not a little halting action and commonplace motivation."

general biographical and chronological treatment of the earliest work.[8]

ABORTION

This play was copyrighted but never produced during O'Neill's lifetime. In keeping with the analytic presented in the first chapter, let us begin by asking the first question. What kind of human experience is this play imitating? "Convention", perhaps, is the keynote, for the characters are as familiar as daily headlines in the newspapers.

The action begins with Herron, Lucy, and Mrs. Townsend entering Jack's and Herron's darkened study which is part of their suite of rooms in a dormitory of a large, eastern college. They switch on the lights and indulge in some harmless holiday banter, centering around Lucy's sharp tongue and Herron's stature.

At this point, Joe Murray enters looking for Jack and is told by Herron to wait outside; more banter.

Jack enters with Evelyn, his sweetheart, and there is more banter. Herron tells Jack that Murray is looking for him. Lucy, Herron, and Mrs. Townsend leave to join the victory parade for the big game in which Jack has been pitcher and captain.

Evelyn and Jack indulge in expressions of love, Evelyn praising Jack's ideal, heroic qualities, Jack demurring. They kiss. Mr. Townsend enters saying, "Caught in the act".[9] Evelyn leaves with father's and son's promise to join the parade when it comes by. Jack discusses his "trouble" with his father. Jack hints that his father did not have a spotless record while in college. Jack attributes his own fault in making Nellie Murray, an innocent town girl, pregnant, to inherited racial beastliness, while his father insists it is Jack's responsibility. Jack indicts the faulty ethics of his society. He tells his father the girl (Murray's sister) is all right and thanks him for his generosity in paying the two hundred

---

[8]   Clifford Leech, *O'Neill* (London, Oliver and Boyd, 1963), pp. 1-19.
[9]   O'Neill, *Lost Plays* . . . , p. 20.

dollars for the abortion. Jack is truly repentant. The father leaves to join the others as Murray enters. Jack motions his father out reassuringly.

Murray confronts Jack with the truth of his sister's death. Jack is stunned. He begs, not for himself, but for the sake of his parents and his sweetheart to have the thing kept quiet. He offers money to Murray. Murray, misunderstanding, thinking Jack wants to pay for Nellie, threatens him with a gun. Jack takes it away from him and puts it on the table. Murray maneuvers out the door telling Jack he has found a better way to fix him than to shoot him as Jack has asked him to do. Murray leaves for the police station to reveal the scandal.

Students burst into the study looking for Jack to carry him to the carnival, but he has taken refuge in the bedroom of the suite, and they leave.

Cheers and shouting are heard outside as Jack rushes distractedly back into the room. As the crowd sings "For He's a Jolly Good Fellow", he grabs the revolver Murray left, puts it to his temple and pulls the trigger. The report is drowned by the singing.

Evelyn rushes in to find Jack dead and faints beside him as the crowd outside marches away and the curtain falls.

A minimum amount of time is spent on moralizing or reflecting in this action. The thing that grips us is the breakneck speed with which everything happens, which is all in keeping with the quickened and giddy holiday atmosphere. There is little time for reflection on anyone's part. Most of it occurs during Jack's talk with his father. Our suspense is early aroused by the entrance of Murray during the first few minutes of the play's unfolding.

Yet, we are hard put to find any of the characters lacking in dimension. For example, Evelyn's ethereal, ideal beauty is quickened by her convincing animal desire for Jack, which is balanced against her admiration of his skill and his seemingly noble athletic behavior. Mr. Townsend's thought is as much for the girl, Nellie, as it is for his son, and he tells Jack that it was a mistake not to write to the girl and reassure her on her sickbed. Jack agrees, and he is convincingly remorseful. His whole explanation to Murray on hearing the truth centers around sparing the feelings of his family and his betrothed, Evelyn.

Jack is a character better than most in his milieu. He truly is not predominantly selfish, though we know and he knows, that his generally good behavior is marred by a selfish moment, and further complicated by later selfish acts of omission when he refuses to comfort the girl on her sickbed. Murray tells him, "She might 'a lived if she thought yuh cared, if she heard from yuh; but she knew yuh were tryin' to git rid of her".[10] Everyone in the action, in the terms in which it is cast, is convincing and three dimensional. As Lawrence Gellert says of *A Wife for a Life* in the introduction to this volume, "The O'Neill opus has no villain!"[11] O'Neill avoids polarizing his characters into good and evil. His characters give the illusion of being like real men, capable of both good and evil, caught in the web of their own actions and the inertia of circumstance, not simply in the toils of one or the other.

What kind of human experience is this play imitating? We may say, having looked at the facts, that this experience involves action chiefly as its formal principle, and that action may best be described as a quick and complete change in the main character's situation, determined by character and thought. The change brings death to the protagonist; and as the whole action has involved us in the fortunes of the other characters, a real sense of pity and fear for him and the other characters whose lives will be shattered by the impending revelation of his suicide and of the reasons for it.

Now we must answer the second question preparatory to arriving at an immediate view of the essential form of the work with which we are dealing, wherein it may be said to have its mode of existence. By the use of what possibilities of the poetic medium is the experience presented here being imitated? We have singled out action as the center of the play, with character and thought contributing to its development.

Let us consider some of the possibilities of the patterns of

---

10   *Ibid.*, p. 29.
11   *Ibid.*, p. 10.

action that could have been employed. In terms of exposition and development, Jack and Herron could have entered first and exposed the whole situation, and Murray could have been made to enter at some time close to the crisis to reveal the truth of the situation. But then the factor of fast moving events, giving the illusion of unfolding naturally in the course of action would have been slowed down by the exposition. O'Neill saves this exposition till just before the crisis and has it take place between father and son, a stronger position, and a more critical relationship. The holiday giddiness of the whole situation, the almost frantic pace of the action pressing the main character would have been sacrificed, and his violent act of suicide would not seem plausible in the slowed temporal quality of the movement that would have resulted from the placing of our suggested exposition.

Suspense, too, would have been qualified to the extent of "waiting to see what happens eventually", rather than "wondering exactly what will happen next". O'Neill chose the more economical course of gradually revealing the situation, almost fully exposing it, and bringing the action just before the reversal and simultaneous discovery to a strong crisis with the final revelation of the truth. Then, having put the revelation at this point, he makes the heavier beat of the climax, closely following a partially unexpected crisis, hit with more force and more plausibility. The way in which O'Neill arranges the action builds the pressure on the protagonist gradually to such a sure breaking point that we are better prepared to accept his final and violent act of suicide. Without this gradual and steady increase of tempo, the character's suicide would seem arbitrary rather than plausible and convincing. He is not allowed to have time to think in the final moments. Everything rushes in on him at once.

His sense of shame and remorse seems so heavy and crushing, especially when the students begin to cheer him, and the irony seems so shattering that we expect him to do something violent. Perhaps O'Neill might have had him shoot Murray out of fear, and then have had the crowd enter with his parents, friend, and sweetheart; but this would have been no release for the character, and certainly not in keeping with his essentially good, though

faulty, makeup. This would have made him seem merely monstrous. The imitated facts of the situation are ineluctable. The
girl is dead, and the hero has not only been partly responsible
for her death, he has refused her comfort and recognition through
a further act of selfishness. He does not kill himself to avoid
scandal. Remember that he asks, quite convincingly, that Murray
shoot him so that he may be relieved of the pain of his remorse,
and leave the facts of the case a secret in order to spare the
living. This shows more than a desire to be punished, a recognition of implacable error; it shows, too consideration for those
who must live on.

Given many other possibilities of action, it appears O'Neill
has chosen the best course in terms of all the factors of the
situation: characters, crisis, climax, and denouement, and most
important of all, the best course in terms of the temporal magnitude to which he obviously desired to limit himself. He could,
however, have chosen to alter temporal magnitude, and thus
easily have changed many of the other factors and perhaps have
written a drama that would be entirely different in its formal
nature.

Even his denouement, which might be thought to be "over-
done", by some critics, seems right. We expect Evelyn to come
looking for the protagonist when the others cannot find him.
Her physical attraction to him, her sense of possessing him, makes
it seem only natural that instead of screaming and running from
the room that she should move quickly toward him to touch him,
and that the shock of her discovery should cause her to faint.
Her loss of consciousness seems a symbolic parallel to Jack's
own death and extends the significance of Jack's death immediately to those characters associated with him in the play. We
are made to sense their loss directly – remembering his concern
for them.

O'Neill could have had his friend, his father, his mother, his
sister, or simply a student discover the suicide, but any one of
these other choices would have seemed weaker in dramatic effect;
and in the case of his friend or a student, might have involved
anticlimactic action. That Jack is released from his torment, and

that his death is most directly known by the character closest to him in the play, ironically fulfilling his fear of hurting her, seems to be the strongest climax and denouement possible considering those factors which the given particulars make dramatically necessary.

Since so much of Jack's *ethos* as a character in the play depends on his position in the university milieu, even the final "For he's a jolly good fellow, which nobody can deny",[12] seems dramatically appropriate as a third aspect of the crushing irony of the action presented. The death of the girl, Nellie, is opposite to what Jack expects to be the outcome of the action in which he is involved. Evelyn's knowledge of his suicide defeats his desire to spare her pain.

The university community worships a shallow image of Jack that no man can live up to. "For he's a jolly good fellow" is a polarized image of what most of the characters are in the special context of the structure of this play. Jack discovers too late that he is forced to play a role, the standards of which allow little room for the whole man to exist. Nor can he find through that role an equitable relation to himself. His polarized role, we may assume, has been played so long and so thoroughly that he has had no chance to prepare himself to deal with those other real aspects of himself he discovers. Unable to deal with those other and more "terrible" aspects of his nature, faced by the horns of this dilemma – what he is expected to be and what he actually is – he throws himself upon death. He finds that he cannot keep his real identity and his false identity in any distinguishable balance within himself.

It can be said that Jack is not simply (1) morally better than we, nor (2) like us, nor (3) in some sense worse. He seems in some respects better than most men but not preëminently virtuous and just (as most of us are not), and in the case of his refusing to comfort the girl, Nellie, he seems worse than most of us. So he is a combination of all three moral qualifications, not simply the essence of one. This partially puts him in the category of the

---

[12]   *Ibid.*, p. 34.

Aristotelian tragic hero: "There remains, then, the intermediate kind of personage, a man not preëminently virtuous and just, whose misfortune, however, is brought upon him not by vice and depravity but by some error of judgment, of the number of those in the enjoyment of great reputation and prosperity; e.g. Oedipus, Thyestes, and the men of note of similar families." [13] In some respects Jack does not fit Aristotle's requirements. He is not of so illustrious a lineage as Aristotle seems to suggest. He is closer to us in that respect. And he seems in one respect to be worse than most of us, and that is in his failure to respond to the girl's plea for comfort or her need for it. He errs in judgment when he supposes that an abortion will settle the affair without pain to anyone. Perhaps he did not know the risks involved. Such ignorance would likely be in keeping with the sort of ignorance of these matters his polarized role has forced upon him. Not comforting the girl when she asks to see him is not so explainable an error, however. It is possible, as Murray suggests, that this cruelty on Jack's part destroyed her will to live.

Now we must ask the third question involved in our analytic: Through what mode of representation is the experience being imitated? This answer is clear. Since all the characters speak "in scene" [14] without the interpolation of a narrator, we may safely call this mode the dramatic mode. The action depends primarily on the manipulation of casual, realistic surfaces. All of this is accomplished in prose dialogue, with the exception of the singing of the students, which includes verse and music. The whole of the action involves the use of a "complex" plot.

Now, perhaps, we come to the most difficult of the four questions: For the sake of evoking and resolving what particular sequence of expectations and emotions relative to the successive parts of the imitated object is the experience being imitated? We are presented with the climax of a day of ideal triumph in the

---

[13]   Aristotle, *Poetics* 13. 1453 8-12. trans. Bywater, ed. Solmsen, pp. 238-239.
[14]   Wallace A. Bacon and Robert S. Breen, *Literature as Experience* (New York, McGraw-Hill Book Company, Inc., 1959), p. 222. "A play exists entirely in *scene*."

life of an ideal college senior surrounded by his family, sweet-heart, and roommate. The major part of his triumph seems to consist of his social standing at the college, which has been directly influenced by his athletic prowess. Little reference is made to his intellectual achievements except perhaps as vaguely suggested by the interest in his parents and himself taken by a Professor Simmons, who never appears on stage but accompanies Jack and his father from the Inn after dinner as they follow the others to the rooms.[15] We take a certain delight in the hilarity and general good spirits expressed in the banter among Mrs. Townsend, Lucy, and Herron, when they appear on the scene. But this general merriment is interrupted by the shadowy figure of Mur-ray, who enters and asks for Jack. He is very surly, and we cannot suppose that his mission is a pleasant one. Yet we do not know what it is, and suspense of a minor kind is introduced in the first few minutes of the action. Thus, our general participa-tion in the merriment and our sharing of the hero's triumph is qualified by curiosity and a vague sense of danger for him. Jack enters; his humility and general good sense and pleasantness of manner are attractive. And again the ominous note of Murray is introduced when Herron tells Jack that a "townie" is looking for him, further building our curiosity and suspense. His demur-ring in the face of Evelyn's praise after the others have gone makes us wonder, however, for he seems to refer to something other than her praise:

JACK. (*His face suddenly grown serious, as if at some painful memory*) 'Please Evelyn! You make me feel so mean – and contemptible when you talk like that.'[16]

In the scene with his father, after Evelyn has gone to join the others, our curiosity is satisfied and we find out that this perfect specimen has made a serious error, however unintentional, that is made more distressing by his refusal to even communicate with the ailing girl. We think back on Murray's presence and wonder if, as Jack says, everything is all right, what Murray

15   O'Neill, *Lost Plays* . . . , p. 17.
16   *Ibid.*, p. 19.

wants. Murray enters as Jack's father is leaving, and soon we know the terrible facts of the case.

From here on the action grows more and more painful as the hero is torn further on the horns of his dilemma, and his steadily increasing suffering is felt by us until it is almost too much for him and for us. What we want, I believe, more than anything, is the hero's release from the tremendous agony he suffers as his conscience and the facts of the case grow more painful. We do not want him to suffer, for basically he is good, though he has committed two errors. We feel as he does that the situation has no solution. His death by suicide releases us, with him, from its pressure.

Still Jack's release is not a total release for us. The terror we feel at his psychological struggle is eased by his death, but pity for those he holds most dear is enforced by Evelyn's discovery. Somehow we feel a kind of anger at the stupidity of the crowd for we know, though they do not, that "Jolly Good Fellow" may have deep suffering of which they are not aware. The foregoing sequence of expectations and emotions evoked by the imitated action involve the purgation of pity, terror, and like emotions to a limited extent: the purgation of the intense terror and suffering of the hero. But pity, if anything, is magnified rather than purged and is mixed with the stimulation of intense regret at the waste of so many fair possibilities. That seems to be the end emotional result of the aesthetic pattern we witness in O'Neill's *Abortion*.

Perhaps the most outstanding quality we notice in this early piece is *economy*. This complicated aesthetic structure seems brought to fulfillment by an exactness and sureness that is in itself pleasing to behold.

The four questions of fact have now been answered. The remaining task is to synthesize from these facts a description of the form wherein the play may be said to have its mode of existence.

If we combine and condense the above four aspects of the form we arrive at something like this: The form of this play consists of the imitation of a swiftly paced action of approximately twenty minutes in length that occurs near the triumphant end of a happy day for the protagonist, involving him in a sudden reversal of fortune resulting from the discovery of his responsibility for the death of a girl. All of which is accomplished in the most expedient and probable manner of dramatic action, utilizing a complex plot, the manipulation of casual, realistic surfaces, and prose dialogue. This evokes from us a series of emotional responses to the protagonist's struggle that may be described as terror regarding the outcome of his unbearable pain as he is faced with the ineluctable facts, release from this terror when the protagonist releases his own suffering through suicide, but no release from our own pity which is magnified by his suicide and its discovery by his betrothed; which in turn fills us with regret at the waste of the situation, and anger at the ignorance of the crowd, who, in spite of themselves, seem to mock the sorrow aroused in us by our superior knowledge of the situation.

If we attempt to describe the role of Nemesis as justice-in-action in regard to the four categories set up in the definition of Nemesis in the first chapter, perhaps the least difficult category to begin searching for will be the *lex talionis,* for it is most closely connected with subjective emotion, one of the prime materials of drama.

Joe Murray's feeling of Nemesis (righteous anger),[17] at Jack's treatment of his sister is the clearest example within the structure of this play of a desire for blood vengeance according to the *lex talionis.* But O'Neill utilizes this aspect of Nemesis in a very special way. He makes Nellie's brother the agent of retaliation, true, but he also uses Murray as a device to build suspense. On his first entrance Murray appears surly, threatening. Mention is made again of him after Jack enters and just as we think the situation will work itself out equitably as a result of Jack's con-

---

[17] Greene, p. 19. "Nemesis, in particular, involves a sentiment of disapproval, in varying degrees, of all violations of duty or any excess or disproportion, of all temerity or presumption; it is quick to emerge at the sight of undeserved misfortune, or at the triumph of the wicked. It is a moral sentiment, in that resentment is felt against the offender even if one is not personally offended by him. And if men feel *nemesis* at overweening acts, so also do the gods."

versation with Mr. Townsend, he enters again as Mr. Townsend leaves, and the full destructive force of his significance in the drama is unleashed. But, as he talks to Jack, Murray conceives an even more horrible retribution which he may exact from Jack, and that is public disclosure of Jack's mistreatment of Nellie. Here the idea of vengeance becomes modified from one of private retaliation to one of greater suffering involving the public disgrace of the hero. This modification on Murray's part involves Jack additionally in the intense suffering that such exposure will work on those he holds most dear: Evelyn, his parents, and his sister.

Murray begins as the agent of a personal Nemesis, the law of the claw, fully intending to take the life of the man responsible for his sister's death, but discovers as a result of the dramatic action, that he can work greater pain on the hero by resorting to legal retribution or socially reasoned justice.

And we must agree in the special terms the drama presents that in this case, at least, what Jack says to his father is partially true:

JACK. (*Scornfully*) Restraint? Ah, yes, everybody preaches but who practices it? And could they if they wanted to? Some impulses are stronger than we are, have proved themselves so throughout the world's history. Is it not rather our ideals of conduct, of Right and Wrong, our ethics, which are unnatural and monstrously distorted? Is society not suffering from a case of the evil eye which sees evil where there is none? Isn't it our moral laws which force me into evasions like the one which you have just found fault with? [18]

The society presented in the play (imitated in it) makes no provision for the darker side of the nature of the characters that inhabit it. Appetency simply is not accorded any public recognition either in law or custom. But as a matter of fact it exists in this imitated social milieu, as it did in the actual society which was the object of the imitation of the dramatic milieu. Jack fears the Nemesis of his society, but even more strongly he fears the Nemesis such a society will wreak on those he really loves, shame,

---

[18] O'Neill, *Lost Plays* . . . , pp. 24-25.

dishonor, embarrassment, and scorn. He thinks an abortion will solve the threat of society's Nemesis; but since it must be performed in secret under improper conditions, it involves the risk of death for the woman. That even death must be risked to avoid exposure is monstrous; that Jack's training apparently had deprived him of the knowledge of contraceptives is probably the final absurdity. But once his acts have gotten him so far into this tangle of progressively complicated mistakes, Jack commits a cruelty which is not really excusable in reference to the twisted sense of correct behavior enforced on him by his society. He becomes as inhumane as the social customs and legal statutes he has been trying to circumvent and imitates in effect what they amount to. He refuses to pay attention to Nellie and proceeds to ignore her humanity, as society in turn has ignored through its unreal maxims of behavior his own individual needs. That this is a fine piece of dramatic logic is unquestionable. That the hero is without responsibility here, as he tries to tell his father, is questionable. He knows how wrong his society is, but he is unable to see how wrong he himself has been in refusing to recognize the plea of the girl written to him from her sickness. It is this realization that finally drives him to suicide. He knows that by any standard his failure to go to the girl and comfort her is supremely cruel. It is in this ultimate realization of his withdrawal of human sympathy, his own inhumanity, that we may see the working of tragic justice-in-action in the terms this play presents. Final justice in this view depends not on vengeance, not on reasoned social justice which has been shown to miscarry when it becomes the servant of a personal hatred, but on the individual relationships between human beings, on their acceptance of the personal responsibility involved in contact privately with one another.

The Nemesis wreaked on Jack is self-inflicted. The idea of social and reasoned justice is shown to be abortive in the play as it becomes the instrument of Murray's personal hatred, and thus is equated with the *lex talionis* or personal vengeance. Tragic justice seems rooted in the need for common human sympathy, outside the demands of an eye for an eye, or reasoned justice (the society's code being inadequate in this situation), and outside the divine (significant dramatic considerations of which never occur in the play); so that we are finally left with a justice or retribution based primarily on the "unwritten law" of common human decency.

"Common human decency" is precisely what the social milieu in the plays does not demand of its imitated characters. The social milieu demands maintaining the false, polarized image of man presented in the play at all costs, and its lack of *real* concern for humans as humans, minus their social tags, is partially responsible for the protagonist doing just what the code does and that is blinding himself to the essential human needs of those around him, especially in the case of Nellie.

Perhaps, as Murray suggests, Jack destroyed Nellie's will to live. This moral failure seems rooted not in outward behavior alone, but basically in the lack of an inner syntax, an inner moral code, without which no outward style of behavior is possible.[19] Jack, finding himself without these inner resources, is unable to resolve the tremendous conflict such a discovery explodes within him; and truly unable to support consciousness on these overbalanced terms, destroys himself, which really does not resolve anything in terms of the whole social milieu the play imitates, but which does dramatically restore the balance or justice within the character through imitated death.

That this Nemesis or restoring of proper balance should come from the character himself is perfectly just in two ways. The milieu in which the character is imitated provides no machinery for restoring the character to some semblance of a stable existence, hence it must come from within, from his own hands. And since the society is partially responsible for creating one-sided distortions, or aborted personalities incapable of sustaining a whole life, it seems only natural and just that such incomplete

[19]   Jean Cocteau in *Cocteau on the Film: a Conversation Recorded by André Fraigneau*, trans. Vera Traill (New York, Roy Publishers, 1954), p. 126. "All this shows that minds and souls live without a syntax, that is to say, without a moral system. This moral system has nothing to do with morality proper, and should be built up by each of us as an inner style, wihout which no outer style is possible."

things should cease to live as it becomes more and more obvious they haven't the resources to support life on their own. The real Nemesis that pursues Jack is his awakening inner moral conscience. Once it is fully awake and once he recognizes the image it throws back at him, his despair is so great he destroys the distorted thing he has become.

Yet he knows that despite his blindness he is directly responsible. He admits this to his father and agrees with Murray that perhaps he is what Murray has called him – a murderer.

True, the girl did not necessarily have to die; but then, neither did Jack necessarily have to risk her life with an abortion. Nemesis seems to be a result of two factors, not simply of one determined one: his own conscious acts, and the inertia of circumstances partially beyond his control once he has of his own free will made the fatal choice; even then, the action spells out for us, he could possibly have avoided the net gathering around his wayward feet by comforting the girl, but he chooses for selfish reasons not to and the girl dies. In this case then, as Leach says, "the fate that overtakes the hero is no alien thing, but his own self recoiling upon him for good or evil". Which is in fact Nemesis.

If we look at the above conclusions in the light of the *lex talionis*, reasoned social justice, and tragic justice we come to further and even more interesting conclusions. In the light of distributive justice the girl dies, so the boy must die. In the light of retributive justice the girl dies as the result of the boy's breaking the social code (both written and unwritten), so the boy must suffer public exposure and possibly death as an accessory to her death. But in the light of tragic justice as Myers so shrewdly says:

Following the tradition which conceives of the notions of equilibrium, balance, and equality as lying at the center of the idea of justice, tragedy denies that this equality can be found in the relation of the citizen to the state (as in Plato's *Republic*), or in the relation between individual and individual (as in the *lex talionis*), but affirms that it can be found in the relation of the individual to himself, in his perfect self-equality.[20]

[20]   Myers, pp. 26-27.

As Myers says, the first two categories appealing to graspable factors, capable of being objectively balanced, have no final significance in the face of the imitated inner subjectivity of tragic character. Such factors are capable of being manipulated like figures in a column. But the tragic factors of experience as they are imitated in an aesthetic form truly do not submit to manipulation, for in the aesthetic framework presented they are ineluctable (since the play is an ended, finished form), and are not subject to further manipulation in the quiddity, the absoluteness of their position.

This ultimate awakening of Jack stems from a new conception as to where his responsibilty lies – not in the social code, not in any external manipulation in the physical world – but in the common human responsibility that exists privately between individuals (a seeming modification of the *lex talionis* as it influences his public and private behavior). This does not reduce all tragic character to one limited maxim; the tragic manipulation of these ineluctable factors, as must be obvious by now, can be extended and proportioned in many ways this play does not use, and in many ways other plays do not use.

Yet it must be noticed that this seems to contradict Myers to some extent. Myers would go so far as to rewrite Aristotle's definition, reducing tragedy to studies in justice:

'Tragedy', *he* [Aristotle] *might then have said*, 'is an imitation of an action that is serious, complete, and of adequate magnitude – in language embellished in different ways in differing parts – in the form of action, not of narration' – *revealing a just relation between good and evil in the life of a representative man.*[21]

Although Professor Myers' discussion is of invaluable aid in the discussion of Nemesis and related ideas, it appears that his replacing of the term "catharsis" with the idea of "justice" is no more final than Aristotle's definition. It is a good working definition, but, obviously, if the critic happens to find a play which demands another description of its operative form, it will have to be modified, in the way the description of the form of O'Neill's

[21]   *Ibid.*, p. 53.

Abortion has been modified in this study. Myers would substitute "justice" for "emotion" in his definition of tragic form. The writer asks why it is necessary to categorically include or exclude either, since it is only reasonable that the possibility exists that both materials – ideas of "justice" and "emotional" significances – may be interrelated in any given tragic form; and what is most important is that the two may be further interwoven with a great many other materials. The real problem, then, as this study envisages it, is to *see what is there* in regard to the several forms with which the study is committed to deal. Clearly, three material ideas of Nemesis stemming from the *lex talionis,* social justice, and tragic justice have been shaped and formed to serve special dramatic functions in *Abortion.*

THIRST

What kind of human experience is this play imitating? The type of experience imitated in *Abortion*, as we saw, was primarily an action involving a sudden reversal in the situation of the main character. This play certainly seems different. Perhaps the best place to start would be to attempt to describe what happens in the play.

Three characters, victims of shipwreck, are shown close to death due to exposure, starvation, and thirst; they are adrift on a small life raft in the midst of a tropical sea. They are "A Gentleman", "A Dancer", and "A West Indian Mulatto Sailor".[22] The Gentleman wears the remains of evening dress, has scanty black hair, a bald spot badly sunburned, and a once dyed but faded and drooping mustache. Between the Sailor and the Gentleman lies a once gaily costumed Dancer, her costume now in tatters, her slippers swollen and pulpy, and around her throat she wears an elaborate and expensive diamond necklace. Her hair is blond and long but spoiled by sea water and lack of attention. She is weeping and her makeup is litte more than a collection of

22   O'Neill, *Thirst* . . . , p. 6.

streaks and smudges. The Sailor wears a blue uniform with "Union Mail Line" in red letters written across the back of his jersey. He "croons" a continuous, monotonous melody, and the quality of his voice gives the impression that he is troubled by an odd speech defect located in his throat. The Gentleman has just been on the first vacation of his life and has recently sailed from Buenos Aires on the ill-fated ship for home. The Dancer happened to be on board for the fatal cruise to New York on her way home to fame and money. These people need water more than anything else. The whole play seems sprung on their mad desire for it. The Gentleman thinks the Sailor has stolen and hidden water from them. The Dancer and the Gentleman plot to get this imagined water from the Sailor. First they try to buy it from him with the Dancer's necklace. When that fails the Gentleman gives up, and the woman, close to madness, tries to make herself "attractive" and offers her body to the Sailor. He has no water, of course, but she does not believe him and driven to utter madness commences to dance, recalling a performance she had given for the duke who had given her the necklace, which now lies discarded and glittering on the raft. The Gentleman urges her on. The effort of the dance kills her and she falls to the deck of the raft. The Gentleman rushes to her, shocked by her death. But the Sailor tells the Gentleman that now they will eat and drink and begins to sharpen his knife on the sole of his shoe. The Gentleman, horrified, throws the Dancer's body to the sharks. The Sailor, enraged by what is to him a stupid waste, plunges his knife into the Gentleman's breast; and as the Gentleman topples overboard he clutches the Sailor's jersey, and they both fall into the sea and are devoured by the ever present sharks. "The sun glares down like a great angry eye of God." [23] The necklace glitters in the intense sunlight.

Action does not adequately describe this imitated human experience. Action is involved, yes, but something else appears to be the center of this experience as it is imitated. The situation of the characters does not change much. It is fixed and hopeless as

[23] *Ibid.*, p. 43.

the play begins. Thought, Crane's third Aristotelian category, does not seem to be the center of the experience either. According to Crane's three types of plot: plots of action, plots of character, and plots of thought, the second seems most adequately to describe the imitated experience we have just examined.

According to Crane the plot of character involves complete alteration in moral character – brought on or controlled by action, made apparent in itself and in thought and feeling. Much of what actually takes place in the play has necessarily been deleted in the above brief. Most of the deletions consist of long character speeches in which the characters react to their present situation, their past experiences, and each other. Thus, a full description of what happens would include many incidents of character recall, reaction to the present situation, and reaction to the other characters. This is particularly true of the Dancer and the Gentleman. The mulatto is characterized by his comparative lack of reaction – his seemingly resigned quality of character. Only once during the whole piece does he react violently and that is, as we have seen, at the climax when he kills the Gentleman who has deprived him of his "food and drink". On the strength of the above evidence we may safely call this imitated experience an imitation that uses as its central, controlling, or formal principle the revelation of an almost complete change in moral character, brought on by action and made apparent in itself and in thought and feeling.

Now we must attempt to answer the second question of fact: By the use of what possibilities of the poetic medium of character is the experience being imitated? Clearly these characters have no normal environment provided for them. They are isolated on a desolate raft in the remotest sector of a vast tropical sea. With this given setting the characters can be revealed only by what they say, what they are, and what they do, without reference to any *immediately* related social milieu. When the play opens they have been in this situation long enough to bring them close to the brink of madness and death. These are the given factors of the situation. And they are what they are. So far we have no right to consider other possibilities, for these are the specific factors the poet has set himself to deal with. What we have to think about is what the characters *become* in this situation through the limited action they are allowed to perform by the restricting circumstances. We know that they are out of the traveled sea lanes, for the Gentleman says:

I know little of navigation, yet I heard those on board say that we were following a course but little used. Why we did so, I do not know. I suppose the Captain wished to make a quicker passage. He alone knows what was in his mind and he will probably never tell.[24]

Many other lines of the play add to this impression that a chance of rescue under the present conditions seems hopeless. The only hope they have is to drift close to a small tropical atoll. Rescue is such a remote possibility in view of the given dramatic factors that it would seem almost ridiculous to us if O'Neill had the characters rescued. It would not seem dramatically probable. The possibility of discovering an atoll offers faint enough hope to "keep the characters going", for if they had no hope the reason for all their activity would be arbitrary. But the dimensions and limitations of the legitimate theatre make the chance of their drifting to an atoll unacceptable as a dramatically feasible possibility.

Had this experience been imitated in another form – narrative or film – the action of the characters happening upon an atoll would not seem forced. But in the stage milieu it does not seem to be a very likely or workable solution.

The drive to get the imagined water plus the *hope* of drifting near an atoll are enough to motivate the characters forward in the dramatic action. It is the dramatic probability of the characters that must really be examined in this instance.

Possibilities other than the ones O'Neill has used are obviously numerous. The Gentleman and the Dancer suspect the Sailor of concealing water. O'Neill might have had them discover their suspicions to be true. The Sailor might then have given them the water, or a struggle for it might have ensued. In that case the

²⁴   *Ibid.*, pp. 16-17.

play would end much sooner than it does and it would have become a play of action rather than one of character; for such an eventuality would have precluded the final insane and character revealing performance of the Dancer. The shock produced by her death returns the Gentleman to a pattern of fastidious, civilized behavior.

A precipitated struggle also would have made impossible the more gradual reversion of the Sailor to cannibalism. The blush of civilization he has only leaves him in O'Neill's action when the Dancer dies of natural causes. If he had killed both the Dancer and the Gentleman in our supposed fight and begun to eat them, the effects of civilization would seem to have a weaker hold on him than we normally expect. Handling the development of his character through the action O'Neill projects appears less obvious, more complex, and effects a more sensitive portrayal of the Sailor's character in terms of what we know of the deep seated effect civilization does have on the savage removed several generations from his savagery – whether the savage be Ainu, Mongolian, Caucasian, or West Indian.

The same gradual effect could have been accomplished, it should be observed, through other patterns of character revealed through action. But the important point here is that O'Neill did choose this less precipitous pattern. One cannot think of a better specific pattern than the one O'Neill has used to obtain this effect.

Since the Dancer and the Gentleman constantly revert to lucid moments of civilized compassion as the action progresses, it seems only probable that the Gentleman should revert to his fastidious civility when the Dancer dies in this special dramatic context. The shock of her death is convincingly strong enough to bring him back to sanity. Given the Gentleman's character as it is developed up to the crisis of the Dancer's death, the Gentleman's participation in the Sailor's cannibalism would have been difficult to accept. We know from reliable reports that civilized people on life rafts have eaten each other, but this is not life. It is a limited aesthetic structure that presents limited, structured characters.

O'Neill's Gentleman, as presented with his weakness, his age, his fastidiousness, his essentially formal patterns of behavior and speech, his sentimentality, his real sensitivity to the predicament of others, his attitude toward death, and his fundamental despair, simply could not have eaten another human being's dead body. Had O'Neill chosen to have him do so, it would have seemed to us a bland denial of everything the character was in terms of aesthetic and cumulative detail. One cannot divorce character in drama from the spectrum of detail the dramatist provides in his cumulative structure of characteristic traits, actions, and attitudes.

When it occurs to the serious student of this early play of O'Neill's to wonder why the Dancer happens to be here in the first place, he discovers that the artistic reasoning for her presence on the raft as it is evidenced in the lines of the play is adequate until he reasons back to the motivation provided her for boarding the ill-fated ship as it left port. The Gentleman is on his first vacation trip after many years of hard office work. The Sailor is a member of the ship's crew. But the Dancer's reason for being involved with the ship and its misfortune seems gratuitous. She has, this writer feels, no solid, specific, dramatic reason for getting on the ship in the first place. And, unlike the Gentleman, who expects to return home to New York and retirement, she isn't going there for any specific reason. She says:

I was coming home, home after years of struggling, home to success and fame and money. And I must die out here on a raft like a mad dog.[25]

But where she is coming home from we do not know. It must be from Buenos Aires, but what she was doing there we do not know. The Gentleman, on the other hand, refers to a banquet given in his honor by the "United States Club of Buenos Aires".[26] We must suppose that she had a successful engagement in Buenos Aires, but we can only suppose. We can assume that the Gentleman is coming from some specific place and going back to do what he had always done:

25   *Ibid.*, p. 26.
26   *Ibid.*, p. 19.

After twenty years of incessant grind, day after weary day, I started on my first vacation. I was going home. And here I sit dying by slow degrees, desolate and forsaken. Is this the meaning of all my years of labor? Is this the end, oh God? So I might wail with equal justice. But the blind sky will not answer your appeals or mine. Nor will the cruel sea grow merciful for any prayer of ours.[27]

The Dancer recalls a specific engagement in London many years before during which she had played before the Duke who gave her the necklace, but immediate and clear reasons for her having been on the ship are lacking.

Now in the spectrum of the dramatic possibilities of her character this may not seem too important. But her immediate situational motivation breaks down in a similar fashion. Most of what the Gentleman does seems in keeping with his character. Even when he suspects the Sailor of having water and wants to "buy" it with the "real property" of the Dancer's necklace, we accept his actions as consistent with the character of a "businessman". When this fails, he simply gives up. But the Dancer suddenly decides to sell her body to the Sailor for water, as she has previously sold her body to the Duke for the necklace. The degree of her thirst, and the subsequent madness, appear at first to provide her with solid enough motivation for this lowering of herself. Yet something about the quickness of her decision – the lack of preparation for it – does not seem in keeping with her character as it has been presented. She has sold herself before, and she has loved the Second Officer of the ship; but the Duke was rich, and the Second Officer handsome. The Sailor almost responds to her offer but sinks back into his quiescence. The logic of repetitive action on the Dancer's part is there, but the general physical wretchedness of all three characters at this point in the action makes the Dancer's behavior appear highly improbable. Had the play begun before the characters' physical condition became so emaciated, perhaps the Dancer's scheme would be more dramatically probable; and had she not been quite so delicate, so sensitive, but a little more earthy (like the Sailor) perhaps, and not quite so ethereal a character, we could

[27] *Ibid.*, p. 26.

accept her action as more in keeping with the dramatic necessities of her characterization. This is not to suggest that her character is a complete failure. It can hardly be denied, however, that it would have been better in her case for the playwright to have developed the possibilities of the poetic medium of character more fully in terms of her exposed motivation for being on the ship in the first place, and in terms of her offer of sex to the Sailor in the second place.

The reader might answer that in the rush of the action of the play on stage such an objection would not occur to anyone. But this must be denied, for in the rush of reading the play through for the first time with the strict object in mind of "enjoying" the play as one imagines it being acted on a stage, one is affected by a vague but nagging disturbance at this point in her development as a character, and the dramatic illusion seems spoiled as one ceases to be completely absorbed in the action and notices his retreat from the poetic object. What has been done, then, is to try to trace in afterthought exactly what causes this lack of enjoyment at this point in the play's unfolding. Since Aristotle tells playwrights to visualize the characters as acting in scene, and also to take the parts of the characters while writing as fully as possible, in attempting to discover the problems faced by the writer based on the concrete evidence of the text one could do no better as a critic than to try to simulate at second hand that which Aristotle suggests should be a part of the playwright's activity.

As stated in the first chapter of this study, and as Professor Crane says, the use of Aristotle should entail an *extension* of his critical thinking, not a slavish imitation. Aristotle's suggestion to playwrights has been modified into a critical tool which may be used for the purpose of examining O'Neill's plays.

As we have seen, O'Neill used possibilities of character development that are more or less satisfactory in the cases of the Gentleman and the Sailor. In the case of the Dancer we see that he did not handle the possibilities of her characterization as fully as he might have had he given her some specific reason for being on the ship originally; nor did he seem to skillfully match her moral decay under pressure with the given cumulative spectrum of her character as he established it from the beginning through to her act of offering her body to the Sailor.

The next question of fact to answer is: Through what mode of representation is this experience being imitated? Clearly it is again the dramatic mode, but with a difference. As observed in *Abortion* the play seemed geared to a sense of actual time and a sense of real action. With *Thirst* the dramatist's selection of setting, odd juxtaposition of characters, and fabrication of such an extreme situation pushes his dramatic mode well past the "normal" occurrences of everyday life. So extreme does this limitation and selection appear that we begin to see the characters as symbols of universal qualities invested in man. The Sailor perhaps functions as a symbolic agent of the dormant savagery in all men; the Gentleman functions as a symbolic agent of the practical civilized world; and the Dancer functions partially as a symbolic agent of the aesthetic and spiritual qualities in all men. The setting is representative of the macrocosm, while the creatures on the raft in the center of it may represent the micro cosm in the macrocosm. Here are seen the three contending elements of most human personalities; and further, the dramatist faces them with the problem of survival. All three die, but in different ways. The Dancer dies totally mad. The Gentleman dies attempting to cling to and uphold the formal values of society. And the Sailor dies, a victim of his own savagery, because of his anger at the Gentleman who has deprived him of what is most essential to him: survival at any cost, even the reversion to the behavior of an animal – feeding on the flesh of his own kind.

One does not deride this extremity of technique, for it allows the dramatist to get directly at the ultimate problems facing his imitations of human character in a modicum of space and time. The action, because of the less casual sense of character and significance, allows a broader and more vivid kind of dramatic object to be presented than would have been possible in characters geared more closely to particular reality.[28]

---

[28]   Eugene O'Neill, "Strindberg and Our Theatre", *Provincetown Playbill*, No. 1 (Season 1923-1924). "Strindberg still remains among the most modern of moderns, the greatest interpreter in the theatre of the characteristic

Perhaps it is unfair to demand that so symbolic a play provide the kind of concrete connections found lacking in the character of the Dancer; but the play does achieve this extreme kind of tone through the use of carefully selected concrete detail in the cases of the other two characters, even to the "Union Mail Line" written across the Sailor's jersey, which realistic detail itself seems very symbolic.

We may say, then, the mode of representation through which the experience is being imitated is a highly universalized image of those major currents of behavior found in human character and projected through dramatic action in scene, which is, with the exception of the Dancer, intricately supported by probable actions and behavior and by carefully selected realistic detail utilizing a simple plot and prose dialogue.

Now let us ask the fourth question of fact: For the sake of evoking and resolving what particular sequence of expectations and emotions relative to the successive parts of the imitated object is the experience being imitated? This play presents an object that evokes a realization of suffering in the characters; yet this suffering has different effects on each of them.

As the play opens, the characters fear for their lives, and we in turn fear for them and pity their suffering. We are successively aware of degrees of fear, pity, hope that they may find an atoll, and that the Sailor will give them water, which involves suspense over the outcome. As soon as it is clear that the Gentleman's suspicions of the Sailor are obviously mad, we return again to a state of pity for the characters and begin to fear for their precarious states of mind for we have come to like them through their many previous character speeches. In other words, we have come to know them, and our fear is directed primarily at the grim possibilities threatening their established characteristics; and we are further thrown into suspense involving fear as we see their characters begin to disintegrate.

---

spiritual conflicts which constitute the drama – the blood! – of our lives today. He carried naturalism to a logical attainment of such poignant intensity that, if the work of any other playwright is to be called 'naturalism', we must classify a play like 'The Dance of Death' as 'supernaturalism' and place it in a class by itself. . . ."

Perhaps the most painful moment is the final disintegration of the Dancer's morality when she offers her body to the Sailor, because her thirst has become so great as to deprive her of further desire to maintain her moral relation to her environment. We are actually relieved by her final death, and our desire for moral stability is partially satisfied when the shock of her death restores the Gentleman to his pattern of civilized behavior as he rejects the Sailor's notion that they eat her. This is undercut by our realization of the unavoidable logic of the Sailor, and we are in partial agreement with him, even though against our will; for we know that if his suggestion is followed the two men may be able to sustain life for a while longer.

We are cast into a state of extreme anxiety, pulled one way then another as we see the Gentleman uphold morality by throwing the Dancer's body overboard because the Sailor's savagery is a threat to the Gentleman, and because we are partially sympathetic toward the Sailor. (It must be remembered here that these civilized beings have treated him rather badly, and that up until this point he has remained innocent of becoming involved in their neurotic fantasies – which might be a result of their very refinement, which refinement does not always appear attractive to us.)

The terrible state of anxiety produced in us by these conflicting factors (our sympathy for savage innocence balanced against our desire for morality) is released as the characters destroy one another.

The victory of either one in this situation would have been very dissatisfying, and would have left us in a state of turmoil. The balancing of the two basic forces (savage innocence and civilized morality) in death at least provides a resolution for our anxiety, as the death of the Dancer has released us from the pain of seeing the artistic sensibility suffer in its own peculiar way. Into this resolution of anxiety there flows a great sense of pity for the common lot of all men faced by the ineluctable dilemma of this imitated situation. This pity is not purged, but is magnified in us, and conditioned this time by an anger at the inertia of the recalcitrant environment imitated in the play.

Whereas the characters in *Abortion* are pitied because of their lot in society, in this play the characters are pitied because of their lot in the environment of earth; and by an imaginative leap to the universal significance of this highly symbolic play we feel pity for the common lot of man in the cosmos. And we agree with the above quotation from the Gentleman: "Nor will the cruel sea grow merciful for any prayer of ours."

On the strength of the above evidence it is safe to call this imitated experience an imitation that uses as its central controlling or formal principle the revelation of a practically complete change in the moral character of the Dancer; revelation of comparative stability in the moral character of the Gentleman; and a partial change in the moral character of the Sailor, utilizing a reversion to the innate savage elements present in his character when the play opens. All this being brought on by action, and made apparent in itself and in thought and feeling. In the case of the Gentleman and the case of the Sailor the possibilities of the poetic medium of character are realized in a probable and coherent manner; whereas in the case of the Dancer, the possibilities of her characterization are not as fully realized as they could be, and her moral decay under pressure is not as skillfully matched as possible with the cumulative spectrum of her character at the final point of its disintegration. The mode through which this experience is being represented is a highly universalized dramatic imitation of those major currents of behavior found in human character, utilizing a simple plot for the most part intricately supported by probable actions and by carefully selected realistic detail, which is accomplished in prose dialogue. Pity for the characters is induced by their attractive qualities and by the progressive disintegration of the Dancer and the Sailor; and great anxiety is induced by the struggle between the morality of the Gentleman and the savage innocence of the Sailor, which is resolved in the death of both, giving rise to an even greater pity for them, and, perhaps by universal extension, pity for the lot of all men in the cosmos. This is qualified by an emotion of anger at the inertia of the ineluctable hostility of the environment of the characters and again, by extension, the ineluctable hostility of the cosmos toward all men.

The above statement regarding the form (mode of existence) of this play involves the method of the "multiple working hypotheses" as it was described in Chapter One.

A general description of the role of Nemesis in this structure may now be inducted from the above particulars. After factually describing what this play is in terms of structure and form, it appears that Nemesis as a material idea is even more prominent here than it was in *Abortion*. The *lex talionis* (distributive justice) seems the most important material element of Nemesis employed in the structure. The distribution and attainment of water, a basic life sustaining ingredient, is the central problem faced by all three characters. But O'Neill uses this in a special way. In this tragedy of character there is actually no water to be justly distributed, yet the Dancer and the Gentleman, maddened by their need for water, suspect the Sailor of concealing it. It is quite certain that the Sailor has broken the law of the sea, however, for though he has no water now, the Gentleman tells the Dancer:

THE GENTLEMAN – (*With mad eagerness to prove his fixed idea.*) 'No he has no food. There has never been any food. But there has been water. There was a whole small cask full of it on the raft when I came. On the second or third night, I do not remember which, I awoke and saw him draining the cask. When I reached it, it was empty.' (*Furiously shaking his fist at the negro's back.*) 'Oh you pig! You rotten pig!' (*The negro does not seem to hear.*) [29]

The rules of disaster survival on the sea are rigid. All life sustaining goods, such as water and food, are to be strictly and equitably rationed among the survivors by someone appointed to administer the distribution. The Sailor has broken this law, the observance of which might have sustained not only himself but all three of the characters until they might drift near an atoll where water and food might have been had in abundance. As pointed out in the discussion of the play's structure, the characters are isolated from any contact with retributive justice which may be exacted from them on the basis of social or reasoned forms. They are thrown directly on the law of nature, the law

[29]   O'Neill, *Thirst* . . . , p. 30.

of survival, in this case depending upon the equitable distribution of life materials (really an extension of social or reasoned justice that may apply in such emergencies), and they are subject to retaliation, a primitive kind of retribution. Thus, the bad treatment and abuse the Sailor suffers from the two other characters is partially justified.

The Sailor's breaking of the law has destroyed the possibility of establishing the emergency or survival system (which, as said, is an extension of retributive social, reasoned justice), and through having put the characters in this situation O'Neill has intensified and reduced the *lex talionis* to terms that effectively isolate the individuals and force them to the most basic terms of the law of the claw, each man for himself – or dog eat dog. The artist and the savage are the first to fall to this level of animal survival; but the Gentleman retains, even at the cost of his life, his essentially human pattern of behavior, however empty we may think his code is.

Looking at the whole situation, the Nemesis visited on the characters is not justly a balancing of accounts; for though the characters are not perfect, they are not totally depraved and only two of them become so as their characters are subjected to the particular action with which the play deals.

Their Nemesis then, in terms of their whole lives seems to go beyond what is just, or what is deserved. But in analyzing their particular character development with the focus on how they behave in this particular dramatic situation, we see that (in a qualified sense) the Nemesis visited on the Dancer is partially deserved, and in the case of the Sailor partially deserved, whereas in the case of the Gentleman, the upholder of civilized behavior and morality to the bitter end, his death at the hands of the Sailor seems (from the standpoint of retributive, socially reasoned justice) to be wholly beyond what is just. But considering the terms to which O'Neill has reduced the situation – survival of the fittest – ironically enough the Gentleman has opposed himself as violently to that law as the Sailor has opposed himself to the emergency extension of social justice. In that sense then, the Gentleman has broken the most basic law, survival of the fittest (for the Dancer has died of natural causes before the other two men and should provide sustenance for them according to the reduced system in which O'Neill has placed his characters); therefore, according to the dramatic logic of the special way in which O'Neill has utilized and shaped the material idea of Nemesis in this play, even the Gentleman's death is partially deserved, for his actions have gone beyond what is just in these special circumstances.

From the standpoint of the above analysis we may say that the *lex talionis* has been reduced by the shaping pressures of O'Neill's dramatic technique to the most cruel and basic form imaginable, and that it forms the greatest element of Nemesis in the play in terms of sheer material quantity. Through other dramatic pressures O'Neill has destroyed even the emergency survival extension of retributive or social justice, and at the same time has not employed ideas of divine justice directly in his text.

Thus we are forced to conclude that tragic justice resides in the absolute quality of the most brutal form of the *lex talionis* in this play, the law of the survival of the fittest, the law of the claw, which only the Gentleman breaks effectively as the shock of the Dancer's death returns him momentarily to sanity. But this return reëstablishes at the last moment social justice in the person of the gentleman, who, inadvertently, brought face to face with the law of the claw in the character of the Sailor, destroys and is destroyed by the *lex talionis*. Tragic justice, the final Nemesis, then, is a perfect balance established between the symbolic representatives of the two extreme forms of law in their mutual destruction. Balance is restored in death, the final Nemesis, and neither form of justice triumphs.

The characters call on God in the play, but God and the environment appear bent on the destruction of the characters. The environment is totally hostile. The symbol of distributive justice, the "real property" of the Dancer's necklace, is stared down upon by the sun which seems "like a great angry eye of God".[30] Ultimate justice, then, in the sense of divine Nemesis, is served

<hr>

[30]   *Ibid.*, p. 43.

on the characters through shipwreck before the play begins. This Nemesis cannot be called poetic justice, for it appears the characters are meted out a punishment that goes beyond the exact degree of their sin, though each in his own way is partially good and partially evil. Their imperfection *qua* imperfection without reference to any possible or established good in them is reason enough for so horrible a Nemesis to catch them in its nets; and from this it may be seen that the ultimate source of Nemesis stems from a "jealous God", or *phthonos*,[31] for man's insolence and satiety – a truly Greek idea.

THE MOON OF THE CARIBBEES

This play is perhaps one of the most intriguing O'Neill wrote. It appears to be unconventionally structured on first sight. It seems to make its own rules of form, and for that reason it will be more difficult to describe than the two plays just dealt with.

Before answering the question of the kind of human experience this play is imitating, let us look first at what seems to happen in the play. The Glencairn, a British tramp steamer, lies at anchor off an island in the West Indies, suffused by the radiance of the full moon. The setting consists of the forward section of the ship about which seven seamen are lounging. They are Yank, Driscoll, Olson, Davis, Cocky, Smitty, and Paul. With them lounge Lamps, the lamp trimmer, Chips, the carpenter, Old Tom, the donkeyman, and four of the ship's firemen. The firemen are Big Frank, Dick, Max, and Paddy. Later the sailors are joined by four West Indian Negro women: Bella, Susie, Violet, and Pearl. Two other seamen are also there, Scotty and Ivan; and the other sailors are present but not identified by name. The First Mate of the Glencairn appears toward the end of the action. In all there are twenty-one characters named plus several extras not named. This is quite a difference from the previous two plays studied, which

---

[31]   Greene, p. 6. "Indeed he may for a time suppose that mere prosperity, apart from any misdeed, may involve a man in such *ate* because it has aroused the jealousy* (*phthonos**) of the gods. . . ."

had many fewer characters: seven, in the cast of *Abortion* (plus a crowd of students); and three in the cast of *Thirst*.

As the action opens most of the sailors are sitting on the forward hatch, which is covered with canvas and battened down for the night. "A melancholy Negro chant, faint and far off, drifts, crooning, over the water." [32] The sailors are engaged in several group conversations and are smoking as the curtain rises.

Their conversation lulls into silence shortly thereafter, and the singing from the land stands out clearly.

Smitty is immediately recognized through his response to Driscoll as a "touchy fellow". Smitty speaks the second line in the play in which he indicates the singing makes him sad. Cocky indulges in some horseplay, slapping Smitty on the back and telling him not to worry, because "She loves yer".[33] Smitty resumes his dreamy-eyed musing, seemingly unconscious of his surroundings.

The men, led by Cocky, indulge in more playful conversation and tall tales.

Driscoll informs the crew that Bella and her girls have promised to bring rum. The men settle down, relight their pipes, and wait in anticipation of the fun.

While waiting for the women and the rum, Smitty again voices his irritation at the native songs.

The men get Driscoll to sing a sea chanty. He chooses "Blow the Man Down", in which everyone joins, except Smitty who broods alone on the forecastle head.

The women are heard approaching. The men grow tense with anticipation while the women are aft on the bridge clearing with the Captain. We learn that Bella has brought the Captain two high-color women.

Cocky makes some bragging comments about women, and Paddy calls him "A 'airy ape. . . ." [34] Cocky puts his hand on his sheath-knife, but they are separated by the crew.

Driscoll comes forward, having helped the women aboard and

---

[32] O'Neill, *The Plays of* . . . , I, 455.
[33] *Ibid.*, p. 456.
[34] *Ibid.*, p. 461.

to the bridge, tells the men the price of a pint of rum, and the men complain bitterly about Bella's price cheating. He pulls out a bottle and all begin drinking.

Bella (old and ugly), Susie, Violet, and Pearl enter, giggling and whispering. The liquor is distributed with Bella's warning that the Captain has given strict orders against it.

They all start into the forecastle to divide up the women and liquor to avoid detection by the Captain. But Pearl (the prettiest) on Yank's arm stops, attracted to the young mustachioed Englishman, Smitty. Smitty rebuffs Pearl's advances, and she goes into the forecastle in a huff.

Smitty begins consuming the rum purchased from Pearl and complaining to the donkeyman about the mournful chant of the Negroes again, which is still plainly heard. A long discussion of Smitty's troubles ensues (consisting of haunting memories of a woman, brought on by the music). Smitty winds it up with his characteristic bluntness: "I'll trouble you not to pry into my affairs, Donkeyman." [35]

Pearl and Yank come out of the forecastle, and an exchange takes place between Smitty and Pearl over his remaining alone, the kernel of which is found in Smitty's words: "Thinking and (*he indicates the bottle in his hand*) – drinking to stop thinking. (*He drinks and laughs maudlinly. The bottle is three-quarters empty*.)" [36] A flirting scene follows between Pearl and Smitty, with Pearl taking the initiative. As Smitty prepares to leave with her, Yank stumbles drunkenly toward them; Smitty says with characteristic suddenness and lack of tact: "Right it is, Yank. But you're wrong about this girl. She isn't with me. She was just going back to the fo'c's'tle to you. (*Pearl looks at him with hatred gathering in her eyes.*)" [37]

Engaging people into his confidence and then thoughtlessly rebuffing them seems to be Smitty's one preoccupation in the play. He does so first with Cocky, then with the donkeyman, and

---

[35]   *Ibid.*, p. 467.
[36]   *Ibid.*, p. 468.
[37]   *Ibid.*, p. 469.

now with Pearl. This is exactly what he has done with the woman
who is so much in his memory.

The whole crowd now pours out on deck and begins to dance,
accompanied by Paul's accordian on which he plays "You Great
Big Beautiful Doll". The crowd gets louder. Someone smashes
a bottle on deck. Pearl and Yank pass Smitty who has remained
aloof, and Pearl slaps his face with real vehemence. Smitty only
smiles bitterly when he sees who has slapped him. Paddy trips
Cocky and Susie, who are dancing. They fall flat on the deck.
Cocky rises and springs at Paddy, who knocks him down. Driscoll
hits Paddy and Big Frank hits Driscoll. The stage is inundated
in a roiling brawl with everyone fighting, though it seems to be
generally the seamen against the firemen. A knife flashes high
in the moonlight. Someone yells with pain, while another shouts
that the Mate is coming. Everyone scurries toward the forecastle
to hide. Yank and Driscoll remain, bending over the still form
of Paddy, wondering who has knifed him.

The Mate enters, discovers Paddy's wound is only a flesh
wound, and detects the scent of liquor. Driscoll and Yank carry
Paddy off. The Mate orders the women off the ship without their
money, for the Captain has orderd that if they bring the men
liquor they are not to be paid. Everyone leaves except Smitty
(who has continued daydreaming all this while) and the donkeyman.

The crooning of the natives on shore becomes plainer. The
donkeyman bids Smitty good night telling him he will not be
able to hear the Negroes crooning in the forecastle, and that
there will be more liquor there in which to drown his melancholy.
Smitty says good night. The donkeyman enters the forecastle.

Smitty "gets wearily to his feet and walks with bowed shoulders,
staggering a bit to the forecastle entrance and goes in. There is
silence for a second or so, broken only by the haunted, saddened
voice of that brooding music, faint and far-off, like the mood of
the moonlight made audible." 38

What kind of human experience is this play imitating? In the

---

38   *Ibid.*, p. 474.

case of *Abortion* the experience of action was the controlling principle of the imitation; in the case of *Thirst,* character seemed central. It will be recalled that Crane says there are mainly three kinds of plots: action, character, and thought. But he also says "for what he must do and can do at any point will differ widely according as he is imitating a character, a state of passion, or an action".

The writer proposes to solve this dilemma for his own purposes by adding a fourth type of plot to Crane's categories, the plot of *passion*. Surely "passion" is closely related to "character", but on the evidence presented above in regard to what happens in *The Moon of the Caribbees,* we cannot say it involves primarily "complete alteration in moral character, brought on or controlled by action, and made apparent in itself and in thought and feeling". Rather, the type of experience being imitated in this play involves primarily complete alteration in subjective passion, brought on and controlled by character, made apparent in itself in action and in thought. But Smitty's "subjective passion" does not undergo "complete alteration". It does not even change significantly. What is actually seen is a sustained state of subjective passion, brought on and controlled by character, and made apparent in itself in action and in thought.

A consideration of the possibilities of the poetic medium of passion, through which the experience is being imitated, will indicate that many other courses were open to O'Neill in accomplishing his imitation of the experience of the particular degree and kind of passion with which he deals.

Smitty's maudlin melancholy could have been more clearly verbalized. He could have been given long speeches expressing the faintest nuance of his melancholy. But, given Smitty's characteristic action, such a verbal display would not seem dramatically probable on his part. Smitty does not see that the reason he is isolated first from the woman he is remembering, then from the crew, and finally from the woman Pearl exists in his selfish bids for sympathy, which he characteristically follows by blunt, sudden, tactless, cruel, and senseless rejection of the familiarity he establishes through his maudlin appeals. O'Neill has chosen to have him say very little, and to show successive withdrawal at critical points in the action, and to make him brood alone and aloof, while his aloneness and aloofness are contrasted against the busy activity of the crew.

It is not likely that a man so blind, so insensitive to the effect his actions have on those around him, would be intelligent or sensitive enough to delicately or completely verbalize his melancholy.

O'Neill has also employed spectacle in terms of the setting splashed with moonlight and the melody of the continuous crooning of the Negroes on shore (contrasted with the rowdy "Blow the Man Down" the crew sings) to fully mirror the watery sadness, the pastel blue passion of which Smitty is capable internally.

But these elements also, because of their omnipresence, provide a further contrast in relation to which Smitty's little blueness seems quite insignificant. The characters all seem worse than most men. Smitty's sadness appears insignificant beside the brooding melancholy of the setting: the crew's activity seems pointless, and both are contrasted against the "immense, immeasurable, emptiness of things".[39]

Considering the many possibilities open to O'Neill for sustaining this mood or passion in the character of Smitty as it is contrasted against the larger, ineluctable sadness of the moon, the sea, and the land in conjunction, his technique seems highly satisfactory within the given necessities of his medium.

The mode of course is dramatic, all characters speaking in scene, and contributing more or less to the imitation of the passion of melancholy. But unlike *Abortion*, in which the dramatic mode was geared to a semblance of actual time and action unfolding with a giddy swiftness, and unlike *Thirst*, in which the situation was so extreme as to seem in violent contrast to actual experience, *The Moon of the Caribbees* sustains, through what seems a casual and complex selection of realistic detail, a delicate and phantasmagoric mood utilizing a simple plot and prose

---

[39]   Theodore Roethke, "The Dying Man: in Memoriam: W. B. Yeats, '5 They Sing, They Sing' ", *Words for the Wind* (Garden City, New York, Doubleday & Company, Inc., 1958), p. 190.

dialogue. This technique does not employ obvious and violent contrasts of seemingly symbolic proportions; but rather it employs an intricate selection of detail that gradually builds a specially qualified mood wherein the borders of contrast appear to fade magically into one another, as Smitty's aloofness and little blue passion are contrasted against the hectic activity of the crew and the immense panorama of the setting.

For the sake of evoking and resolving what particular sequence of expectations and emotions relative to the successive parts of the imitated object is the experience being imitated? The melancholy activity of the crew as the play opens, and the quiet and warm somnambulance of the scene intrigue us. The withdrawal of Smitty is at once made apparent, and as the mood builds with his further withdrawal and the contrasting noise and hectic activity of the crew, we are less inclined to become excited over the outcome than to realize the insignificance and isolation of Smitty and the other characters. They probably do not excite our pity. Rather, we take on their essential melancholy (apparent even in the pointless and frenetic quality of their attempt to escape through physical activity – sex and liquor).

The overall sadness of the play as poetic object steadily builds to the climax of intensity of mood in the few seconds remaining in the play after Smitty goes into the forecastle. The sudden emptiness of the stage and setting heightens the intensity of the passion of melancholy, which is underscored by the moonlight and the return of the melancholy chant of the Negroes, making us aware of the "immense, immeasurable emptiness of things" restored to what seems its proper dignity – the dignity of grandeur and peace (effected through the cessation of the crew's insignificant noise and the disappearance of Smitty's little blue passion).

The sustained passion is not resolved; it is steadily built and brought to a moment of the most intense beauty, as those factors which have marred it (the noisy crew, the little blueness of Smitty) are magically erased from the scene by the dramatist's removal of the crew and Smitty from the stage.

From the answers to these four questions of fact we must now synthesize a description of the mode of existence of the play, in other words a description of the play's form. The form of this play consists of a sustained state of subjective passion, brought on and controlled by character, and made apparent in itself, in action, and in thought. This involves characters that seem worse than most men; the protagonist's melancholy seeming insignificant beside the melancholy of the setting; the crew's activity seeming pointless. The protagonist and crew are contrasted against the "immense, immeasurable, emptiness of things". All this is accomplished through what appears a casual selection of realistic detail in the dramatic mode that sustains a delicate and phantasmagoric mood utilizing a simple plot and prose dialogue, wherein the borders of contrast seem to fade into one another. The sustained passion is not resolved, but steadily built and brought to a moment of the most intense beauty when the noisy crew and the little blueness of Smitty are removed from the scene. This in turn qualifies the passion of melancholy by returning the scene to its original dignity and grandeur.

Nemesis in this play, as in *Thirst*, seems closely related to the laws of the sea. The "little" acts of Smitty beget his continual melancholy and loneliness, his Nemesis; but the crew are soundly brought to task when one of their members is wounded by a knife. This seems to be a direct result of their breaking the Captain's orders regarding the prohibition of liquor on board.

Social or reasoned justice, retributive justice, is exacted from the women in their not receiving pay as a result of their having broken the command of the Captain – the supreme administrator of law at sea. O'Neill utilizes the law of the claw (a feud between Cocky and Paddy) to bring an end to the crew's merriment, the actual riot resulting from the crew's breaking the command of the Captain not to drink liquor while on board.

Nemesis in terms of the *lex talionis* is clearly exacted as Cocky stabs Paddy because Paddy has first tripped and then knocked Cocky down – this final precipitation having been foreshadowed by Cocky's putting his hand on his sheath-knife earlier, when Paddy called him a hairy ape.

Yet the Captain's social retribution, the Nemesis that overtakes the women, is clearly spelled out by invoking a retributive Nemesis or justice in the case of the women by depriving them of their pay, material goods. But, as is made quite clear, the source of this social Nemesis, the Captain, is as imperfect as the crew; for, we learn, he commits adultery with the two women Bella brings especially for him.

Tragic Nemesis, Smitty's continual isolation and helpless melancholy, seems to stem from his inability to relate to others – some internal flaw in him, some flaw in his will; yet the mood depends on the contrast of Smitty's maudlin isolation, the crew's pointless activity, and the women's ruined savage innocence, as all three factors are significant when considered in the light of the omnipresent moon, sea, and land. The ultimate punishment of these creatures seems to be their contributing to their own insignificance, frustration, and deprivation by their fruitless interest in money (Bella and the girls), escape pleasures (the crew), and solipsism (Smitty).

Their ultimate Nemesis resides in their continued insignificance, to which they contribute and for which they are partially responsible. The ultimate justice of the cosmos, symbolized by the land, the sea, and the moon seems to be in remaining intensely beautiful when it is not marred by the presence of such insignificant creatures as those this play imitates. When the stage is empty of them, the grand beauty of the cosmos is restored and Nemesis enacted on the creatures who marred it.

This environment, unlike the environment imitated in *Thirst,* is not hostile but beautiful, and its beauty is marred by the imitated characters. The comparatively innocent crooning of the natives, sad and melancholy, is "like the mood of the moonlight made audible".

O'Neill has created here a truly delicate dramatic form, one that is neither properly tragic nor comic, but somewhere in between; and the fine shading of this dramatic form as O'Neill has been able to realize it is nowhere even envisaged or suggested in Aristotle, though Aristotle's complex system of analysis, as further refined by Crane, can be extended to accurately describe that which the form is.

CONCLUSION

The writer has now examined the three plays selected from the three collections of O'Neill's earlier efforts. It will be helpful to discover whether or not this formal analysis of the plays in terms of the role of Nemesis in them is in agreement or disagreement with the criticism already published on the plays.

There is no thoroughgoing, careful criticism of the *Lost Plays*. There are only quick, book review estimates of the collection as a whole, and of course Lawrence Gellert's preface written especially for the volume, which has already been cited. Gellert's estimate of the plays is the most favorable, but he seems to think that *Abortion* is excellent because the young playwright "can fashion a sociological capsule".[40] A better basis for this evaluation, however, would be O'Neill's practically perfect handling of dramatic technique, especially in terms of probability of action and character.

There is also Clark's completely negative position on the plays:

As I said, the "Lost Plays" adds nothing of importance to the study of O'Neill. In O'Neill's book *Thirst* you will find early plays that are immature and not very interesting. Intrinsically, the "lost" plays are dull, and my hope is that no one already familiar with the later work will get his first impressions of O'Neill by looking at them.[41]

After the analysis of *Abortion* this writer finds it impossible to agree with the above estimate of the *Lost Plays*. They have been important to this study of O'Neill, and they are anything but "dull". Certainly this was not Clark's opinion of one of the *Lost Plays, The Sniper*:

I read a script of *The Sniper* when I was going through the files at the office of The Provincetown Playhouse, perhaps the only one in existence. It is far better than most of the plays in *Thirst*. . . . Sentimental though much of the writing is, *The Sniper* is none the less an exciting little scene.[42]

---

[40]   O'Neill, *Lost Plays of* . . . , "Introduction", by Lawrence Gellert, p. 8.
[41]   Clark, "Lost Plays of Eugene O'Neill", *Theatre Arts*, p. 7.
[42]   Barrett H. Clark, *Eugene O'Neill: The Man and His Plays* (New York, Dover Publications, Inc., 1947), p. 54.

Clark had either drastically changed his opinion of *The Sniper* when he published his review of the *Lost Plays*, or under the pressure of his friend's distress at their publication allowed his estimate of *The Sniper* to go by the board.

This writer's critical estimate of the *Lost Plays* as a whole follows point by point Saul Colin's:

And all, despite understandable limitations and weaknesses and being somewhat dated, not only are interesting historically, in light of the author's subsequent development, but also are interesting intrinsically and are extremely stageable.[43]

As a matter of fact, *Abortion* appears to be superior in technique to anything in the *Thirst* volume, and with the exception of *A Wife for a Life*, all the plays in the *Lost Plays* seem to this writer far superior to the plays in the *Thirst* volume (though it must be remembered that *The Sniper* came a full year after the publication of the *Thirst* collection).

The one review of publication *Thirst* received was Clayton Hamilton's:

Another playwright of promise is Mr. Eugene O'Neill – a son of the noted actor, Mr. James O'Neill – who has recently published five one-act plays under the title of *Thirst*. This writer's favourite mood is that of horror. He deals with grim and ghastly situations that would become intolerable if they were protracted beyond the limits of a single sudden act. He seems to be familiar with the sea; for three of these five plays deal with terrors that attend the tragedy of ship-wreck. He shows a keen sense of the reactions of character under stress of violent emotion; and his dialogue is almost brutal in its power.[44]

It is striking in the light of subsequent criticism (which practically always attacks O'Neill's dialogue) that the first review of his published work should point to the "brutal power" of O'Neill's dialogue, which is certainly true of some of the dialogue in *Thirst*, especially of the Sailor's speech, "We shall eat. We shall drink".[45]

---

[43]   Saul Colin, "Without O'Neill's Imprimatur", *New York Times*, June 18, 1950, p. 4.
[44]   Hamilton, *Bookman*, XLI, 182.
[45]   O'Neill, *Thirst* . . . , p. 42.

Clark said much later of *Thirst*:

The play is written in an exaggerated, violent and rhetorical style, but there is undeniably an air of sincerity about it.

· · · · · · · · · · · · · · · · · · · ·
The best that can be said of *Thirst* is that it is a forthright and daring melodramatic scene.[46]

Clark seems to object to the violence and rhetoric of the style primarily because he does not accept the extremity of O'Neill's technique in this particular play, which moves, as it does, in a highly wrought, symbolic dramatic world, which is yet supported by a more or less skillfully executed selection of realistic detail in the best Ibsen tradition. One thinks especially of Ibsen's *When We Dead Awaken*. Even Strindberg's violence is supported in this plausible manner in *The Father* and *Miss Julie*.

In this writer's opinion, the most sensitive criticism of *The Moon of the Caribbees* comes from an Italian, S. d'Amico:

Ne *La luna dei Caraibi* il dramma non nasce da un intrigo purchessaia: consiste unicamente in un sèguito di scene descrittive, sulla tolda d'un piroscafo inglese ancorato al lido d'un isoletta dell' Indi occidentali, fra marinaie femmine di colore salito abordo, sotto la luna che imbianca il mare e la barbara terra, di cui si sento il respiro.

· · · · · · · · · · · · · · · · · · · ·
Da questi drammetti dove il mare, invisibile e onnipresente, s'è come assunto la parte del Fato, s'esprime un senso d'attrazione, e, insieme, di repulsione, d'incanto maledetto, di schiavitù deprecata e ineluttabile, che gia aveva ispirato il citato Synge nei suoi belissimi *Cavalcatori a mare,* ma che qui risulta da un disegno, se non più perfetto, più ampio, in insistenti motivi sinfonici, d' una tremenda risonanza.[47]

George Pierce Baker also recognized the tremendous mood power of this piece resulting from O'Neill's brilliant imitation of the little blue passion of Smitty as contrasted against the overwhelming beauty and melancholic charm of the tranquil moon, sea, and land in conjunction.

---

[46]   Clark, *Eugene O'Neill: . . .* , 1947 ed., p. 51.
[47]   S. d'Amico, "I primi drammi di O'Neill", *Nuova Antologia*, CCCLXV (January 16, 1933), 298, 299 respectively. This item does not appear in Miller's bibliography referred to on page 6 of this study.

When in "The Moon of the Caribbees" the atmosphere of the place, the sounds, became almost a force, even a character, it was clear that as situation had led O'Neill into character, now character was leading him to think of the forces, the subtlest influences, which work compellingly on men and women who believe themselves free agents.[48]

Thus we find O'Neill, Baker, and d'Amico generally concurring about the overwhelming quality of the mood of this piece which comes from the controlling form of the piece, the imitation of a clearly delineated state of passion, of the most delicate hue in Smitty, and just as delicate but of much more vast a magnitude in the setting (see the quotation of O'Neill's letter to Clark and the subsequent note, page 19, this study). *The Dial* reviewer pretty well concurs with the above cited criticism (see note 7, page 28, this study), but finds the action "halting" and the motivation "commonplace"; as well they have to be considering that O'Neill is not primarily imitating an action, but a passion, and also considering the fact that he is imitating "commonplace" characters rather than heroic ones.

We find C. Jones also concurring on the power of the mood established in *Moon* when he says:

The dramatist uses the sea to produce moods, as he uses drums in *Emperor Jones*. His tone is always serious, even the moonlight in *Moon of the Caribbees* gives a ghostly pallor, the surf on the beach is a mocking whisper.[49]

It seems accurate to say at this point that O'Neill was on the road to world-wide recognition with the publication of his collection of plays *The Moon of the Caribbees, and Six Other Plays of the Sea* (New York, Boni and Liveright, June, 1919). The above critical commentary represents only a small portion of the reception given these plays on publication, and on the subsequent re-issues of the volume.

The structured form of *Abortion* seems quite Aristotelian and

[48]   George Pierce Baker, "O'Neill's First Decade", *Yale Review*, XV (July, 1926), 790.
[49]   C. Jones, "A Sailor's O'Neill", *Revue anglo-americaine*, XII (February, 1935), 228.

utilizes a complex plot in his sense of the word. Action is the controlling principle, and this action involves as a synthesizing principle a complete and quick change in the main character's situation which is determined by the nature of his character and by the quality of his thought. Jack is not, however, exactly like an Aristotelian tragic protagonist as his lineage is not so illustrious. This play further departs from Aristotelian form in that terror is purged in Jack's suicide; but pity is not purged, it is magnified. The probability of the action is amazingly consistent within itself in view of the fact that the playwright was comparatively inexperienced. The whole emotional impact of the play is further qualified by the inducement of a certain kind of anger at the crowd because of its ignorance of the situation.

Thirst seems an imitation of an experience that uses as its central controlling, or formal principle, the revelation of a comparative stability in the moral character of the Gentleman, and a partial change in the moral character of the Sailor, utilizing a reversion to the innate savage elements present in his character when the play begins. All this is accomplished through the creation of a simple plot, and a highly universalized dramatic imitation of those major currents of behavior found in human character supported by more or less probable actions, and by carefully selected realistic detail and prose dialogue. Pity is aroused for the characters, which is then followed by anxiety about which code of behavior will be victorious: savage innocence or civilized morality. This anxiety is resolved in the death of the Sailor and the Gentleman, for neither code is victorious. But pity is magnified by the ultimate phthonos of the cosmic God personified in the setting, and perhaps a universal pity for man in an angry cosmos is achieved.

The form of *The Moon of the Caribbees* consists of a sustained state of subjective passion brought on and controlled by character and made apparent in itself and in action and thought, involving characters that seem worse than most men, Smitty's little blue melancholy seeming small and insignificant against the melancholy dignity and grandeur of the cosmos imitated in the moon, the sea, and the land. This all seems accomplished through a casual selection of realistic detail in a manner that sustains and magnifies a delicate and phantasmagoric mood, utilizing a simple plot wherein the borders of contrast seem to fade into one another, as the sustained passion is not resolved but steadily built to a moment of intensest beauty.

The Nemesis wreaked on Jack in *Abortion* is self-inflicted. The idea of social justice is shown to be abortive in the play as it becomes the instrument of Murray's personal hatred, and is thus equated with the *lex talionis,* or personal vengeance. Tragic justice seems rooted in the need for common human sympathy, outside the demands of an eye for an eye, or even social justice (the society's code being inadequate in the play), and outside the divine (significant dramatic considerations of which never occur in the play), so that we are finally left, as in Sophocles' *Antigone,* with a justice, Nemesis, or retribution based primarily on the demands of the "unwritten laws" of common human decency, the knowledge of which exists in the individual.

In *Thirst* we see the *lex talionis* has been reduced by the shaping pressures of O'Neill's dramatic technique to the most cruel and basic form, survival of the fittest, and that this forms the greatest material element of Nemesis in this play; and we see also that through other dramatic pressures O'Neill has destroyed even the emergency survival extension of retributive or social justice, while at the same time not using the idea of divine Nemesis *directly* in the action of his play. *Phthonos,* the jealousy of God at the imperfection *qua* imperfection of the characters without reference to any good that may be in them, seems the source of ultimate Nemesis of this play.

The Moon of the Caribbees utilizes the *lex talionis* in conflict with retributive social justice. This is represented respectively by the commands of the Captain (social law at sea), by the breaking of his command, resulting in the personal vengeance of Cocky being enacted on Paddy, by the Captain's subsequently punishing the women (invaders from the land) and invoking a retributive justice on them (related to the *lex talionis*), through depriving them of their money which was to be paid for their goods. Smitty is visited with the Nemesis of isolation, stemming from his breaking the "unwritten laws" of decency between human beings. All this is balanced against the ultimate Nemesis of the cosmos, which in the tranquil beauty of its melancholy seems to visit the Nemesis of insignificance on these characters, who contribute actively to their own insignificance, frustration, and deprivation through their fruitless interest in money, escape, and solipsism.

Abortion, primarily an action in its formal nature, utilizes the tragic Nemesis of the "unwritten laws"; *Thirst,* primarily a play of character in its formal nature, utilizes the ultimate Nemesis of *phthonos,* not involved in its character development but imitated in its setting; *The Moon of the Caribbees,* primarily a play of passion in its formal nature, utilizes the ultimate Nemesis of continual insignificance actively brought on by the characters themselves as they are contrasted with the eternal *dike,* or just beauty of the cosmos.

III

THE HAIRY APE[1]

With this chapter the examination of O'Neill's major work begins. The order of this examination, as it turns out, will be chronological, embracing a cross section of the work. There has been no attempt here to rigidly classify the playwright's work, nor any attempt to find a strict relation between the chronology of the work and its classification into types. No such relation exists so far as I can ascertain.

Roughly, the principle I have followed may be described as follows. O'Neill had an early period in which he produced successful works of major proportions. In this early period he produced several successful works quite conventional in nature, and interspersed between the production of these conventional works were his (equally successful commercially) experimental works which are usually called "expressionistic". The principle of selection here has been an aesthetic one based primarily on excellence of structure.

Two experimental plays stand out in this period from this point of view as being the best of the experimental plays: *The Emperor Jones* and *The Hairy Ape*. I have, rather arbitrarily, selected *The Hairy Ape* for analysis.

From the group of conventionally naturalistic plays of this

---

[1] The edition of *The Hairy Ape* to which I shall refer throughout this chapter appears in *The Plays of Eugene O'Neill* (New York, Random House, 1955), III, 206-254. All subsequent references to the texts of the plays will refer to this edition, with the exception of *Long Day's Journey into Night* (New Haven, Connecticut, Yale University Press, 1960). Hereafter references to the texts of the plays will be indicated by "Random House" or by "Yale".

first period this writer has selected, again using the general principle of structural excellence, *Desire under the Elms.*

The second period of O'Neill's success is marked primarily by the exceptionally long experimental plays, which again were produced not in a lump but interspersed with the continuing production of experimental normal length plays, and more conventional plays of normal length. From these longer plays *Mourning Becomes Electra* has been selected as inestimably superior.

After *Days Without End* there was a twelve year silence in terms of publication. This was broken with the publication of *The Iceman Cometh,* and continued through the posthumous publication of *More Stately Mansions.*[2] This is often referred to as the "later period" in O'Neill's career, and again, experiment was interspersed with convention. One experimental play, *The Iceman Cometh,* has been selected from this period; and one more conventional play, *Long Day's Journey into Night,* in keeping with the previous principle of cross sectional analysis.

There will be no "summary" of criticism for this chapter. The researcher has discovered that enough of the criticism of the major work is of sufficient depth and complexity to be used as evidence in developing the "multiple working hypotheses" this study employs. Thus, pertinent published criticism of the plays will be integrated from this point on in the development of each chapter.

Beginning as previously in examining the earlier work of the playwright, a brief of *The Hairy Ape* is presented below.

Scene one takes place in the fireman's forecastle of an ocean liner one hour after sailing from New York. Yank brags about his towering strength. Someone breaks into a sentimental love ballad. Yank silences him, saying that the work they do, though it is done in a hellish place which they must call home, can be done only by men. Long starts a social protest speech, using Yank's words for ammunition. Yank cuts him off. The men hoot Long down. Paddy begins to reflect on the dignity of men who went down to the sea in sailing ships. Yank takes up this chal-

---

[2] (New Haven, Yale University Press, 1964).

lenge and attempts to out argue Paddy. Paddy merely laughs at
Yank and sings two lines from the "Miller of Dee", which state
"I care for nobody, no, not I, / And nobody cares for me". Yank
essentially agrees with this song's message. But Paddy answers
that he is not a slave like Yank. Paddy says he is content with
his dreams. Yank condemns him for this and strides out as the
scene ends.

Scene two opens in the morning two days out on a section of
the promenade deck. Mildred Douglas and her aunt recline in
two chairs. In contrast to Yank's ferocious and brutal strength
she is white, wan, and an anemic girl. Mildred tells her aunt she
is going into the stokehole in search of a fresh thrill, and because
she "wants to see how the other half lives". We learn that her
father is president of the Steel Trust and owner of the ship. The
second engineer comes along to take her on her tour of "hell".
Mildred tries to embarrass him, but he laughs it off. Her aunt
calls her a poser. Mildred slaps her face and walks gaily off.

Scene three opens in the stokehole. The great furnaces loom
in the background. The men are resting. Paddy complains that
his back is practically broken. Yank chides him again and leads
the men in another opening and feeding of the massive furnace
mouths. He praises his task and the great ship he is driving on.
Finally they rest from their stoking, but almost immediately the
engineer's whistle hurries them back to more feeding of the
furnaces. Curses are uttered. Yank shouts up at the engineer.
The men urge him on. He indulges in a harangue about engi-
neers, their general worthlessness, cowardice, et cetera. They all
turn back to stoking. But at this instant Mildred, in her white
dress, accompanied by the engineer, enters behind the men. All
are turning back to get more coal; just then the whistle sounds
insistently, insultingly. Yank stops in mid-turn, looks up into the
darkness without seeing Mildred, and begins a violent stream of
abuse directed at the engineer above. The other men have all
turned around and have stopped, dumbfounded, at the spectacle
of Mildred in her white dress. Yank, unaware of her presence,
continues to hurl his abuse at the engineer overhead somewhere
in the darkness. Suddenly Yank becomes aware of a presence

behind him and whirls with a snarl. When he sees her, he freezes, too shocked to do anything, or say anything. She is crushed by this image of utter and abysmal brutality and, on the point of fainting, calls Yank a *filthy beast,* and asks the engineer to take her away. As the door shuts behind them, Yank, having recovered from the shock of the apparition of Mildred, throws his shovel at the door which it hits with a resounding clang. Yank curses with rage. The insistent whistle sounds again as the scene closes.

Scene four returns to the fireman's forecastle. The men are glum. Something is seriously wrong with their hero Yank. He is brooding, and has not eaten nor washed. He tells them he is thinking. When they chide him, he silences them with a threat. Someone taunts him, suggesting he has fallen in love. He assures them he has fallen, not in love, but in hate. Long reveals that the girl is the daughter of the owner of the Steel Trust, who also owns the ship; he begins another socialistic harangue which is quickly put down. Paddy tells Yank that Mildred looked at him as if he were a hairy ape escaped from the zoo. Yank asks if that is really what she called him, but Paddy explains that she "looked" it at him if she didn't actually say it. Yank is stung by this and tries to explain that he had thought Mildred was a ghost and that she had actually frightened him. Yank decides to revenge himself, to go immediately on deck and kill the girl with his bare hands. The men hold him down by main strength. The scene ends with Yank screaming from beneath the pile of men restraining him that he will show her who's an ape.

Scene five opens on Fifth Avenue, New York, three weeks later. Yank, still driven by his intense desire for personal vengeance, has been brought to this place by Long. He waits till the people come out of the church. They look at the monkey-fur coats in the shop windows which have huge price tags. Yank attempts to assault them, but bounces off as if they were made of steel and his strength fades before their façade. He finally attacks a gentleman, but only succeeds in causing the gentleman to miss his bus. The gentleman, unharmed, but irritated, calls the police, who swarm on stage and beat Yank to the pavement.

Scene six takes place the following night in the cell block of the prison on Blackwell's Island. In the cell block an exchange takes place between Yank and the other prisoners. One of them tells him about the I. W. W., amid catcalls and jeers. He is given a paper in which a Senator Queen attacks the I. W. W., accusing them of being violent incendiaries. Reflecting on this, Yank comes to the realization that he is not the great man he had thought himself, and that this world of speed he bragged about belonging to in the first scene is actually a cage in which he is trapped. Madly he grasps the bars of his "cage" which give way under his tremendous strength. The guard, thinking only the insane have such strength, turns a fire hose on him as the scene ends.

Scene seven shows the street outside an I. W. W. union office, and the interior of the office. Yank comes down the street, enters, and tries to join the union. He promises to blow up factories if necessary. The bureaucratic secretary of the local suspects Yank of being a spy attempting to trap him and has Yank summarily thrown out. Yank is lying on the street trying to recover himself when a policeman comes along and tells him to stop loitering as the scene closes.

Scene eight opens at twilight of the next day. Yank stands in front of a gorilla's cage in the city zoo talking to the gorilla and commiserating with him about their relative states of imprisonment. Finally Yank decides that Paddy, who had told him that the good old days of sailing were best, was right. He opens the cage to shake hands with the gorilla. The gorilla promptly steps out of the cage, crushes Yank, throws him into the cage, shuts the door, and shambles off into the darkness as the other smaller monkeys set up a frightened chatter. Yank regains consciousness, pulls himself to his feet, and addresses an imaginary audience, telling them to look at the one and only Hairy Ape from the wilds of ———, but he falls to the floor of the cage and dies before he can finish the sentence as the play ends.

What kind of human experience is this play imitating? If we were to formulate a fifth kind of experience that may be imitated, fantasy, we might be close to describing the central synthesizing principle (formal principle) of this play.

Aristotle mentions the tragedy of 'Spectacle' as the fourth type of tragedy. The *Prometheus* of Aeschylus he considers a tragedy of 'Spectacle', and all tragedies with scenes "laid in the nether world".[3] The element common to both experiences embodied in these two designations seems to be fantasy, because Prometheus is a mythic figure, and because we cannot *experience* events in the nether world in the ordinary sense of that word. Certainly there seems to be something "hellish" about Yank's experience, and certainly the "spectacle" of *The Hairy Ape* plays a great part in generating its total effect. But stokeholes can be *experienced* by men, and the quality of the events that happen to Yank is *probable* if the unlikely aspects of the spectacle are seen as they were intended to be seen: as distortions projected by the inner subjectivity of Yank's character. William S. Clark, II, writing of *The Hairy Ape* says this:

> Expressionism is so called because it casts aside representation of outer reality in order to give expression solely to inner significances. These subjective values, arising either from a state of mind in the playwright or in the human objects of his study, are made concrete by means of symbols especially adapted to the stage. The words and actions of external reality may still be used, but they no longer control the meaning. Usually the scenes and characters are stylized, or distorted in an arbitrarily fantastic manner.[4]

It appears from the above that the elements of fantasy so evident in *The Hairy Ape* are contributory factors, serving to make some other poetic object fuller and clearer. Margaret Gump makes quite plain that object which the exaggerated and seemingly fantastic elements of the play create for us:

> The cage which runs as a leitmotiv through the whole play is not so much a symbol of social oppression as it is a symbol of a much more

---

[3]   Aristotle, *Poetics* 18. 1455b 32-39, trans. Bywater, ed. Solmsen, p. 247. "There are four distinct species of Tragedy – that being the number of the constituents also that have been mentioned: first, the complex Tragedy, which is all Peripety and Discovery; second, the Tragedy of suffering, ... third, the Tragedy of character. ... The fourth constituent is that of 'Spectacle', exemplified in *The Phorcides*, in *Prometheus*, and in all plays with the scene laid in the nether world."

[4]   William S. Clark, II, *Chief Patterns of World Drama* (New York, Houghton, Mifflin, 1946), p. 1009.

general oppression and bewilderment, that metaphysical anguish which Kafka's heroes experience.[5]

Ira N. Hayward makes this object of the play clearer still:

... particularly in 'The Hairy Ape', and 'The Emperor Jones', the author sinks deep shafts into human souls for the purpose of laying before his audiences their inarticulate feelings and motives. In the latter two this is accomplished by the use of rigid economy. The structure is essentially that of the dramatic monologue. All of the other characters are scarcely more than wraiths that flit into and out of the consciousness of Yank or the Emperor.[6]

The above evidence indicates that fantasy is not the human experience this play ·is centrally concerned with imitating. Fantasy in the play serves to create and emphasize a more central object. The evidence all tends to point to character, but not the externals of character. The externals are there, as Mr. Clark points out, "but they no longer control the meaning". For the purposes of this study Mr. Clark's word "meaning" should be expanded to include every aspect of "the object of the play's imitation".

Perhaps the greatest objection made to *The Hairy Ape* by critics is what is generally referred to as the "lack of verisimilitude, or humanity" in Yank Smith. The validity of this objection is questionable, as Una Ellis-Fermor points out:

But the distinction between the presentation of character in terms of statement and its indication by means of the evocative technique remains within the province of dramatic aesthetics. Since, as we have demonstrated, the technique of statement cannot reveal so much or so profoundly as can the evocative technique, the method, even in the hands of Ibsen, is a hindrance to drama, and, so far, undramatic. It appears to present reality, only to provoke the accusation that 'character' in drama is an illusion. Whereas in fact, even with the realists, the illusion is all in the technique and the 'character' imagined (and in part transmitted, despite the technique) is an aspect of imaginative truth. But in the great poetic dramatists, who proceed by evocation, there is, rightly understood, no attempt to present a likeness to the surface of character. Speeches, phrases, single words even, are all

[5]   Margaret Gump, "From Ape to Man and from Man to Ape", *Kentucky Foreign Language Quarterly*, Vol. IV, No. 4 (1957), pp. 182-183.
[6]   Ira N. Hayward, "Strindberg's Influence on Eugene O'Neill", *Poet Lore*, XXXIX (December, 1928), 600-601.

indications, leading the imagination to an awareness and comprehension for which the intelligence has no words, to comprehension of processes of emotion, of hitherto unperceived depths and complexities of character which the dramatist himself has discerned.[7]

In Aristotle's first sense of plot, then, we may say that the type of experience being imitated in this play is the experience of character, which involves complete alteration in moral character, brought on and controlled by action, and made apparent in itself in thought and feeling, which give rise to subjective fantasy, such fantasy being a mirror of the internal experience of the character.

To obtain a statement of the second "multiple working hypothesis" we must consider what possibilities of the poetic medium of character *The Hairy Ape* employs in imitating the experience of that character. If we ask ourselves whether Robert "Yank" Smith is morally better than we are, like ourselves, or in some sense worse, the obvious answer would be that Yank is morally worse than we are. However, if we look strictly at the characters with whom he is grouped in the play, we must conclude that in some respects he is better than most men, but not preëminently virtuous and just, and is brought to his catastrophe, not by depravity or vice, but by an error in judgment, and a flaw in his character. The error in judgment (thinking his lot superior to most men) is directly caused by his flaw, which is a limitation in the lexical ability inherent in his character. But when we look at his capacity for feeling, we see that he is capable of depths and heights of feeling no other character in the play possesses, and a capacity for feeling few of us in real life possess. He is a savage innocent, much like the Negro sailor in *Thirst*. He represents a part of all men, the brute that is in all of us.

Symbolically considered, "the hairy ape" is the blind cyclopean Demos that cannot build but only destroy; malformed, powerful – when he stirs fair cities topple – thick-witted, dangerous, ugly.[8]

---

[7] Una Ellis-Fermor, "The Nature of Character in Drama, with Special Reference to Tragedy", *English Studies Today*, eds. C. L. Wrenn and G. Bullough (Oxford University Press, 1951), p. 21.
[8] Desmond MacCarthy, "Hairy Ape or Bronze Ajax?", *New Statesman & Nation*, I (May 23, 1931), 462.

But he is at the same time made a very particular stage person, a dramatic character, and it is apparent that O'Neill intended this elasticity of character imitation. We may ask, however, in considering the possibilities employed by the playwright in his imitation of character whether or not a more equitable balance of symbolic and particular detail might not have been employed. There is such a thing in dramatic technique as making an ambivalence in character perfectly clear.

The obvious reason for the critical split expressed in Margaret Gump's statement as opposed to Desmond MacCarthy's can be explained in the following way. In Clark's definition of expressionism above he says, "These subjective values, arising either from a state of mind in the playwright or in the human objects of his study, are made concrete by means of symbols especially adapted to the stage." At times the subjective values in the play arise from a state of mind of the characters. An example would be Yank's speech toward the end of scene one in which he says:

It – dat's me! – de new dat's moiderin' de old! I'm de ting in coal dat makes it boin; I'm steam and oil for de engines; I'm de ting in noise dat makes yuh hear it; I'm smoke and express trains and steamers and factory whistles; I'm de ting in gold dat makes it money! And I'm what makes iron into steel! Steel, dat stands for de whole ting! And I'm steel – steel – steel! [9]

But at other times (and at many fewer times), as in this passage from scene four, the subjectivity of the playwright seems to be expressed:

LONG. . . . We kin go to law –
YANK. (*with abysmal contempt*) Hell! Law!
ALL. (*repeating the word after him as one with cynical mockery*) Law! (*The word has a brazen metallic quality as if their throats were phonograph horns. It is followed by a chorus of hard, barking laughter.*)
LONG. (*feeling the ground slipping from under his feet – desperately*) As voters and citizens we kin force the bloody governments –
YANK. (*with abysmal contempt*) Hell! Governments!
ALL. (*repeating the word after him as one with cynical mockery*) Governments! (*The word has a brazen metallic quality as if their*

[9]   Random House, III, 216.

*throats were phonograph horns. It is followed by a chorus of hard,
barking laughter.*)
LONG. (*hysterically*) We're free and equal in the sight of God –
YANK. (*with abysmal contempt*) Hell! God!
ALL. (*repeating the word after him as one with cynical mockery*)
God! (*The word has a brazen metallic quality as if their throats were
phonograph horns. It is followed by a chorus of hard, barking
laughter.*) [10]

O'Neill tugs us one way and then the other in regard to our
interest in Yank. At times it seems we must be totally involved
in the expressionistic imitation of Yank's inner subjectivity. At
other times Yank seems to be a symbol for the expression of
O'Neill's own subjectivity. Obviously, O'Neill had three clear
choices in avoiding such confusion. He could have kept our
interest centered on the inner experience of Yank; or he could
have kept it centered on Yank's symbolic dramatic value; or he
could have established a perfectly clear interest in both Yank's
symbolic value and his inner dilemma. He chose none of these
three possible courses, and consequently his structure (since the
controlling formal principle is character) is marred by a lack of
clarity in the technique of his imitation. This does not, of course,
mean that the play is without great power and depth.

Yank is at times what MacCarthy calls him in the above cited
quotation. Yank is also what Margaret Gump tells us he is
above. But he is not *always* clearly one or the other or both.
That is the difficulty. But it is clear that he is *primarily* what
Gump describes him to be, and not *primarily* what MacCarthy
tells us he is. He is less a symbolic vehicle for the playwright's
point of view and more a particular character with a particular
dilemma imitated through the expressionistic mode of dramatic
imitation. The final effect of his character, despite the flaw that
has been pointed out, is well put in Gump's further comment:

Yank arouses our pity; despite his crudity, despite the fact that he
has been likened to a hairy ape, he remains very human to the end
in his tragic search for his place on earth.[11]

[10] *Ibid.*, pp. 228-229.
[11] Gump, *Kentucky Foreign Language Quarterly*, IV, No. 4, 183.

O'Neill himself supported the view of this study in regard to the primary dramatic identity of Yank's character:

The individual life is made significant just by the struggle, and the acceptance and assertion of that individual, making him what he is [,] not, as always in the past, making him something not himself. As far as there is any example of that in "The Hairy Ape" it is his last gesture, when he kills himself. He becomes himself and no other person.[12]

The answer to the third question, through what mode of representation is the experience being imitated, has been suggested partially in answering the previous two questions. The mode of dramatic character imitation being employed in this play involves "subjective values, arising either from a state of mind in the playwright or in the human objects of his study" in order to give expression primarily to the inner significances of character. This is what has been termed expressionism. Clearly this technique need not be limited to dramatic imitation. It could be employed in narrative or lyric imitation as well. But here the characters are not seen through the eyes of an interpolated narrator. Everything happens in scene.

One vivid difference of mode stands out in this play, however, when thought of in relation to the three plays previously considered. They were completely in prose, verse entering in only in incidental songs in *Abortion* and *The Moon of the Caribbees,* while in *Thirst* no verse was used. In *The Hairy Ape* verse is employed in the songs "Whiskey Johnny" and "The Miller of Dee". But the use of verse does not end there. A kind of choral verse is used in the stokehole scenes:

VOICES. He ain't ate nothin'.
  Py golly, a fallar gat to gat grub in him.
  Divil a lie.
  Yank feeda da fire, no feeda da face.
  Ha-ha.
  He ain't even washed hisself.
  He's forgot.
  Hey, Yank, you forgot to wash.

[12] Eugene O'Neill, in an interview with Harold Stark, published in Stark's *People You Know* (New York, Boni and Liveright, 1923), p. 246.

YANK. (*sullenly*) Forgot nothin'! To hell wit washin'.
VOICES. It'll stick to you.
        It'll get under your skin.
        Give yer the bleedin' itch, that's wot.
        It makes spots on you – like a leopard.
        Like a piebald nigger, you mean.
        Better wash up, Yank.
        You sleep better.
        Wash up, Yank!
        Wash up! Wash up! [13]

The above choral verse occurs at the beginning of scene four. A similar kind of verse occurs in scenes one, three, four, five, and six. In scene five the free verse becomes much more sophisticated and complex in imitating the cosmopolitan chatter of the crowd coming from church on Fifth Avenue:

VOICES. Dear Doctor Caiphas! He is so sincere!
        What was the sermon? I dozed off.
        About the radicals, my dear – and the false doctrines that
            are being preached.
        We must organize a hundred per cent American bazaar.
        And let everyone contribute one one-hundredth per cent of
            their income tax.
        What an original idea!
        We can devote the proceeds to rehabilitating the veil of
            the temple.
        But that has been done so many times.[14]

It is free verse, of course, but the verse return of lines and the heavy patterning of cadences and figures of sound is quite evident in these passages.

Verse is joined with a heavily patterned prose, the most striking examples of which occur in the first scene in an exchange between Paddy and Yank. Paddy says in part:

Oh, to be back in the fine days of my youth, ochone! Oh, there was fine beautiful ships them days – clippers wid tall masts touching the sky – fine strong men in them – men that was sons of the sea as if 'twas the mother that bore them. Oh, the clean skins of them, and the clear eyes, the straight backs and full chests of them! Brave men

13   Random House, III, 226-227.
14   *Ibid.*, pp. 236-237.

they was, and bold men surely! We'd be making sail in the dawn, with a fair breeze, singing a chanty song wid no care to it. And astern the land would be sinking low and dying out, but we'd give it no heed but a laugh, and never a look behind. For the day that was, was enough, for we was free men – and I'm thinking 'tis only slaves do be giving heed to the day that's gone or the day to come – until they're old like me.[15]

And on this speech goes, rolling like the sea to a crest where it breaks in a climax of nostalgia. At the conclusion of this speech Paddy asks Yank: "Ho-ho, divil mend you! Is it to belong to that you're wishing? Is it a flesh and blood wheel of the engines you'd be?" A part of Yank's vicious and effective response has already been quoted on page 83. Here, in part, is more of Yank's answer:

Sure I'm part of de engines! Why de hell not! Dey move, don't dey? Dey're speed, ain't dey? Dey smash trou, don't dey? Twenty-five knots a hour! Dat's goin' some! Dat's new stuff! Dat belongs! But him, he's too old. He gets dizzy. Say, listen. All dat crazy tripe about nights and days; all dat crazy tripe about stars and moons; all dat crazy tripe about suns and winds, fresh air and de rest of it – Aw hell, dat's all a dope dream! Hittin' de pipe of de past, dat's what he's doin'. He's old and don't belong no more. But me, I'm young! I'm in de pink! I move wit it. It, get me! I mean de ting dat's de guts of all dis. It ploughs trou all de tripe he's been sayin'. It blows dat up! It knocks dat dead! It slams dat offen de face of de oith! It, get me! De engines and de coal and de smoke and all de rest of it! He can't breathe and swallow coal dust, but I kin, see? Dat's fresh air for me! Dat's food for me! I'm new, get me? Hell in de stokehole? Sure! It takes a man to work in hell. Hell, sure, dat's my fav'rite climate. I eat it up! I git fat on it! It's me makes it hot! It's me makes it roar! It's me makes it move! Sure, on'y for me everyting stops. It all goes dead, get me? De noise and smoke and all de engines movin' de woild, dey stop. Dere ain't nothin' no more! Dat's what I'm sayin'.[16]

O'Neill's skill with diction goes still further in this play. He takes the rough, ungainly diction and syntax he has given to Yank in this powerful speech and transforms it into a dramatic medium capable of the deepest pathos in scene eight:

15 *Ibid.*, pp. 213-214.
16 *Ibid.*, pp. 215-216.

But me – I ain't got no past to tink in, nor nothin' dat's comin', on'y what's now – and dat don't belong. Sure, you're de best off! You can't tink, can yuh? Yuh can't talk neider. But I kin make a bluff a talkin' and tinkin' – a'most git away wit it – a'most! – and dat's where de joker comes in. (*He laughs*) I ain't on oith and I ain't in heaven, get me? I'm in de middle tryin' to separate 'em, takin' all de woist punches from bot' of 'em. Maybe dat's what dey call hell, huh? But you, yuh're at de bottom. You belong! Sure! Yuh're de on'y one in de woild dat does, yuh lucky stiff! (*The gorilla growls proudly.*) And dat's why dey gotter put yuh in a cage, see? [17]

Yank lets the gorilla out of the cage; it crushes him, throws him into the cage, and shuffles off in the darkness. Yank regains consciousness and says:

Say – dey oughter match him – with Zybszko. He got me, aw right. I'm trou. Even him didn't tink I belonged. (*Then, with sudden passionate despair.*) Christ, where do I get off at? Where do I fit in? (*Checking himself as suddenly.*) Aw, what de hell! No squawkin', see! No quittin', get me! Croak wit your boots on! ... In de cage, huh? ... Ladies and gents, step forward and take a slant at de one and only – ... one and original – Hairy Ape from de wilds of – (*He slips in a heap on the floor and dies. The monkeys set up a chattering, whimpering wail. And, perhaps, the Hairy Ape at last belongs.*) [18]

This most sensitive criticism of dramatic dialogue comes from Hugo von Hofmannsthal:

Let us assume a distinction between literature and drama, and say that the best dialogue is that which, including the purely stylistic or literary qualities, possesses at the same time what is perhaps the most important of all: the quality of movement, of suggestive mimetic action. The best dramatic dialogue reveals not only the motives that determine what a character is to do – as well as what he tries to conceal – but suggests his very appearance, his metaphysical being as well as the grosser material figure.[19]

Hofmannsthal's criticism gets to the heart of the matter in a way that no other criticism of O'Neill's dialogue this researcher has

---

[17]   *Ibid.*, p. 253.
[18]   *Ibid.*, p. 254.
[19]   Hugo von Hofmannsthal, "Eugene O'Neill", trans. Barrett H. Clark, *Freeman*, VII (March 31, 1923), 40.

read to date manages to do. Hofmannsthal finds O'Neill's plays lacking in these respects. Looking at the above presented evidence from the text of the play, *The Hairy Ape,* one must be aware, however, that Hofmannsthal's description of what dialogue should be exactly coincides with what O'Neill's dialogue generally proves itself to be in *The Hairy Ape;* if we accept the play as it is: an expressionistic imitation of character in the dramatic mode which involves complete alteration in moral character, brought on and controlled by action and made apparent in itself through thought and feeling, which give rise to subjective fantasy (primarily on the part of Yank), such fantasy being a mirror of the internal experience of the character. The major flaw within the play, as pointed out earlier, lies in the lack of clarity of the play's intent with regard to its delineation of the final effect of the character – not specifically in its dialogue.[20]

One final statement must be made about the mode of representation in this play. It concerns the arrangement of the incidents. In both Crane's and Aristotle's first sense this play utilizes a plot of character with the attendant effects described above. In the second sense, regarding the arrangement of the incidents or substrate, the play utilizes a complex plot. The major peripety (reversal) occurs in scene three when Yank is confronted with Mildred. Whereas previously he had been perfectly content with his lot, after this confrontation his confidence dwindles progressively until it leaves him completely in scene six, which takes place in the cell block. Yank says, speaking of Mildred's father, Douglas, the president of the Steel Trust:

He made dis – dis cage! *It* don't belong, dat's what! Cages, cells, locks, bolts, bars – dat's what it means! – holdin' me down wit him at de top! But I'll drive trou! Fire, dat melts it! I'll be fire – under de heap – fire dat never goes out – hot as hell – breakin' out in de night – [21]

The major discovery (*anagnorisis*) occurs at this point. Yank

---

[20] For a clear and rigorous examination of O'Neill's skill with dialogue in the body of his work see John Henry Raleigh's *O'Neill* (Carbondale, Illinois, Southern Illinois University Press, 1965), pp. 208-238.
[21] Random House, III, 244.

finally realizes his true position in the scheme of the society imitated in the play. But in this discovery there is also a reversal and a further complication. Now Yank, realizing fully how unimportant he is (discovery and reversal) makes a complete change of plans. Instead of a personal vendetta against Mildred, he decides he wants to destroy the whole system. There was also a discovery (though partial) connected with his previous reversal in scene three which, too, was a complication. Scene six may be called the crisis of the play. It leads inevitably to the climax of Yank's death in the arms of the gorilla.

This play does not adhere to unity of time in its succession of scenes, but it clearly has unity of action, involving Yank's continuous effort to resolve the conflict set up in his character by Mildred. The progression of action in which Yank consistently rejects "social, reasoned solutions", as ways of getting the justice he desires, points to an emphasis on Yank's particular dilemma and character; though this issue, as pointed out, seems clouded. Perhaps the dramatist's subjective references to the state of man in the imitated society the play presents are meant to provide a contrast to Yank's individual dilemma. If that is the case, the fault pointed out previously seems mitigated, and, perhaps, future investigations may be able to demonstrate that in reality it works to further unify the play.

When we come to answer the fourth question about this play we begin to realize O'Neill's originality. Yank is the lowest of the low with respect to his station in life, intelligence, and physical appearance. He is not of noble lineage – not even of important lineage. He seems morally worse than most men, taken in relation to his mates and most of the other characters we encounter in the specifically limited milieu of this particular play's imitation. However, he does have tremendous physical power and heroic emotional vitality. Allowing his protagonist only these two virtues – strength and courage – O'Neill has attempted to create a tragedy, a tragedy that goes against practically all dramatic tradition.

O'Neill shapes his character and the incidents that occur in the play to arouse pity and terror in the audience as they witness the bizarre and overwhelming suffering of Yank (a brutal creature whom we ordinarily would not expect capable of such suffering). How positive O'Neill was concerning the worth of man in this play is indicated in his attempt to show that even the most limited sort of human being may have the ennobling ability to suffer greatly, and through that suffering arrive at knowledge about himself and the world of which ordinarily we would suspect him incapable.

Sure. I seen de sun come up. Dat was pretty, too – all red and pink and green. I was lookin' at de skyscrapers – steel – and all de ships comin' in, sailin' out, all over de oith – and dey was steel, too. De sun was warm, dey wasn't no clouds, and dere was a breeze blowin'. Sure, it was great stuff. I got it aw right – what Paddy said about dat bein' de right dope – on'y I couldn't get *in* it, see? I couldn't belong in dat. It was over my head. And I kept tinkin' – and den I beat it up here to see what youse was like.[22]

Thought is difficult for Yank, but we wonder at this point whether he lacks the capacity to think, or whether it is not simply a question of the motivation to think, an opportunity for which (until this time) he has been deprived, partly by the imitated milieu of the society in the play and partly by his own pride in his physical strength. Yank's insight in this scene is prepared for by the magnitude of his emotional response to Mildred's unwarranted disgust. We are presented with a sensitivity (an ultimate human value) crushed, brutalized, and all but extinct in the character of Yank. As this sensitivity progressively emerges from brute emotion into the light of understanding, with its consequent suffering, the agony such a Herculean labor costs the protagonist is pitiable. We pity him still more, for we realize, as he plainly does, that the knowledge thus gained through suffering cannot overcome a lifetime of progressive and brutal numbing. The knowledge will destroy him rather than liberate him. He knows this in his clumsy way, and so do we. This is a great irony, a fit subject for tragedy. We generally believe that the light of understanding liberates, but in this case (contrary to poetic justice, but consistent with tragic justice) light annihilates Robert "Yank" Smith. As the gorilla (symbolic of all the brutality inflicted on

22   *Ibid.*, p. 252.

Yank by his society and by his own pride) crushes Yank, the only thing that is purged in us is the tremendous suffering that is lifted from Yank in death – the ultimate balance. Pity is magnified, because the evil that has created this distorted soul is ineluctable and cannot be overcome.

William Perry tells us O'Neill's chief flaw is:

... that his characters lack the necessary nobility; and this may be a flaw in his philosophy of composition. It may well be that he who would write great tragedies should seek his protagonists elsewhere than among 'the most ignoble, debased lives'.[23]

But O'Neill is not interested in creating a traditional kind of tragedy in *The Hairy Ape*. *The Hairy Ape* is no more like *Oedipus* than *Macbeth*; this play departs even further from Aristotle's definition of tragedy. Nor is O'Neill the only writer in this century who has endeavored to extend the tragic form of drama to be more inclusive of the modern milieu. Many critics have insisted that fit subjects for tragedy have been changing since the days of Aristotle. One of the best expositions of this position concerning what may now be considered tragic is given by Erich Auerbach in his *Mimesis*:

In modern literature the technique of imitation can evolve a serious, problematic, and tragic conception of any character regardless of type and social standing, of any occurrence regardless of whether it be legendary, broadly political, or narowly domestic; and in most cases it actually does so.[24]

Joseph Wood Krutch tells us further, particularly of O'Neill:

They [most modern playwrights, sociologists, and moralists] are, to put it somewhat differently, concerned with problems properly so called, while O'Neill, like most great tragic dramatists, is concerned with dilemmas.[25]

The play does not exalt us nor the character. It does release the

[23] William Perry, "Does the Buskin Fit O'Neill?", *University of Kansas City Review*, XV (Spring, 1949), 287.

[24] Erich Auerbach, *Mimesis*, trans. Willard R. Trask (Princeton, New Jersey, Princeton University Press, 1953), p. 31.

[25] Joseph Wood Krutch, "O'Neill's Tragic Sense", *American Scholar*, XVI (Summer, 1947), 286.

terrible suffering of the character, and in turn we feel relieved from the terror of his situation and his suffering. O'Neill is charged constantly with a kind of nihilistic pessimism. It seems likely that every tragic playwright would have to have the same charge leveled at him on that basis. The most accurate statement this researcher has discovered concerning this problem is made quite succinctly by George Kimmelman:

What happens during the aesthetic experience is that we are reliving those tragic emotions which are always part of us, their sharpness being mitigated because they are being projected toward an integrated pattern. This projection enables us to experience them 'objectively', as it were, and to be relieved from the tensions which the tragedy is imposing on us. Any attempt to include here a theory of catharsis which merely stresses the purging of 'archaic desires and fears' is entirely uncalled-for. We can no more accept the therapeutic than the religious, metaphysical, or moral explanations for tragedy. We do not read or contemplate tragic art as a purifying aperient, an immunizing toxin, or an emotional stabilizer.

A great deal of 'exaltation' which the critics have attributed to the moralistic or cosmological conceptions of the writer actually derives from the mere subject-matter and its transmutation into the magic of pure art.[26]

Drawing partially from the particulars included in the brief and from additional passages of the text, we have answered our four questions of fact. In answering these questions we have formulated four "multiple working hypotheses". In order to describe the form of the play, its mode of existence, we must further induct a condensed description of that form from the hypotheses.

In Aristotle's first sense of plot, then, it may be said that the kind of experience imitated in this play is *primarily* the experience of a particularized character, involving a complete alternation of his moral character, brought on and controlled by his own actions and made apparent in himself, his thoughts, and feelings, which give rise to subjective fantasy that is a mirror of

[26] George Kimmelman, "The Concept of Tragedy in Modern Criticism", *Journal of Aesthetics and Art Criticism*, IV (March, 1946), 156. For the discussion of the critical dilemma sometimes referred to as the "decline of tragedy", Mr. Kimmelman and Mr. Auerbach present informed, interesting, and creative resolutions.

his internal experience. The character is low on the social, intellectual, and moral scale the play imitates, but has great physical strength and emotional vitality which cause him to struggle to find his own identity. Through this struggle against the tremendous odds of his situation he takes on a kind of worth that tends to make him in many respects better than the characters imitated in the play with him. All this is accomplished through a unity of action, but not a unity of time, utilizing a complex plot and verse joined to a heavily patterned prose which point *primarily* to the inner dilemmas of the character. In the above fashion we are presented with a sensitivity (an ultimate human value) that has been all but crushed, brutalized, in Yank's character. And as we witness the progressive emergence of this sensitivity from brute emotion into the light of understanding, with its consequent suffering, we pity the agony this labor costs the protagonist. Our anger at the imitated social forces of the play is mitigated, for we realize, as does the protagonist, that he is partially responsible for his predicament. Suffering is purged as the gorilla crushes Yank, but pity is magnified because the evil that has created this distorted soul is ineluctable and cannot be overcome.

Il fine che O'Neill assegna al teatro tragico, è di far rivivere il mito della fatalità e del destino.[27]

Many critics agree with this statement from the Italian critic, Salvatore Rosati, but few include "myth" and "destiny". Again we see O'Neill utilizing a Nemesis involving both the inertia of circumstance (fate in the limited sense), and the operative volition of his protagonist (the internal, intrinsic nature of man being part of the cause of his action). It is not enough here to say that "character is destiny" as Smyth insists. As we see in this play the character is up against his environment as well as himself. Caught in his greatest moment of luxuriating in his animal vitality, his Gargantuan pride is deflated by an ineffectual girl in a white dress. O'Neill has presented a myth here. He has done it so skillfully that the audience is aware at practically every moment of

[27] Salvatore Rosati, "Eugene O'Neill, pessimista eroico", *Nuova Antologia*, XLD, No. 89 (January, 1954), p. 65.

the precarious position which Yank Robert Smith is maintaining. It is clear that inevitably such a creature must be crushed by the titanic forces that surround him. The difference is, of course, that the audience does not know in advance the particular circumstances of his end. As Baum says in *Tempest* and *Hairy Ape*: "The Literary Incarnation of Mythos", "The structural principle of the play is contained in the cosmology",[28] or the world view.

Nemesis, in the guise of the *lex talionis*, propels the play forward. The revenge motive of Yank drives him to seek physical retribution against Mildred, and then against her father, who seems to Yank to symbolize the whole system that has, as he finally realizes in the cell block, made of him the distorted creature he is – unfit for heaven or for earth, fit only for hell.

Nemesis stemming from social justice is shown to be a mockery in the play. His attempts to align himself with social forces, mainly the I. W. W., result in his being thrown out of the union hall. His drive to fulfill his personal Nemesis against Mildred and against his society is constantly thwarted by the usual sources of social redress. This is because his personal outrage blinds him to the fantastically complicated and ineffectual systems of social justice.

Nemesis stemming from the divine is shown to be a sham in the play. Religion is a mockery, and as the play imitates it, the idea of God is dead. There is no recourse in the play to divine Nemesis.

As in *Abortion*, the tragic source of Nemesis exists within the individual himself. God and society can provide no balance for the individual. He must provide it for himself. Tragic Nemesis consists in the character's self realization. When he realizes what he is, he seeks out that image and directly permits it to destroy him. Nemesis becomes an image of himself, within and without. Here again O'Neill returns to the idea of a personal justice (part of the *lex talionis*) and extends it beyond the strict meaning of the possibility of a self equality based on distributive ideas which

---

[28] B. Baum, *Modern Language Quarterly*, XIV (1953), 260.

may be manipulated to control things external to the self. In Henry Alonzo Myers' words:

There is in it no question of the distribution of material goods for the achievement of justice, for such goods are meaningless to an Oedipus, a Lear, an Antigone.[29]

This study essentially agrees with Stamm who says O'Neill's "interest had become concentrated in the struggles within individual souls", but does not agree with Stamm's observation that "In his first phase, when he composed his short plays, the last-mentioned problem did not trouble him yet".[30]

The structure of O'Neill's play, involving primarily an expressionistic technique that allows a portrayal of the inner experience of the character, seems well suited to utilizing the form of Nemesis it ultimately expresses. That is, a Nemesis inflicted on the character by himself in relation to the dramatic imitation of his internal characteristics.

This play expresses a classic sense of Nemesis which shows the character brought to his ultimate doom, not primarily by external forces impinging on his character (though that is part of it here), but primarily by the dramatic return of the character recoiling upon himself – which is, in fact, Nemesis.

---

[29] Myers, p. 25.
[30] Rudolf Stamm, "The Dramatic Experiments of Eugene O'Neill", *English Studies*, XXVIII (1947), 9.

IV

DESIRE UNDER THE ELMS

In *Desire under the Elms* O'Neill continued his constant experiments with the "quantitative" arrangement of the incidents in his plot. *Beyond the Horizon,* written in conventional three act form, experimented with outer scenes contrasted against interior scenes in each act. *Desire under the Elms* departs from the conventional division of its quantitative parts into "acts" in the ordinary sense. It is written in three "parts", each divided into four scenes. The scenes throughout are not of equal duration in time. This tends to disturb the reader, but if it is imagined smoothly staged the objections disappear. It should also be noticed that the interior and exterior scenes are effectively made to function as a unity, rather than being played off against one another as in the earlier play, *Beyond the Horizon.*

Continuing our pattern of analysis we must first ask ourselves what kind of human experience this play is imitating. The brief here presented has been carefully derived from the Random House text. It is the hope of the writer that the contacts with the briefs, presented before the analysis of each play, appears by this time in the study to make a real contribution to the inductive nature of the study. The writer has noticed that his final induction of the role of Nemesis from the structure of each play selected for analysis and from the inducted description of each play's form, or mode of existence, is significantly affected by the method of analysis.

PART ONE

Part One opens early in the summer of the year 1850. The first
scene takes place outside the farmhouse of Ephraim Cabot. Eben
Cabot enters from the house and rings a bell. He then admires
the sunset, spits on the ground, and returns to the interior of the
farmhouse. Simeon and Peter enter from the fields, speaking of
their resentment for their tyrannical father, Ephraim, and consider going west for gold. Peter suggests they could have Ephraim
declared incompetent in court and get the farm for themselves.
Eben, who has been listening from the dining-room window,
sticks his head out and tells them sarcastically to honor their
father, and in the next breath says he prays Ephraim has died.
They smell the bacon Eben has prepared, and bumping together
like two friendly oxen, they go into the house to eat.

Scene two takes place in the kitchen as twilight is falling. The
three sons are seated around the table eating. Eben reveals that
he knows of their secret desire to go to California. Then he expresses his intense hatred for his father, whom he blames for
working his own mother to death. He also holds Peter and Simeon
partly responsible for his mother's death (she was stepmother to
Eben's brothers), because they did nothing to prevent it. The
"something" the two brothers see in Eben's eyes is his smoldering
desire to avenge his mother's death. Conversation turns to
Ephraim's reasons for leaving the farm that spring. Apparently
he had gone to seek a mate. Eben gets up from the table indicating that he is going up the road to see the local prostitute,
Min. Simeon and Peter agree that Eben is the spitting image of
his father, Ephraim, and they go to bed as Eben leaves for his
visit with Min.

Scene three opens just before dawn with Eben returning from
his all night stay with Min. He hurriedly wakes up his brothers
to tell them the news that the village talk has it that Ephraim has
married a pretty young woman of thirty-five. Peter and Simeon
realize they are about to be disinherited and speak seriously of
going to California. Eben tells them he can get them money if
they will agree to give up their share of the farm for it. They are

not sure exactly what they will do, as Eben goes to make their breakfast.

Scene four opens in the kitchen as Simeon and Peter are finishing breakfast, while Eben, his food untouched, sits frowning at them. They indicate they might be willing to give up their share of the farm for the thirty twenty-dollar gold pieces Eben has offered them. He runs to the barn to milk, leaving his brothers to talk.

Simeon and Peter decide to accept the gold when Eben returns, and let dog (Eben) eat dog (Ephraim). Eben rushes back from the barn with the news that he has just seen Ephraim and his new bride coming up the lane in the buggy. This news causes the brothers to decide to leave at once. Eben asks them if they have signed the deed paper he has drawn up for them. They reply that they will when they see the color of the old man's money and go upstairs to pack. Eben rushes furtively to a special floor board in the kitchen, lifts it and takes out the bag of gold his mother had told him of before she died (thus his mother reaches in vengeance from beyond the grave to deprive Ephraim of his miser's hoard). The brothers come downstairs into the kitchen with their carpet-bags packed. Eben demands to know if they have signed the paper. They answer they have, count the money, and give Eben the paper as they clump out to go to California. They reach the gate, decide to wait and mock Ephraim and his bride, and lift the gate off its hinges.

Ephraim and Abbie enter. Simeon and Peter engage in some very rude and dismaying horseplay, insulting Abbie, who goes into the house. They dance around Ephraim, loud in their triumph. He thinks they are mad. They go a few paces out of the gate, pick up stones and throw them through the parlor windows, and Ephraim, enraged, chases them off then returns. Abbie sticks her head out of the bedroom window saying she is glad they are gone and asking if the bedroom is hers. Ephraim insists angrily that it is not *hers* but *our'n*. Abbie, with distaste, pulls herself back into the bedroom and shuts the window. Ephraim suddenly fears that his two mad sons may have done some harm to the stock before they left and races anxiously to the barn.

Abbie enters the kitchen where Eben has been seated sullenly all this while. They are immediately attracted to one another despite the conflict of ownership apparent between them. Abbie tries to win Eben's confidence, tellling him the only reason she married the old man is for a home. Eben threatens to tell his father this, but Abbie counters that she can convince Ephraim that Eben lies. Cabot enters cursing his sons. Eben calls him a hypocrite. Ephraim demands to know why Eben is not at work. Eben counters by demanding to know why Ephraim isn't working. They leave matter of factly for the barn to get to work as Abbie washes *her* dishes.

PART TWO

Scene one opens on a hot Sunday afternoon two months later, with Abbie sitting on the porch and Eben just coming out the door. He is going to Min and tries to leave without speaking to Abbie. She taunts him, and he tells her Min is prettier than she is and that he will fight Abbie to the end for his mother's farm. They quarrel, and as Eben stalks off up the road Ephraim enters from the barn. He complains that he is getting ripe on the bough. Abbie tells him Eben thinks he is getting soft. He is angry at this. Abbie prods him on, telling him Eben has tried to make love to her. He is furious, but she calms him, telling him it was only a boy's foolishness. He calms somewhat, but still insists on horse-whipping Eben off the place. Abbie says that wouldn't be smart as Ephraim couldn't run the farm by himself. He admires her good sense but complains that he has no heir to leave the farm to. She intimates that maybe they will have a son. Ephraim is excited and promises to leave the farm to her if she bears him a son.

Scene two opens about eight o'clock the same evening with Abbie and Ephraim sitting on the edge of their bed discussing their mutual desire for a son; while Eben, in the next room, sits on the edge of his bed. Ephraim gets up to go down to the barn where he can be at peace.

Abbie and Eben sit in their separate rooms, fighting the attraction that is drawing them together. Finally Abbie makes the first move, rushes into Eben's room and begins kissing him. He flings her away angrily, fighting his attraction, remembering how she has replaced his mother. Abbie insists Eben will give in to his desire, because she is stronger than he. She tells him she is going down to the parlor to await his courting. He tells her she cannot open that room, which has remained closed since his mother had been laid out there for her funeral. She repeats she will be waiting for him in the parlor.

Scene three opens a few minutes later in the parlor which Abbie has opened and filled with lighted candless. Eben enters, and a strange courtship scene ensues in which Eben tells Abbie that he can feel that his mother's spirit approves of her and of the love between them. The scene ends with Eben capitulating completely, throwing his arms about Abbie, telling her he has loved her madly these two months.

Scene four opens the following dawn with Eben coming from the house dressed for work. He seems chipper and satisfied, almost jaunty, at his conquest of his father's wife. It is evident he is enjoying this as revenge as well as enjoying his conquest for its own sake. Abbie puts her head out of the parlor window, calling adoringly to Eben. She gets him to say he loves her, and a short passionate love scene ensues. Eben hears Ephraim coming from the barn where he has spent the night with the cows. He cautions Abbie to get up to her bedroom so the old man won't be suspicious. She tells him not to worry as she can pull the wool over the old man's eyes. She goes upstairs. Ephraim enters, struck immediately by his son's jaunty air. Eben tells Ephraim he is the cock of this walk and goes off toward the barn. Ephraim, wonderingly, goes into the house.

PART THREE

Scene one opens on a night in late spring of the following year. A party is in progress in the kitchen. Ephraim is celebrating the birth of his son (which is really Eben's). Abbie is seated wearily at one end of the kitchen and asks where Eben is. Ephraim is out dancing everyone in the room. But the neighbors know instinctively that the child is not his. He comes over to Abbie, but she brushes him off and goes upstairs to the baby where Eben has been all this time looking at his son. She enters the room and is pleased to find Eben there admiring their child. They kiss, and Abbie tells Eben that the child is exactly like him. But Eben is furious that he must pretend his child belongs to Ephraim.

Cabot, on the porch outside, decides to go to the barn, as the Fiddler in the kitchen tells the neighbors to dance in triumph over the old fool Ephraim.

Scene two opens half an hour later with Eben standing by the gate outside the house. Ephraim approaches, gloating over having what he thinks is his son, and begins to taunt Eben with disinheritance. Eben laughs at him. Ephraim becomes so angry he reveals that Abbie has wanted the son in order to disinherit Eben and tells Eben the farm is now hers, and that the dust of the road is Eben's. Eben, not realizing that Abbie now truly loves him, thinks she has tricked him into having a son with her for her own nefarious purposes. They fight. Ephraim is choking Eben as Abbie rushes from the house shouting to Ephraim to let Eben go. Ephraim flings Eben to the ground. Abbie bends over Eben fearing Ephraim has hurt him. Ephraim tells her he isn't going to get hanged for such a fool, and with a whoop goes to join the merrymakers.

Eben castigates Abbie for her trickery. She explains that that was before they had loved one another, and that now she truly loves him. But Eben is adamant. He says he wishes the baby were dead. Mysteriously Abbie says she will prove she loves Eben, if Eben thinks that the child stands between them and their love. Eben says he is going away to the gold fields.

Scene three opens just before dawn the following morning with Abbie bending over the cradle in her bedroom having just smothered the child as Ephraim sleeps soundly in the bed; Eben sits below in the kitchen with his carpetbag already packed for the trip to California. Abbie rushes down to the kitchen and tells Eben he does not have to leave now, for she has murdered the child that stood between them. Eben is shocked, almost mad with grief, for he has come to love the child. He rushes out to get the sheriff.

Scene four opens in the kitchen an hour later. Abbie sits at the table listlessly. Ephraim comes down from the bedroom, and she tells him she has murdered the child. Ephraim hurries up to the bedroom, sees what she says is true, and rushes down again demanding to know why she has killed their son. She discloses that the son was not his, and that she should have murdered him (Ephraim). He is overcome for just a second, but he hardens and becomes like a rock of judgment. He starts for the sheriff, but she tells him Eben has already gone. Calmly then, Cabot tells her he is going to get to work since Eben has saved him the trouble. He goes out and runs into Eben just returning. He shoves him, telling him to get off the farm when the sheriff takes Abbie, or he'll murder him. Eben, regretting his haste and anger and finally realizing he loves Abbie, rushes into the kitchen and they embrace desperately. Eben decides to go to his death with Abbie. She tries to prevent this, but Eben insists. Cabot returns from the barn and withers them with abuse, telling them the sheriff is coming. He says he is going to burn the farm and use the gold he has hoarded to go to California. He looks for it, but finds it gone. Eben tells him what he has done with it. Ephraim says that it is his hard God forcing him to stay on the farm, and that he will listen now to his hard God and never leave. The sheriff enters to take Abbie, but Eben tells him he must go with her. Cabot says, resentfully admiring Eben, that that is pretty good behavior even for Eben. He stalks off unconcerned toward the barn as the sheriff leads the two united lovers away to be hanged.

This play provides great difficulty for analysis. The kind of experience this play is imitating is not at once obvious. This difficulty is reflected in the existing criticism of the play. Winther apparently thinks it is a play of action that has a central protagonist, Ephraim Cabot, and that Ephraim is the tragic protagonist without flaw.[1] Roger Dateller thinks the play is a play of

[1] Sophus Keith Winther, "Desire under the Elms: a Modern Tragedy", *Modern Drama*, III (December, 1960), 327.

passion "which races towards a tragic disaster"[2] in which Eben and Abbie are the dual protagonists. The play clearly does not "race" to a tragic conclusion, and there is as much justification for seeing Ephraim as the protagonist if the play is one of action. Nathan sees this play as composed primarily of actions and emotions manipulated in the manner of Strindberg.[3] Let us look at the play inductively to see what may be arrived at, and supported, in terms of the play itself.

If the play is a play of action, then it should show a complete change, quick or slow, in the main character's situation (determined by character, thought, and passion). It will be difficult here to single out the play's main character, or protagonist, for the interest is more or less evenly divided among three characters, Ephraim, Eben, and Abbie. Ephraim's situation is not appreciably changed. Abbie's and Eben's situations are changed, but the process takes a year; since both of them are more or less dispossessed when the play begins, the change in their situation is not really complete at the play's close, it is merely made more severe.

If the play is a play of character, then it should show complete alteration in moral character, brought on or controlled by action, and made apparent in itself through thought and passion. But their *moral character* is not really *altered*; they are both rapacious and grasping from the beginning. They do change completely at the end, but their change is not primarily a moral one.

The play is obviously not a play of thought, for that would involve a change in thought of the main character, or characters (and in their feelings subsequently), controlled and formed by character and action.

Nor can this play be called a play of fantasy, which would involve a sustained milieu of the impossible, employing any of the patterns of plot described above.

If the play is a play of passion, it would involve either a sustained state of subjective passion or a complete change, quick

---

[2] Roger Dateller, *Drama and Life* (London, Rockliff, 1956), p. 128.
[3] George Jean Nathan, "The Theatre", *American Mercury*, IV (January, 1925), 119.

or slow, in the passion of the main characters, brought on or controlled by character, and made apparent in itself through thought and action.

It appears that this most accurately describes *Desire under the Elms*. In the case of Ephraim, the passion is sustained and perhaps simply qualified into a kind of metaphysical desire; whereas with Eben and Abbie the passion of desire is completely altered in them to the passion of love. That love destroys them both – a singular tragic irony. They no longer wish merely to acquire. Their acquisitive impulses are transformed into impulses to share and to give. That their actions in this direction result in a knotted kind of irony and reversal is tragic. Abbie gives up her child to Eben through infanticide. Eben, who wanted to share the child, is deprived of this sharing and thinks first of punishing Abbie, but finally realizes that his selfishness has driven her to the deed. Since he cannot share the child with her, he decides to share death with her. All of this is motivated by the passion of love, and all the love acts of the two, whether we think the acts acceptable or not, are blinded by the passion of love and operate to bring swift destruction to the two, while Ephraim continues to survive, never loving, simply desiring.

Love should bring happiness and life. Here it brings only death, as light and understanding brought death to *The Hairy Ape*.

The possibilities of the poetic medium of passion the poet has employed in *Desire under the Elms* are manifold. The central passion employed is, of course, desire in all its varied forms. First is the desire of the characters for the earth. This is split in the play into two main categories: a kind of innocent and noble passion to possess the land, and, growing out of this, the passion of greed on the part of Abbie, Eben, and his brothers. Ephraim's passion for the land never seems to be the kind of greed expressed frequently by the other characters. Abbie's desire for a home is still another type of desire the play imitates. It sometimes seems more like the narrower passion of greed.

Sexual desire is the second most significant passion expressed by the characters in the play. This centers within a triangle consisting of Ephraim, Abbie and Eben. Ephraim desires Abbie, but he seems to confuse her with the land and does not appear to desire her as an individual. Abbie desires Eben as an individual, as Eben desires her. But up to a certain point in the play the sexual desire of Eben for Abbie and her desire for him, though it appears to stem from an individual desire, seems a part of their general desire for possessions. As the French critic, Catel, says, Abbie's desire for Eben is mixed with the terrific romanticism of Phèdre for Hippolite in Racine's *Phèdre*.[4] But Ephraim is not the attractive figure Theseus is, nor is Abbie torn by any scruples in her desire for Eben. Sexual desire is treated as a simple appetite in the play until the final development of the sexual attraction between Abbie and Eben.

The desire for children is another important passion imitated in the play, but for the most part it is treated by Abbie and Ephraim as an extension of their desire to possess, though Abbie ultimately sees it as an expression of her love for Eben.

The less significant desires for creature comforts are imitated in the play and given a certain animal quality in practically every part of the stage milieu. An example of this is evident in the behavior of Simeon and Peter in the first scene of Part One, where, according to the stage directions, they shoulder each other *"their bodies bumping and rubbing together as they hurry clumsily to their food, like two friendly oxen toward their evening meal"*.[5]

The passion of desire in practically every conceivable form is imitated in the play. I cannot think of one passion the play does not imitate in one form or another, though the passion for the land and the sexual passion seem to be central in the play; and at times, as in the case of Ephraim, they appear merged into one.

Out of the concatenation of these two basically selfish passions O'Neill imitates the growth of the passion of love, which is more than merely acquisitive. Love is a balance of, and exchange between, the passion for possession and the passion to give of the self. O'Neill has his characters, Eben and Abbie, express it in its simplest form – the desire to share – which expression on the

[4]   J. Catel, "Critique", *Mercure de France*, CLXXIX (May 1, 1925), 836.
[5]   Random House, I, 206.

part of the characters he imitates seems well suited to the comparative simplicity of their natures. "Sharing" implies giving and taking in an equitable balance.

It should be noticed, too, that Eben's desire for children is a much different sort of passion from that same passion expressed by Ephraim.

If this development of the passion of desire into the passion of love is seen as the central controlling principle (formal principle, *dynamis*) of *Desire under the Elms*, the other structural peculiarities of the play fall into their proper perspective. The odd length of scene is utilized to this end, as is the year of time, and the special selection of incidents from that year. The growth of life in Abbie's womb parallels the growth of love. That this love destroys, partly because of a series of misunderstandings between the characters, is ironic – the irony of tragedy.

This leads to a discussion of the mode of representation through which this experience of passion is being imitated. The play seems a kind of "supernaturalism" in mode. O'Neill does not return here to the casual, realistic surfaces he had employed in *Abortion*, nor does he return wholly to the violently selective technique employed in *Thirst* and *The Hairy Ape*, nor simply to the super-subtle selection of realistic details he employed in *The Moon of the Caribbees*. He seems, to this writer, to carefully fuse into a balanced whole all three of the techniques employed in the one act plays previously considered in this study. The interior of the characters seems mirrored perfectly in his slightly emphasized setting so that the two elms brooding over the house contribute to a revelation of the characters without calling an overbalancing degree of attention to themselves. They function as an organic part of the whole milieu. They are rooted in the earth, but brood over the house. They *express* the actual bridge or connection between the earth and the house, or between the animal qualities of the characters and their humanity. They express "taking" and "returning", an arch, a unity, desire and love, which are a taking and a returning. They are strong, and yet they bend.

The characters themselves contribute to this depth and scope of the dramatic milieu. They are aware of the existence of love in the past, as is Eben with his animal or primitive belief in the friendly "mana" of his mother's spirit, in which Abbie comes to believe, also. And as the setting expresses a unity between the interior and exterior, the characters come to this kind of unity between their exterior actions and their interior feelings – the unity of love.

The dialogue, which has been heavily criticized, is intended to mirror the simplicity of this final relation of the characters of Abbie and Eben to themselves, to one another, and to the environment in which they live. Even Ephraim knows something extraordinary has happened at the climax of the play when he says to Eben, who insists on sharing Abbie's lot, "Purty good – fur yew!" [6] The dialogue does not seem strange or forced if viewed as contributing in an organic way to the play's whole nature. We would not want the smooth dialogue of a Williams in this play. It would seem incongruous. The affectation of verse would soon become distracting in a play of this nature. Poetry in dialogue does not depend on its being in verse or prose, nor in "beautiful" language. Poetry in dialogue depends on the accuracy with which it imitates the established characters of the dramatic speakers. I cannot find in this carefully wrought play many places where the dialogue seems not to do just what it should do.

Concerning the plot, which is single and complex, and the relation of the dialogue to it, Una Ellis-Fermor has put my observation of these elements in this play perhaps as well as it can be stated, though she is speaking of plot and dialogue in a general sense.

Character, plot, imagery, language, verbal music are only aspects of the indivisible whole which is the play, and whatever we discover in one of them to be essential to the whole will reveal itself also in others. We separate them by virtue of an agreed convention. But in relation to the whole and to each other they are inseparable; each may in fact appear at times to be an aspect of another. And just as what drama presents to our imagination as character differs from

[6]   *Ibid.*, p. 269.

what life presents, so it is with plot, which is not identical with a series of actual events or even with the groups of events that sometimes seem to emerge in life. Each has a similar relation to its counterpart in what we call the actual world in that in each the artist's imagination has selected from the raw material on which his inspiration worked and revealed a pattern inherent in it. And the nature of this imaginative selection is determined by the mode of the dramatist, so that in every aspect of the technique we may trace a corresponding pattern in harmony with the form of the whole to which it contributes.

.   .   .   .

Such, I would suggest, is the process at work as the action of great poetic drama is embodied in a sequence of events ordered not by demonstrative but by poetic logic.[7]

Sophus Keith Winther in his essay cited above presents Ephraim as the tragic protagonist of this play, and tells us O'Neill goes against Aristotle in imitating Ephraim's character as one without flaw. Actually, as we have seen, Ephraim is not *the* protagonist of this play. There are three protagonists functioning in a love triangle. Abbie's and Eben's passion changes completely from desire to the passion of love. Ephraim remains locked in the not altogether negative state of his inexplicable passion for the earth. His near-sightedness is symbolic of his inability to "see" love – which requires giving as well as desiring. But Winther is accurate on another point in his essay when he writes:

Such substantial critics of O'Neill as Engel, Falk and Eric Bentley make their judgment within the moral limits of the traditional Aristotelian framework. Even when Bentley can not like O'Neill because he can't do a successful stage production, it is quite obvious that his real difficulty lies in his inability to grasp O'Neill's concept of tragedy. Miss Falk's study of 'The Tragic Tension' is penetrating and profound even when it assumes that O'Neill accepted the moral view of *hamartia,* which he certainly did not. On this point he followed Ibsen and Strindberg, and in following them he violated the doctrine so hallowed by tradition that it is very nearly sacred.[8]

Aristotle suggests a way of viewing this play in the *Poetics,* as

---

[7]   Una Ellis-Fermor, "The Nature of Plot in Drama", *English Association Essays and Studies* (London, John Murray, 1960), pp. 65-66, and 80, respectively.
[8]   Winther, pp. 327-328.

this study has pointed out, when he names one of the four types
of tragedy as the tragedy of "suffering". Taking a cue from Crane
and from Aristotle, this study has extended that concept into the
concept of "passion". The arrangement of the incidents (the
substrate in Aristotle's and Crane's sense) of plot contributes to
the presentation of the larger poetic object in the sense of the
totality of the play, or its "soul", or "end", which, as Aristotle
says, is the final cause of the play's existence. Here O'Neill has
created a type of play which does not represent anything that
Aristotle actually formulated. The plot represents, as does the
plot of *The Hairy Ape,* a new departure in tragic form. It is not
an episodic plot, a simple plot, nor a multiple plot, but a complex
plot with a single issue: the transformation of the passion of
desire into the passion of love. O'Neill knew fairly well what he
was doing with this plot when he wrote the following in a letter
to George Jean Nathan (who, incidentally, did not wholly approve of, nor understand the play):

What I think everyone missed in "Desire" is the quality in it I set
most store by – the attempt to give an epic tinge to New England's
inhibited life – but, to make its inexpressiveness practically expressive,
to release it. It's just that – the poetical (in the broadest and deepest
sense) vision illuminating even the most sordid and mean blind al-
leys of life – which I'm convinced is, and is to be, my concern and
justification as a dramatist.[9]

Perhaps the most withering criticism has been leveled at the play
in terms of the emotions and expectations it is designed to evoke
in the spectators. For the sake of evoking and resolving what
particular sequence of expectations and emotions relative to the
successive parts of the imitated object is this experience of passion being imitated?

In O'Neill's letter to Nathan, a portion of which is quoted
above, he also mentions the attempted censorship of *Desire under
the Elms.* The play contains incest, infanticide, adultery, cruelty,
a whole catalogue of human crimes. Part of Eben's attraction for

---

[9]   Eugene O'Neill, in a letter to George Jean Nathan, quoted by Isaac
Goldberg in *The Theatre of George Jean Nathan* (New York, Simon and
Schuster, 1926), p. 158. It appears that O'Neill's use of the word "epic"
here means "elevation" rather than "narrative".

Abbie seems to stem from an Oedipal involvement with his own mother as suggested in the parlor scene by both characters' references to the "ghost" of Eben's dead mother, and specifically by the fact that Abbie is Eben's stepmother. I do not believe, however, that "sensation" is all the play intends to arouse in the spectators. "Sensation" is merely one of the elements that contributes to the whole emotional effect. If the play is reduced to that, it is done an injustice. Abbie is, after all, simply Eben's stepmother, not the mother who bore him.

This play means to keep us in constant suspense over the possible explosion the situation contains. I feel we find the two young people attractive, everything considered, and that we pity the situation they are in; we are terrified as well, as to what might happen to them as a result of the overwhelming passion they develop for one another. But at the same time I think we regret that Ephraim is so deceived and that the community holds him in such contempt, for they suspect Eben is the true father of the child. The suspense is brought to its height when it appears that the masquerade will have to continue, and both Eben and Abbie rebel against it, deprived as they are of public proclamation of their love for one another.

When Cabot reveals Abbie's plot to Eben our fear for the characters is greatly heightened. Abbie had told Cabot that she would give him a son who would disinherit Eben. The son is Eben's and he believes Abbie has tricked him, whereas we know that Abbie now loves Eben and thinks of the son as an expression of her love. The scene in which Eben rejects her love in his anger is one of the most anguishing in American drama, exceeded only by Abbie's subsequent murder of the child and her confession to Eben that she has done so for she thought that would keep them together. Pity for the characters and their plight is at its zenith in this scene.

Fear for both characters is greatly intensified when Eben goes for the sheriff, for Eben's reaction to the child's murder has confirmed that he actually loves Abbie. As the play ends pity and fear are not simply purged but magnified in us for the characters. We know they go to certain death by hanging. But O'Neill introduces the integration of another effect: the sudden mitigation of our fear and pity for the characters through the full expression of their love for one another made explicit in Eben's desire to share Abbie's death, and her effort to dissuade him from that choice. Here the characters turn utterly from themselves to each other, and the full development of the passion of love from the passion of desire is completed. Fear and pity thus are magnified for the characters at the prospect of their certain death, but mitigated by the realization on the part of the characters of the passion of love. There is not a simple purgation here but a partial mitigation of fear and pity.

The effect seems similar to Gassner's notion of the tragic catharsis:

Enlightenment is, therefore, the third component of the process of purgation.
It exists in perfect harmony with the components of "pity and fear", and it is even supported by them, just as enlightenment supports them.[10]

In this play pity and fear are not "purged" in Gassner's sense, but the characters come to the knowledge of love in terms of their actions and their speech. Perhaps terror and fear are purged or released in us to some extent in the observation that the characters will find union in death; pity is magnified, however, partly mitigated through their realization of love.

The validity of the purpose of the play is often questioned on the grounds of Abbie's murder of the child. Many critics see this as a weakness in the play. But Abbie is blinded by her passion – the passion of love – and mistakenly or not gives up for Eben that which she holds dearest after him, the child. Catel finds this scene very convincing and makes a further comment about the final outcome of the Freudian aspects of the play:

Alors, une scène de grande beauté se produit: Eben accuse la jeune femme de trahison. Celle-ci, pour lui prouver la réalité de son amour, étrangle le nouveau-né.

---

[10]   John Gassner, "Catharsis and the Modern Theatre", *European Theories of the Drama*, ed. Barrett H. Clark (New York, Crown Publishers, Inc., 1959), p. 550.

Eben laisse déborder une haine qu'il ne soupçonnait pas, car il aimait l'enfant pour des raisons fort simples, que la psychanalyse ne ferait, en ce cas, qu'obnubiler.[11]

If the *dynamis* of this play is seen as a development of the passion of desire into the passion of love, the play seems perfectly wrought. In that light practically every aspect of the play's structure works toward a unified end. In that light Ephraim's arrested puritanism with its hard God serves to emphasize, by contrast, the worth of the human passion of love.

The form of this play, its mode of existence, may be described in the following fashion based on our answers to the four questions of fact and the "multiple working hypotheses" formulated in answering these questions. *Desire under the Elms* involves a sustained state of subjective passion for the land in the case of Ephraim, which he identifies with his sexual desire and his metaphysical desire for God. In the case of Eben and Abbie a change is wrought slowly in their passion of desire which changes completely into the passion of love. The sustaining of Ephraim's passion, and the changing of Eben's and Abbie's passions are brought on or controlled by character and made apparent in itself through thought and action. Out of the two basic passions of desire for the land and sex, O'Neill imitates the possible growth of the passion of love in Abbie and Eben. This is accomplished in a kind of supernaturalistic dramatic mode that involves the use of casual realistic surfaces blended with a highly selective technique that also uses super-subtle selection of detail fused into a balanced whole. The characters, their prose dialogue, and the setting all contribute to this unity which expresses finally the balanced relation of these characters to their interior motivations, their exterior actions, and the imitated environment in which they exist. A complex plot with a single issue – the transformation of the passion of desire into the passion of love – is employed. This is accomplished to arouse suspense over the possible explosion of the situation between Abbie, Eben, and Ephraim, while pity and fear are magnified by the birth of Abbie's and Eben's son

[11] Catel, p. 837.

and the subsequent strangling of the child, which has become symbolic of the emergence of love. When the characters turn utterly from themselves in love, pity for them is not purged but mitigated by the positive value of their enlightenment. Pity for Ephraim is modified by his lack of emotion at their apprehension by the law, while the certainty of their death magnifies pity – yet partially releases fear for them.

The dramatic role of Nemesis in this play is difficult to describe because the play is so well balanced structurally and formally.

Ephraim represents the viewpoint of a hard and jealous God; Abbie, the point of view of the soft, indulgent, maternal God; Eben represents the point of view of the righteous but forgiving God, and provides the synthesis between the acquisitive puritanism of Ephraim and the equally acquisitive hedonism of Abbie. Eben's strength is the strength of love, and his righteousness is tempered by grace in the final state of his development as a character. If life must end in death for man, that death is made less terrible through the presence of love, which renders the paradox of death a gate of light to peace, the fear of which the entering takes away.

O'Neill's inherent concept of Nemesis seems to be similar to one of the concepts expressed in the *Oxford English Dictionary*:

Penalties inflicted by that Nemesis that is interwoven in the very Law of Nature thus transgressed.[12]

And as Baum says of Prospero:

For him, in the eve of life, there is signalized the elevation of the human spirit in the grace of a judgment of life by death. It is an ultimate grace against the ineluctable brutality of becoming.[13]

Our attitude toward the death of the lovers, the death to which all men are born, is seen partially in this light in *Desire under the Elms*.

The *lex talionis,* one source of Nemesis, is utilized in the play as an instrument of punishment in the case of all three characters. Ephraim keeps material goods from his sons and conse-

---

[12]   *OED*, VII, 87.
[13]   Baum, p. 263.

quently is deserted by Simeon and Peter, cuckolded by Eben, and, finally, isolated – a horrible kind of retribution. Eben's desire for revenge on Ephraim is a form of personal vengeance stemming from the *lex talionis,* the distribution of an eye for an eye and a tooth for a tooth. This aspect of the *lex talionis* is utilized to drive the play forward on its course, and is embellished by Eben's desire to possess the property belonging to his father. The working of this vengeance, as in *Abortion,* creates great suspense. It is finally altered in Eben to a desire to fulfill the tragic justice of love when he decides to share Abbie's lot. The same alteration takes place in Abbie's motivation.

Social Nemesis is visited on all three characters. Ephraim is hated and made foolish by his refusal to treat the other members of the community as equals, and Abbie and Eben pay with their lives for the murder of the child – a life for a life, except in this case two lives. The fear of this impending social justice operates as a suspense mechanism as soon as Abbie murders the child. The impending social retribution functions also as a catalyst in precipitating the final realization of love in the characters.

Tragic justice, or the source of tragic Nemesis, seems to be the result of the concatenation of the two previously mentioned forms: the *lex talionis* and social justice. The desire to fulfill the *lex talionis* drives the characters into a situation where they are subject to social Nemesis or punishment, and directly precipitates the operation of the law of love, which requires that Eben share Abbie's death. The Nemesis of death seems mitigated by the grace of love between human beings, a kind of divine grace, for Abbie says: "I got t' take my punishment – t' pay fur my sin." [14] She wants God's forgiveness for murdering her child but not for loving Eben.

Again we find the characters in this play are not the victims of a blind determinism. They are caught in the web of their own willful desires as well as in the inertia of the circumstances their acts of will create. They are truly free in this play, perhaps freer than the characters in any other play O'Neill wrote. In the final

[14]   Random House, I, 266.

analysis their Nemesis stems from the recoil of themselves upon themselves through the direct exercise of their will, which is in fact, Nemesis.

This study is therefore in total disagreement with the statement of Henry Steele Commager concerning O'Neill's position as it is expressed in his plays:

> It was a new Calvinism, indulged in most recklessly by those who most vehemently repudiated all religion: denying free will to men, it placed responsibility for what seemed evil not on omnipotent and inscrutable God but on an omnipotent and inexorable nature.
>
> . . . .
>
> It speaks the lines in Eugene O'Neill's *Anna Christie* and *The Hairy Ape*, in *Desire under the Elms* and *Mourning Becomes Electra*.[15]

It is the classical balance of *engagement* of the will pitted against circumstances partially created by the will that makes O'Neill's dramatic milieu deeper, wider, and eventually more interesting than the dramatic milieu of all his contemporaries. This of course applies most directly to *Desire under the Elms*. What he has done with Nemesis in *Mourning Becomes Electra, The Iceman Cometh,* and *Long Day's Journey into Night* remains to be seen in the succeeding chapters of this study.

[15]   Henry Steele Commager, *The American Mind* (New Haven, Yale University Press, 1960), pp. 109-110.

V

MOURNING BECOMES ELECTRA

INTRODUCTION

The three plays of this trilogy will be analyzed separately according to the established practice in this study. Analyzing them simultaneously would introduce a great deal of turgidity and lack of clarity in the analysis. Also, there is no reason to suppose that the plays are exactly repetitive in structure nor in the manner in which Nemesis functions in them. This study envisages them as a unit possessing three movements, each movement in turn having its own beginning, middle, and end. Each play will be considered according to this scheme: *Homecoming*, the beginning; *The Hunted,* the middle; and *The Haunted,* the end.

In order to provide a synthesis, an overall view of the structure of the trilogy, and the role of Nemesis in it, this chapter will have a concluding section in which the three separate descriptions will be fused together, and a final induction of the role of Nemesis in the whole trilogy will be undertaken.

PART ONE: *HOMECOMING*

The first act of this play begins with O'Neill's stylized chorus of common folk exposing the expected immediate event, the return of General Ezra Mannon. Through gossip they fill in the background of the terrible secrets of the house of Mannon, including a suggestion of its darkest and oldest secret concerning the cruelty Ezra's father, Abe Mannon, inflicted on David Mannon, Abe's brother. Abe became furious with David when David fell in love with Marie Brantôme, the French Canadian nurse of Abe's children, because Abe also loved Marie. Ezra, Abe's son, whom Marie had nursed, eventually fell in love with Marie, too.

Lavinia enters, and Seth, the old family retainer, reveals that a telegram has corroborated the expected news of the return of her father, General Ezra Mannon, from the Civil War, which has just ended. Seth hints that he has heard strange rumors about Adam Brant (actually Adam Brantôme, son of Marie Brantôme and David Mannon), a sea captain who has been a frequent visitor at the Mannon house during Ezra's absence.

Hazel and Peter Niles enter. Hazel leaves and a short, awkward love scene takes place between Lavinia and Peter in which he suggests she may love Adam Brant. Lavinia denies this. Christine enters and Peter leaves.

Lavinia and Christine have a foreboding conversation about Christine's visits to New York. Before she goes into the house Christine tells Lavinia that Brant will visit them that evening.

Seth enters and confirms his suspicion about the identity of Captain Adam Brant, who turns out to be the son of David Mannon and Marie Brantôme. Lavinia is shocked but put on her guard. Seth sees Brant coming up the drive and leaves.

A scene between Brant and Lavinia ensues in which Lavinia catches him off guard as Seth has suggested, and tricks him into revealing that he is indeed Adam Mannon, son of David Mannon and Marie Brantôme. During this scene the "blessed isles" to which Adam has sailed are fully described, and it becomes apparent that Lavinia finds Brant attractive. It is also revealed that Adam returned from a sea voyage and found his mother ill and deserted (his father having committed suicide years before). Marie had died in Brant's arms. He thinks Ezra as guilty as David and Abe of his mother's death, for Ezra had denied her a loan she so desperately needed. Lavinia says that she knows about the affair between Brant and Christine and threatens Brant with exposure. The first act concludes on this ominous note.

The second act begins inside the house in the study of Ezra Mannon. Lavinia tells Christine that she knows what is going on, drives Christine to an admission and threatens her with exposure.

Christine in turn accuses Lavinia of loving Brant. Lavinia forces her mother to agree never to see Brant again and goes out.

Christine summons Brant to the window of the study and gives him a prescription for poison after telling him of the situation. They agree that murdering Ezra is the only way out. Christine has prepared the town for his death by circulating the story that Ezra has severe heart trouble.

The lovers part as cannons boom from the harbor in celebration of the end of the war. The plot for Ezra's impending death is sealed as Act Two ends.

Act Three begins a week later around nine o'clock in the evening. The scene is the exterior of the house where Lavinia is seated. Seth enters singing the mournful chanty "Shenandoah", the song that had opened the first act.

Seth tells Lavinia that even Ezra had been fond of Marie and reiterates the resemblance between Marie, Christine, and Lavinia. (We know already of the similarity in appearance between David, Ezra, and Adam Brantôme Mannon.) Lavinia tells Seth, who is quite drunk, to go to bed, as they see Christine approaching.

Christine chides Lavinia by asking if Ezra is the beau she awaits in the moonlight. A bitter exchange follows between Lavinia and Christine concerning Christine's affair with Brant.

Someone is heard coming up the drive; it proves to be Ezra. Lavinia and Christine vie for Ezra's favor. Each suggestion Christine offers to comfort the weary traveler is countered by Lavinia's jealous suggestion. Ezra seems changed – kinder, more humane – as a result of his war experiences. They quarrel about Brant's visits, of which Lavinia has informed him. Lavinia finally is sent to bed, and Ezra attempts to woo his wife in a gallant fashion, but she resists. Finally they embrace but are interrupted by Lavinia who comes out of the house. Ezra and Christine go in, Ezra telling Lavinia to go to bed like a good girl. Lights go on in their bedroom, but Lavinia has remained outside talking to herself. She is carried away in her musing on her hatred of her mother and finally shouts, "Father, Father". Her father opens the bedroom window and scolds her to bed.

Act Four takes place at dawn the following morning in the bedroom of Christina and Ezra. Ezra tries to work out his conflict with Christine by talking to her after their night of love, but Christine is intractable. In anger and frustration at his efforts to regain her love in his clumsy way she reveals who Brant actually is. Ezra becomes perilously angry. Christine drives him into a heart attack by revealing that she and Brant are lovers. He asks for medicine, but she substitutes the poison Brant has gotten and mailed to her. The noise of Ezra's struggle brings Lavinia. As he is dying he manages to tell Lavinia that Christine has poisoned him. Christine is about to leave the room when she faints from exhaustion and drops the box of poison which Lavinia discovers and keeps. She throws her arms around her dead father and calls on him to come back and tell her what to do about the discovery of his murder. There the fourth act, and first play of the trilogy, ends.

The play opens at the close of the Civil War, and the general excitement of this event is underlain with the plots that are precipitously developing in the Mannon household: the imminent return of General Mannon and the swift succession of discoveries. The hurried pace of this action has been equaled by only one play considered previously in this study – *Abortion* – in which the action moved at a giddy holiday pace. But *Homecoming* is not structurally similar to *Abortion,* for the characters in *Homecoming* are more fully drawn and their passions more deeply rooted, though this play, like *Abortion,* seems geared to a sense of actual time.

Homecoming, like *Desire Under the Elms,* has three protagonists: Lavinia, Christine, and Ezra. The latter play is not a play of character, thought, action, or fantasy. It is a play of passion. Passion is important in *Homecoming,* as are character, thought, and action; however, the most striking fact about this play is the multiplicity of action. Our definition of the play of action requires a complete change, quick or slow, in the main character's situation (determined by character, thought, and passion). The characters of the three protagonists of *Homecoming* are not altered essentially, nor is their thought or passion essentially changed. It is clearly their situations which are altered, quickly altered. There is no passage of time between Acts One and Two, one week between Acts Two and Three, and a few hours between Acts Three and Four.

As Eleazar Lecky aptly points out:

O'Neill is saying, 'The more everything changes, the more it is the same'. Action, rather than exposition, is the chief method of exhibiting fate.[1]

The fact that psychological attachments are used to motivate this action and to give it the quality of inevitability does not make *Homecoming* a play about psychological attachments in the family. Lavinia's attachment to her father, Christine's attachment to her son (symbolized in her love of Adam who is similar in appearance and mannerisms to her son, but also to her husband!), Ezra's attachment to his nurse (pseudo-mother) Marie Brantôme, in fact all the psychological attachments in the play drive the motivation for action inevitably inward to the immediate source of human action, the struggle of light with darkness, the conflict between the clear commands of the ego as opposed to the chaotic impulses of the id. This is *one* basis for action in the play. It is a material which O'Neill shapes into one aspect of his dramatic action. But *the action* of the play subsumes the psychological significances and orders them to its purpose, which is the imitation of a human action in a certain form. O'Neill was free to utilize whatever materials he chose in shaping his actions. To reduce the significance of the play to a demonstration of Freudian principles of psychoanalysis is just as absurd as to insist that they are not present at all in the play. They are there, but their intrinsic dramatic significance as materials shaped into form is what is most important about them – if we are studying O'Neill's play as a whole.

The passage of a week between Acts Two and Three seems offset by the return of the scene in the third act to the exterior of the house, the place where the play began. This gives the impression of a continuing swiftness of development. And this

---

[1] Eleazer Lecky, "*Ghosts* and *Mourning Becomes Electra*: Two Versions of Fate", *Arizona Quarterly*, XXII (Winter, 1957), 334.

effect of urgency and swiftness is aided by Lavinia's threat to expose Christine and Brant, the impending possibility of Lavinia's personal Nemesis being wreaked on Christine, and the subsequent Nemesis or vengeance that we have been informed Judge Mannon is capable of.

Essentially this is a play with a triangle of protagonists, two bent on disastrous actions (Lavinia on exposing her mother to her father, and Christine on murdering Ezra), while the homecoming of Ezra is held in suspense concerning its consequences for him. It is primarily a play of action involving as a synthesizing principle (*dynamis*) a complete and quick change in the situations of the three main characters (determined by thought, character, and passion). Ezra's action of returning home results in his death; Lavinia's desire to save her father results in defeat; Christine's wish to murder her husband and make it appear as death resulting from natural causes ends in exposure by the dying man warning his daughter, and Lavinia's discovery of the poison.

This play ends successfully with triple reversal in action, and leaves the way open for the second play, which, it is clear, must deal with the apprehension of the murderers, Brant and Christine. Though this is a play primarily of action, none of the characters is polarized into good or evil. They appear to have within them equally distributed the capacity for evil actions or good actions.

In considering the use of what possibilities of the poetic medium of action the play employs, we are struck at once by the complexity of this action and its surprising clarity.

Generally speaking, we would expect a play of action to involve the primary actions of one character. Here O'Neill writes a play of action that involves the actions of three protagonists who assume equal importance in terms of the action, and all three suffer quick reversals. Bonamy Dobrée, referring to this complexity of action and motivation in O'Neill, writes "he seems to set before us stage novels rather than stage plays",[2] and Una Ellis-Fermor agrees that O'Neill made an "attempt to combine

---

[2]   Bonamy Dobrée, "The Plays of Eugene O'Neill", *Southern Review*, II (Winter, 1937), 436.

the privileges of dramatist and novelist".[3] Miss Ellis-Fermor refers specifically to *Strange Interlude,* and Dobré to the body of O'Neill's work in general. In *Mourning Becomes Electra* O'Neill has extended his use of complex action in *Abortion* (involving one protagonist), and has simply multiplied the complexity by three, with an accompanying depth in character, passion, and thought. He has also managed to mirror the internal dilemmas of character without using the expressionistic technique he employed in *The Hairy Ape* by having the characters *act out* their interior preoccupations, and by gradually bringing them to an awareness of the significance of their external actions.

Edward Groff points out:

Because we have taken for granted the 'complete and inveterate objectivity' of the play form, we have not understood sufficiently that experimental point-of-view techniques can operate in the drama as well as in the novel. Like modern novelists, playwrights have become increasingly concerned with the inner life of man and with the loss of a clear 'world picture' which would furnish a comforting certainty for human action.

. . . .

If it [*The Emperor Jones*] seem 'unreal', it is only because the play form has been made subjective . . . an attempt to tell a story from within a man's mind rather than from the parlor. . . .[4]

But in *Mourning Becomes Electra* O'Neill was to go a step further than Mr. Groff suggests he has by having external actions provide a direct demonstration of the internal action of the characters. Thus, we are enabled to get the characters' minds (as we do in the novel) because their external actions are symbolic of the inner qualities of their psychological motivations. *Homecoming* is full of this sort of incident. The best example is the revelation of Lavinia's unconscious attraction to Brant, despite the fact she knows Brant is cuckolding her father. She refuses to admit this when Christine points it out to her, but we are convinced that her motivation for separating Brant and Christine

[3]   Una Ellis-Fermor, *The Frontiers of Drama* (London, Methuen, 1945), p. 122.
[4]   Edward Groff, "Point of View in Modern Drama", *Modern Drama*, II (December, 1959), 270-271.

reflects more than her moral outrage at adultery. She openly voices the fact that she considers her mother her rival in all the love situations in which she has ever been involved. Her hurt and rage demonstrate her affinity for Brant when Christine tells her that she had arranged to have Brant pretend to be interested in Lavinia. Her external rage at this accusation goes beyond mere awareness of insult. It can only be interpreted as jealous rage. In the final play of the trilogy this point is driven home clearly when she calls Peter "Adam". This *lapsus linguae* finally makes clear to Lavinia the truth of her mother's accusation in the first play. The audience has known this all along.

This is perhaps the most outstanding exploitation of the possibilities of the poetic medium of action O'Neill uses in this play. His dexterity in weaving a triple action – involving the fortunes of three characters rather than one – into a perfectly clear and sound drama should also be reiterated at this point.

The action of this first play encompasses all the significances of human action that will be mirrored in the two plays that follow. The action itself is symbolic of the sources of Nemesis within this play. Heinrich Straumann saw this balance of the four sources of justice, or Nemesis, in many of O'Neill's plays. Speaking of *Mourning Becomes Electra* he says:

That this is in essence the conflict between the deterministic pragmatism of the majority on the one hand and the ethico-religious tradition on the other is a fact following inevitably from the history of American thought. ... If he [the dramatic protagonist] obeys his primitive impulses the norms will compass his doom, if he follows the dictates of the norms his repressed vital instincts will turn against him.

.   .   .   .

So all the influences surveyed are found reflected in this tragedy; the deterministic aspect in the uncontrolled human instincts, the pragmatic in the attempt to escape out of the conflict into another sphere of existence, the historico-traditional in the material data underlying the events and the metaphysical aspect in the issue of the conflict.[5]

[5]   Heinrich Straumann, "The Philosophical Background of the Modern American Drama", *English Studies*, XXVI (June, 1944), 76-78.

As the action of *Homecoming* comes to an end, the inevitable Nemesis of deprivation of love is visited on Lavinia through her mother's murder of her father; the determined Nemesis of exposure is exhibited in the case of Christine, who has not the will to control her instinctive passion for release; and the unavoidable death at the hands of the woman he truly loves is visited on Ezra as payment for his years of cruelty and harshness. The action is tragic, because Ezra discovers too late that he will give up his empty pride, in fact anything, for love. In this contrite frame of mind he is viciously and hatefully murdered by his wife. Christine in turn is undone by the very height of her hate, the exhaustion from which causes her to faint short of her goal of freedom. Lavinia, because she does not have the courage to create scandal and thus risk the reputation of her family, remains quiet too long and is deprived of her father.

In more practical terms Roy Battenhouse describes the issue of the action of this play.

Let us note that both dramatists [Aeschylus and O'Neill] describe the history of a chain of crime and punishment. They recognize that the beginning of the evil lies somewhere in the past. An earlier quarrel of some ancestor – that of Atreus and Thyestes, or that of Abe Mannon and his brother Dave – seems to harbor for the present generation an hereditary curse. The factors are so predisposed that crime continues to be committed under the pretext of justice. And new crimes call for new punishments: retribution demands retribution. Can this ancestral blight in no way be helped? [6]

The action of *Homecoming* tends to make atonement impossible. The exercise of the will of the protagonists runs against the blank wall of defeat and prepares the way for the apprehension of the new group of criminals. How will the dramatist ever solve this dilemma? Perhaps he does not.

Now we must discuss the mode in which this action is cast. It is not narrative, though this story could easily be cast in that mode. The opinions of Ellis-Fermor and Dobrée indicate that the dramatic mode used here moves unsuccessfully toward the

[6]   Roy Battenhouse, "Mourning Becomes Electra", *Christendom*, VII (Summer, 1942), 339.

fullness of narrative. There is no narrator in an actual sense; the chorus of townspeople operate as they do in Greek drama, as a kind of collective character, the voice of the community. They manage some exposition, but they do this as characters speaking in scene. It seems clear that we can ascribe a point of view to this drama that will fit all drama: third person, objective observer, effaced. The fullness of character, the depth of action, and its complexity must be ascribed to O'Neill's skill with pantomime and dialogue. This play does not involve the subjective mirroring of the characters' attitudes in distorted images of spectacle as does *The Hairy Ape*.

The plot is complex, involving a triple – not a single – issue: the death of Ezra, the defeat of Lavinia's efforts to avoid his death, and the failure of Christine to murder Ezra without detection. The crisis occurs at the end of the second act when Christine makes the decision to poison Ezra. The climax involves his actual murder, Lavinia's loss of her father, and the exposure of Christine's guilt.

This is all accomplished in prose dialogue that is embellished by the verse and melody of the chanty "Shenandoah". This dialogue avoids the sense of period one might expect in terms of its diction. No great amount of special diction is employed, except the occasional use of New England colloquialisms such as Lavinia's "pesky cold" [7] in the first act. O'Neill had planned this in his notes for the play. He wrote, "Stick to modern tempo of dialogue without attempt at pretense of Civil Wartime lingo. That part of first draft is right." [8] The effect of this dialogue is a kind of bare and uncluttered classical line. By classical is meant a kind of balance and proportion that avoids excessive ornamentation, and attempts to reflect directly the clear dramatic image of the relationship that exists between the internal state of mind of the characters speaking and their external actions and appearance.

[7]   Random House, II, 13.
[8]   Eugene O'Neill, "Working Notes and Extracts from a Fragmentary Work Diary", *European Theories of the Drama*, ed. Barrett H. Clark (New York, Crown Publishers, Inc., 1959), p. 533.

As Hiram Motherwell said in his review of the play in production:

What fascinates is not the story, the acting, or the production merely (these are but faithful expressions of the playwright's idea) but the music which the workaday lines of the play somehow evoke.[9]

Motherwell goes on to say that this particular medium of dialogue successfully mirrors the pent-up emotions of the characters. Tension grows out of the simple words that partially conceal through this very plainness a contrast to the emotional intensity fully revealed in the actions of the characters.

O'Neill was obviously after a "plaintive" music in his tightly wrought and truly poetic dialogue. The stark, yet tragic quality of "Shenandoah" provides a key to the quality of the dialogue employed here. It is as though by understatement more is achieved than would have been possible through a full release of emotion in a more ornate diction. The tone of the dialogue accurately mirrors the inhibited circumstances of the characters. At no time do they communicate *easily* with each other in the dialogue, as, indeed, they do not in the action. The impossible maintenance of restraint explodes into violent action that is productive only of defeat.

The play is naturalistic in the sense that *Desire Under the Elms* is naturalistic. It is a "supernaturalism". The three dimensions used in *Desire* – unobtrusive realistic elements, a very economical technique, and the super-subtle pointing of detail for unique effects – are again welded into an organic whole that demonstrates how the characters are affected by their interior conflicts, their exterior behavior, and the imitated environment in which they exist. Touching on the naturalism of this play Mark Harris writes:

The conflict, then, is seen to be deep and inexorable; not trivial, but rather both great and significant. For Humanism and Supernaturalism combine against the children of the flesh and destroy them. Yet in so doing, they find no victory, since by their vision new-given through

[9] Hiram Motherwell', "*Mourning Becomes Electra*", *Stage* (title varies, i.e., *Theatre Guild Magazine*), IX (December, 1931), 16.

suffering, they see that the laurel lies forever beyond their reach in the hand of nature, who still bestows the crowning gift of life. To many, therefore, who in our day have learned to tolerate the stern message of naturalism, O'Neill seems to project a drama worthy of the ancient goat-song.[10]

The mode of this work is entirely dramatic, utilizing a complex and multiple plot with a triple issue, in dialogue of a peculiarly plaintive tone that helps create a naturalistic milieu involving the use of casual realistic surfaces, a highly selective technique, and the super-subtle selection of detail for special effects; all of which are fused into a balanced whole relating the interior motivations of the characters to their exterior actions and the imitated environment in which they exist.

The purpose of this play in regard to its evocation of a particular sequence of emotions and expectations, and its resolution of them, is clear, clearer perhaps than the previous plays examined in this study. Our curiosity is aroused in the first act and is partially satisfied immediately by the exposition of the chorus of townsfolk. Their subsequent information arouses suspense in us. Our curiosity is satisfied in the scene between Lavinia and Brant, but fear and terror are inspired by the possibility of Lavinia's revealing this knowledge to her father and mother.

Act Two brings a lull, a partial release in tension and suspense, in the scene between Lavinia and Christine where it appears that Christine will relinquish her affair with Brant due to Lavinia's threats. But immediately the suspense and fear are doubled as Christine and Brant plot Ezra's murder.

Act Three inspires our pity for Ezra and for Lavinia, and fear for both of them, which is qualified by our feeling that Christine has been badly used by both her daughter and her husband. Ezra now seems capable of tenderness after his war experience, but we fear that it will be too late to stem the tide of hate he has built up in Christine.

Act Four brings to a conclusion our suspense over Ezra's possible murder, and greatly increases our sense of pity for the

[10] Mark Harris, *The Case for Tragedy* (New York, G. P. Putnam's Sons, 1932), pp. 169-170.

waste of the situation, and our fear of what will happen to Christine and to Lavinia now that Ezra has been murdered. Our greatest pity is for Lavinia; our greatest fear is for Christine. This is qualified by our horror at Christine's brutal action, and the unfeeling attitude of Lavinia, who has done all in her power to keep the husband and wife from having a successful reunion with her puerile and jealous interruptions in the preceding act.

Pity is magnified for Ezra and Lavinia. Terror is inspired by the contemplation of what will happen to Christine. Suspense is released as Ezra dies, but pity and terror are magnified.

This first play of the trilogy takes us into a kind of *purgatorio* of frustrated actions, very similar to Kernodle's general account of modern tragic effect:

I believe we can say that one of the characteristics of the vital plays of the twentieth century is that they do carry the audience through a *purgatorio*, they do face the possibility that nature is cold and indifferent and that man must find his own values, his own relation to the universe, without a warm and friendly earth around him. Even the most assured religious plays gain that assurance after a desperate struggle.[11]

We acquire, too, a sense of the inevitability of the outcome of the play for O'Neill does not depend on surprise or simple suspense effects. We are involved in a kind of intense, almost painful contemplation of events we feel can have no other course than the one we are led to expect very near the beginning. Stark Young called this technique as it is employed in this play "classical suspense":

Knowing how things will end, you are left free to watch what qualities and what light will appear in their progression toward their due and necessary finish.[12]

Synthesizing the results of the hypotheses derived from our four questions, then, we may describe the form of this play in the

11 G. R. Kernodle, "Patterns of Belief in Contemporary Drama", *Spiritual Problems in Contemporary Literature*, ed. S. Hopper (New York, Institute for Religious and Social Studies; distributed by Harper, 1952), p. 190.
12 Stark Young, "Eugene O'Neill's New Play", *New Republic*, LXVII (November 11, 1931), 353.

following manner. This play is essentially a play of action involving as a synthesizing principle a complete and quick change in the situations of the three main characters (determined by thought, character, and passion). External actions provide a direct demonstration of the internal nature of the characters, and we are enabled to get at the characters' minds as we do in novels because their external actions are symbolic of the inner qualities of their psychological motivations. All this is accomplished in an entirely dramatic mode, utilizing a complex and multiple plot with a triple issue, in dialogue of a peculiarly plaintive tone that helps to create a naturalistic milieu involving the use of casual realistic surfaces, a highly selective technique, and the super-subtle selection of detail for special effects; all of which are fused into a balanced whole, unifying the interior motivations of the characters, their exterior actions, and the imitated environment in which they exist. This arouses "classical suspense" in the audience, whose pity is magnified for Ezra and Lavinia, while terror is inspired in the audience for what will happen to Christine, though suspense and fear for Ezra are released at his death. Pity and terror are magnified, not released.

The *lex talionis* reigns supreme in this play. The Nemesis visited on Ezra seems that of an eye for an eye and a tooth for a tooth, though he is in part paying for the sins of Abe, his father, and David, his uncle. Christine is "like" Marie Brantôme, and repulses him as Marie had repulsed his father in favor of someone who looked like him, but who is more tender and not so inhibited. Christine destroys him because he is a threat to her continued happiness with Adam Brant, and because of the long years of brutality he had subjected her to. She also bears him a grudge for sending her son off to war.

The law of society is effectively by-passed in this play. Social justice, or public notoriety, is feared by all the characters, and so it is never brought directly into the picture where they are concerned.

Divine grace, divine justice, is also shown to be ineffectual in the lives of people whose puritanical morality is actually the evil perversion of the laws of God.

The recoil of the willed wrongs of the characters upon themselves is the tragic source of Nemesis in this play. Their character is their destiny, though the threat of social Nemesis is effective as a force that drives them inward to their own resources. Stamm found O'Neill's entire trilogy lacking any possible solution to the terrible Nemesis of an eye for an eye and a tooth for a tooth.[13] This is certainly true regarding the ending of this play as it is of the ending of *Agamemnon*. Both plays imitate this ineluctable chain of evil from the past that overtakes the characters in the present. The sins of their fathers are exactly repeated by the characters themselves in both the classical model and O'Neill's play. The chain of personal vengeance, the law of blood justice, is forged, and is presented as unbreakable by whatever means. But that is only true, in so far as this study has examined the problem, in this play. Perhaps O'Neill follows Aeschylus' pattern and works a redemption for his characters in the succeeding plays. The children must avenge the homicide, we know, and in so doing will spill kindred blood, but will O'Neill end the chain of death and destruction? Aeschylus did it through divine agencies, and a nice point of law. What can O'Neill do to solve his dramatic problem? What will be the source of the solution, divine Nemesis, the Nemesis of salvation?

We must disagree with Francis Fergusson who flatly says no solution is possible to the dilemma O'Neill so adroitly casts in his action.

However, no modern drama embodies values comparable to those of Greek tragedy, for the reason that there is no such publicly established value to appeal to.[14]

There is a clear-cut system of values implied in this first play, and the inevitability of certain behavior is so clearly established in psychological terms that no critic who has written of the play has failed to mention it. A solution is possible to the puritanical

---

[13] Rudolf Stamm, "The Orestes Theme in Three Plays by Eugene O'Neill, T. S. Eliot, and Jean Paul Sartre", *English Studies*, XXX, No. 5 (October, 1949), 253-254.
[14] Francis Fergusson, "A Month of the Theatre", *Bookman*, LXXIV (December, 1931), 445.

and psychological conflict presented here. Our question shall be: "Has O'Neill arrived at a solution, or if not, why? and if so, what is it?" Krutch states the position of this study:

It is no more an exposition or defense of a modern psychological conception than Aeschylus is an exposition or defense of the tenets of the Greek religion, even though it does accept the one as Aeschylus accepts the other.[15]

To deny a solution as Fergusson does is to deny the transmission of culture. We do not expect American ideas to be Greek ideas, though Greek ideas may certainly suggest a point of departure. To deny that they can do so in an absolute statement is to refuse to examine the products of our culture in a responsible way.

PART TWO: *THE HUNTED*

Act One of this play begins two days after Ezra's murder. This time the chorus is not composed of Seth's acquaintances, the ordinary folk; it consists of the town functionaries: the minister, the doctor, and an executive of the Mannon firm. The chorus makes it clear that they and the populace of the town are unaware of the murder, though we know that Lavinia has discovered it.

Christine comes out of the house and is followed directly by Hazel, Orin's sweetheart. Christine is under a nervous strain and tries to persuade Hazel to marry Orin as soon as he returns, for, she tells Hazel, Lavinia may try to keep Orin from marrying. They go back into the house.

Orin enters with Peter Niles and Lavinia. Orin has a heavily bandaged head wound from the war, and he looks strikingly like Ezra and like Adam.

Lavinia gets Peter to go into the house ahead of them so she can talk privately with Orin. She suggests that Orin be on guard against his mother. Orin is impatient, tired from his journey, and strained by the ravages of his wound. He is furious about

[15] Joseph Wood Krutch, "Our Electra", *The Nation*, CXXXIII (November 18, 1931), 552.

Brant's visits, but does not want to continue discussing them. Before Lavinia can reveal the whole story, Christine rushes out and enfolds him in motherly embraces. Lavinia's jealousy interrupts their reunion, repeating her actions in the third act of the first play with her father. Orin is suspicious of his mother. Christine ushers him into the house to see Hazel, leaving Lavinia fuming outside.

The door opens a second later and Christine returns. She attempts to commiserate with her implacable daughter, telling her that the box of pills Lavinia found the night of the death was a sleeping preparation she had used. She asks Lavinia if she intends to try to get Orin to go to the police and report Ezra's murder. She rushes down the steps and takes Lavinia by the arm, shakes her in an effort to get an answer from her, but Lavinia remains silent, pulls her arm free and stalks into the house.

Christine is at her wit's end – not knowing exactly how much Lavinia knows. Orin calls from the house to his mother. She starts, answers him, and goes into the house.

Act Two takes place in the sitting room of the Mannon house. It is cold and austere and hung with portraits of Mannon ancestors. There has been no passage of time between Acts One and Two. Hazel and Peter are discussing the strain Christine is under and are aware of the tension among the family members.

Orin and Christine enter, Orin questioning his mother severely and suspiciously. Orin acts very strangely, talking of his father as if he were still alive, rambling on about the horrors of war, and generally making everyone uncomfortable. He is obviously unbalanced, even suggests that Peter will be as jealous of Hazel as he is of Lavinia. This is innocently countered by Hazel, and Orin takes umbrage at this, indicating he knows Lavinia can be tender if she wants to.

Lavinia enters and commands Orin to come and see their father who lies in state in the study. Christine chides Lavinia for being officious and insists Orin stay and visit with her. Lavinia warns Orin to remember what she has told him, and leaves angrily. Christine nervously demands to know where she is going. Lavinia ignores her mother, and asks Orin to come in a little while. This odd exchange makes Hazel and Peter uncomfortable; they excuse themselves, advising Orin to get some rest.

A long scene takes place between Christine and her son. She tells Orin that Lavinia has been driven practically mad by the loss of her father. She also tells him of Lavinia's suspicions concerning her relations with Brant, cleverly revealing all that Lavinia will surely tell him, and convincing Orin that this is all the mad hallucination of Lavinia. Orin is taken in by this clever device. When Christine has won his confidence, she even goes so far as to tell him that Lavinia suspects her of murdering Ezra. Orin is outraged at this, suggesting Lavinia be put away in an asylum. It appears that Christine has checkmated her daughter, and that Orin will never believe what we know to be the truth.

Having won Orin's confidence, Christine leads him into a long reverie that for her is an expression of her motherly love for her only son; but the truth becomes plain in Orin's reactions to her that his return of her love is more than that of a son for his mother. We are made aware that Orin relates to his mother as a lover to his mistress, though Christine apparently is not aware of the depth of his passion for her. Orin compares her to a blessed isle of sanctuary. His Oedipal involvement with his mother is plain, but at the same time we realize he is not aware of the negative aspects of his love for his mother, just as she is not aware of its incestuous quality.

Lavinia steps calmly into the room and stares at them. She asks Orin if he ever intends to come look at their father. Orin leaves unwillingly to go view his father's body.

Christine tells Lavinia how she has anticipated her by telling Orin everything and convincing him that Lavinia is mad. She threatens to bring out everything in a public scandal if Lavinia continues on her course. She says she will reveal her own adultery, Lavinia's desire for Brant, the old scandal concerning Marie Brantôme, everything. Then she falters and begs Lavinia not to tell Orin about Adam, for she fears Orin will kill him. Lavinia smiles cruelly and grimly. Her mother has inadvertently suggested to her that to have Orin kill Brant would be perfect revenge.

Act Three begins immediately afterward in Ezra's study with Orin speaking to his dead father. Lavinia enters and scolds him having overheard his odd sentiments. Orin tries to explain the horror of war; how the face of each man he has killed seemed to be his own face, as though he were repeatedly killing himself. Lavinia does not comprehend. He discloses that his heroism was the result of a misunderstanding.

Lavinia now tries to convince Orin that her version of what has happened is the truth. She appeals to his honor, to his filial piety, but these are not successful. He wants to forget – tired and weary, worn by the war as he is. But Lavinia taunts him, telling him he is a coward to let his mother's lover escape. Orin's jealous rage is aroused. Lavinia finally appeals to his incestuous jealousy of his mother's affections. She understands his jealousy of his mother. She finally enrages him against Brant, whom he vows to kill if Lavinia can show him his mother and Brant together, which she promises to do. They hear Christine coming. Lavinia cautions Orin to act as if he were not suspicious, and tells him to watch his mother's reactions when she sees the box of poison which Lavinia then places on the dead general's uniform.

Christine reacts guiltily to the poison. Orin is convinced of her relations with Brant, and stumbles out in a jealous rage. Lavinia tells her mother that her actions prove Brant got the poison for her. Lavinia returns the box of poison to the bosom of her dress and stalks out.

Christine looks at Ezra, shouting that only she, Christine, is to blame. She stops, suddenly horrified by Ezra's body, and backs to the door and rushes out.

Act Four is set on a wharf at Boston. A clipper ship is tied up there and Brant is on deck talking to a drunken chantyman. We learn that there have been many robberies in the area.

Christine comes out of the shadows, and she and Brant go into the ship's cabin.

Orin and Lavinia enter, board the ship and lean over the skylight of the cabin.

There is a fadeout in which a few minutes elapse.

As the lights come up we see a section of the ship has been

removed and Brant and Christine are in the cabin, with Lavinia and Orin on the deck listening and watching as before. The lovers expose themselves fully in their conversation. Orin's face is twisted with jealous though silent rage at what he hears and sees.

Brant and Christine eventually go out, Brant escorting her off the ship. Lavinia and Orin take this opportunity to go down into the cabin. There they await Brant. When he returns Orin shoots him twice as he enters the cabin. Lavinia and Orin then arrange the scene to look as though Brant were the victim of a robbery, and they leave.

Act Five takes place the following night in front of the Mannon house. Christine is awaiting the return of Orin and Lavinia from "Blackridge", where she supposes they have gone to visit friends. Hazel is keeping her company until they return. Christine asks Hazel to stay all night with her. Hazel leaves to get her mother's permission to stay, saying she will come back in a little while.

Orin and Lavinia return home. Brutally they reveal Brant's slaying to Christine who is stricken by this information. The murderers tell her they have fooled the police, who think Brant the victim of a robbery. Christine moans to herself. Finally she rushes into the house and commits suicide by shooting herself. Orin rushes in to discover her dead. He comes out distractedly, blaming himself for his mother's death saying he has murdered her with his unnecessary cruelty.

Seth enters, Lavinia tells him to get Dr. Black and inform him that Christine has just killed herself in a fit of grief over Ezra's death. Orin and Lavinia go into the house as the second play ends.

The kind of human experience this play imitates is more difficult to describe than that which was imitated in *Homecoming*. Certainly the play involves a great deal of action. If, however, we attempt to describe it according to that pattern we encounter difficulty. Is this a play of action involving a complete change in the situations of the main characters brought on by thought, character, and passion? That would apply well to Christine and to Brant, who is not, however, a major character. But it does not fully consider the other two major characters, Orin and Lavinia. Their situations are not completely changed, as they manage to forestall detection.

It could hardly be described primarily as a play of thought or fantasy.

It could be a play of character, however. This would involve a complete alteration in the moral character of the protagonists, brought about by action, and determined by thought and passion. That would apply partially to Orin, but does not take into account Lavinia and Christine.

The description of this play that accounts for the greatest number of factors is the one concerning passion. If the play is described as a play of passion (Orin, jealousy; Lavinia, hatred; Christine, fear-love) involving a complete change in the passions of the main characters, brought on by action, and determined by character and thought, we have a description of the play that takes into account the greatest number of the factors contained in the play. Christine's fear for her lover is altered into despair at his death, a despair so deep she commits suicide. Orin's terrible and incestuous jealousy is altered into a shattering remorse when he sees the effect Brant's death has on Christine. His remorse is so great that he considers himself his mother's murderer. Lavinia's hatred of her mother is purged into a kind of calm, satisfied state; she calls her mother's suicide "justice". This is a play that imitates primarily the passions of jealousy, hatred, and fear, which are altered in the characters to remorse, satisfaction, and despair.The Nemesis served on Christine and Orin seems to be a kind of emotional punishment. Orin is paid for his jealousy (which is incestuous) with remorse. Christine is dealt abysmal despair for her adulterous passion for Brant; while Lavinia, though essentially in the right, is again dealt the Nemesis of deprivation of love through her destruction of Brant, whom she secretly desires. She avenges her father's death, but loses him again figuratively.

In this play we find the possibilities of the poetic medium of passion being more narrowly selected and employed than they were in *Desire Under the Elms*. The passion of love (or a passion stemming from love) is the central passion imitated in all the characters. Christine's illicit love passion for Brant, and her intense fear of being deprived of Brant, the love object, who looks like Ezra but behaves entirely differently, is perhaps the least objectionable passion stemming from love that the play imitates. We know that Brant had intended simply to use Christine as revenge against Ezra, but, in spite of himself, he falls deeply in love with her. He is willing to let it go at that, but Christine wants her love to be free, free from the possible financial and social retribution Ezra might have wreaked on them for loving one another; thus, in the first play she initiates the murder of Ezra so that she may be free to love. That part of her motivation is hatred of Ezra cannot be doubted. Ironically, then, Christine has used Brant, the object of her love, partly as an instrument in furthering her hatred of Ezra. Murder for love, it seems, destroys her love rather than freeing it. At great personal risk she attempts to warn Brant of his danger, but too late. She goes against the norms to give vent to her primitive passion for a full expression of her physical love; and the norms, personified in her children, destroy her and her lover.

Orin's incestuous love for his mother is the third clear possible type of love passion imitated in the action of this play. But the passion of incestuous love is illicit also, and Orin's extreme jealousy of his mother drives him to kill Brant, his rival, but inadvertently he is instrumental in casting her into such a state of despair that she kills herself. Orin calls himself her murderer. The tender scene in Act Two between Orin and Christine is a great protestation of the love of mother and son. We become almost convinced that the characters lose contact with their incest motives and ulterior purposes in their expression of love for one another. But the love is too ideal, too much of the past. We never quite succumb to the charm of this scene to the extent that we forget Christine is selfishly attempting to mold her son into a quiescence that will allow her to continue her affair with Brant, nor that Orin's passion for his mother is a passion infinitely less moral than if directed toward his choice of an appropriate mate.

The charm of the scene is underlain by a love relationship that in the case of Orin has been arrested before puberty; and in the case of Christine, a love relationship she is exploiting for her own selfish ends. These people have great sensitivity, great ability to support a productive love relationship. But Orin is stunted, and Christine is too selfish.

Lavinia's love of the dead is the other major possibility of passion imitated in this play. This is mixed with her twisted passion for Brant. Since she cannot have him to love, she would rather see him dead. She feels her mother stands in the way of her desire to love. From this frustration and from her desire for vengeance – not justice – grows her towering hatred, fully imitated in the scene in which the murderers confront Christine with their killing of Brant. Lavinia cares most for propriety, yet is driven by passion. In attempting to conform to the stiff propriety that is part of her puritan heritage she allows her repressed vital instincts to sour and writhe within her. In her external rage for order she denies the equally powerful emotions of pity, companionship, and love – spiritual as well as physical. Through this blindness, or refusal to recognize her vital instincts plus the commands of the norms, she effectively deprives herself of Ezra and, ironically, of Brant. But Lavinia's is a true dilemma, for she has the only moral conscience in this entire group of characters. Christine insists on satisfying her instinctive lusts without conscience. Orin follows her pattern. He weeps, not for his mother, nor because of the pain he has caused her with his incestuous jealousy. He weeps for himself, he mourns for himself the loss of Christine. Lavinia, however, knows that justice, the punishment for murder, must be carried out. She knows that the guilty must suffer. Her sense of propriety is ironclad. Despite her emotional involvement in the necessary course of justice she knows, indeed she is painfully aware of what is right. Had she been the libidinous creature her mother was, she would have sought to have Brant at any cost. But he has helped Christine kill her father, and though she loves him, Lavinia knows he must suffer, as must her mother.

Lavinia's justice is not without flaw, however. She has not

even dreamt of a propriety which tempers itself with a recognition of human failings. Her justice is cruel and unyielding. Her justice requires no sacrifice from the judge, no sympathy for the human beings who transgress her iron dictates. She does not comprehend, as yet, mercy. Her law is the law of the claw, the unbending dictates of the blood strengthened by cruelty. Hence, her passion of hatred for her mother can be in all conscience allowed. Brant must die, and Christine must be punished by being deprived of him, for they have in fact killed her father, whom she loved. That this act of justice also satisfies her own personal hatred and jealousy of her mother disturbs her not the least at this point in the development of her character. But she does have a clearly moral conscience. Any mourning she may do will truly become her, for she is never completely the victim of her selfish instincts. Mourning will become her because she understands, or will understand, exactly what it is she mourns. She will mourn the lack of fruition in her race, not the smaller deprivations to which she alone has been subjected.

Though I do not agree entirely with Battenhouse, his comment clearly and precisely captures the essential pattern of passions O'Neill imitates here:

According to Aquinas, Original Sin arises from the insubordination of the will of man to God, thus disrupting the harmony of original justice. The result is an inordinate disposition – a languor, a sickness of nature, a destruction of the smooth harmony of humanity. The withdrawal of grace has the character of punishment; for our human nature when left to itself, unsupported, develops diverse defects.[16]

Actually, here, in place of a supernatural God, O'Neill has substituted the insubordination of the will of family members to a just pattern of familial behavior: that is, a pattern that will best supply the needs of the family as a whole, and make it a unit that will successfully propagate itself. Ezra in his relations with his wife selfishly takes sexual gratification without considering the needs of his wife. Christine is too bitter to grasp the late development in her husband of the kind of love she needs. Orin

---

[16]   Battenhouse, p. 335.

is a rival for his mother's affections (a relationship which Christine has aided and abetted). Lavinia is in direct competition with her mother for the affections of her father and her brother (situations to which both Ezra and Orin give material aid). Ezra rules without sympathy or understanding. Christine substitutes Orin, and then Brant, for the needs her husband cannot supply, until too late. Lavinia, imitating her parents, and having no model for a balanced love relationship requiring giving and taking, does not extend herself or risk giving of herself, but fastens on that which it requires least effort to love, her father. Orin, too, imitating both his parents, cannot give nor risk deep exterior attachments, and thus selfishly fastens himself to that object which requires least effort to satisfy his possessive love instinct, his mother.

But all this is not to say the characters are purely helpless victims of their distorted family passions, ingrown as they are. Ezra finally does exert his will in an attempt to right his years of brutal exploitation of his wife. His desire to give to her is clear upon his return. She in turn has complete freedom of choice in the matter of whether or not to reach out and take what he tries so pathetically to give her. By a sheer act of selfish choice, she refuses to soften even one jot and murders him. Lavinia and Orin both have the opportunity to give up their puerile attachments to their parents, and to extend their relations with Peter and Hazel. Lavinia simply will not do it and willfully ignores the hope of a healthy love with Peter until it is too late. And Orin willfully refuses to find his need for love in Hazel. He *chooses* incest, and though that choice has been conditioned by many years, nonetheless, it is a choice.

From all the possibilities of the poetic medium of passions he might have chosen, O'Neill chooses to imitate in his characters a pattern of passions that results from the will to love in familial members that is insubordinate to the need in the familial pattern of love relationships that will best maintain the stability of the family as a whole. This insubordination of the love will to the selfish ends of the individual family members in this play results in Christine's fear that her children will murder her illicit lover;

it results in Lavinia's intense hatred of her mother, and is directly productive of Orin's miserable and incestuous jealousy of his mother. During the play these passions run their course and are altered into the passions of remorse in Orin, despair in Christine, and a kind of stability, satisfaction, or emotional emptiness in Lavinia.

The imitation of this particular sequential development of passions in this play depends, of course, on the pattern of action presented in the play preceding this one in the trilogy.

This play is obviously written in the dramatic mode, but the chorus of town functionaries does not have as much exposition here as the chorus had in *Homecoming*. Now they make a significant comment on the action of the preceding play in relation to the action that is to come. Dr. Blake says to Borden, manager of the Mannon shipping company:

I haven't asked Christine Mannon any embarrassing questions, but I have a strong suspicion it was love killed Ezra! [17]

Lecky is aware that the dialogue and the movement of this play, as in the previous play, are so constructed as to provide a clear picture of the internal workings of the characters' psychological rhythms, as well as a picture of their external actions when she writes:

Seldom does O'Neill deceive the audience, even temporarily. Rather, he grants it a kind of omniscience. By introducing an occasional soliloquy or double take and a great many arrested movements (he abandoned the asides or interior monologues of *Strange Interlude*), he renders the characters transparent. We know their secrets, which concern their future plans rather than the past. They are new secrets and the damage which occurs is fresh damage, catastrophe after catastrophe.[18]

As was pointed out concerning the dialogue of the previous play in the trilogy, this transparency is accomplished too through the general tone of the dialogue which perfectly mirrors the inhibited circumstances of the characters. The whole dialogue, then, contributes to this transparent effect.

[17] Random House, II, 71.
[18] Lecky, p. 334.

The plot (in the second sense, the arrangement of the incidents) is complex, all reversal and discovery. It is not as densely
woven, however, there being actually fewer incidents, fewer
complications, and fewer discoveries than were observed in the
first play. This issue still is triple in terms of passion, but the plot
is not multiple, and involves as action the murder of Brant and
the subsequent suicide of Christine.

Harris comments further on the naturalism of the trilogy as a
whole, but his remarks seem to apply especially to the stark outcome of this play:

Again, we find that the naturalistic tragic author is skeptical of the
reality of a moral order of the universe and takes no pains to make
the outcome of his tragedies reassert the validity of that order. He is
more inclined to feel that the universe possesses the non-moral attributes of indifference or even blind malevolence, which, in its very
blindness, is implacable. Consequently, the naturalist not only does
not seek to affirm the moral frame of things, but he rather discredits
both moral order and supernatural agency. And as for the dignity of
the individual, it appears somewhat ridiculous when viewed in direct
comparison with the universe, a comparison frequently employed by
Hardy and Dreiser.[19]

This play, then, is written in a naturalistic dramatic mode, utilizing a complex but single, not multiple, plot, with a triple issue
in terms of passion, and utilizing a peculiarly plaintive dialogue
(extended in depth of passion imitated) that creates a naturalistic
milieu composed of casual realistic surfaces, a highly selective
technique, and the super-subtle selection of detail for special
effects; all of which are fused into a balanced whole, unifying
the interior motivations of the characters, their exterior actions,
and the imitated environment in which they exist.

The purpose of this play in terms of the sequence of emotions
and expectations it evokes and resolves seems, generally, to be
that of showing that the punishment of guilty human beings by
other human beings (as guilty in a sense as the guilty they punish)
is even more cruel to the victims than were the crimes perpetrated
by the guilty against the original victims in the chain of crime

---

[19]   Harris, p. 172.

and punishment. Punishment itself is a horrible business, as criminal in universal terms against humanity as the crimes themselves. The death agony of the officially just is no more pitiable, no less moving, than the death agonies of the condemned. Who will cast the first stone?

"Classical suspense", to use Young's term, is aroused in this play and continues to develop as we watch the particular pattern, the special colors appear, employed in a fabric of which we know the general outline. Pity is aroused for Christine's fear and suffering from the outset. Hope, too, plays its part. We hope that perhaps she can warn Brant in time, though knowing she cannot, and that she struggles pitiably in the encumbering net of circumstances which she is undeniably partly responsible for creating. She is consciously aware that in truth she is more guilty than Brant. She even cries out at the end of the third act:

Ezra! Don't let her harm Adam. I am the only guilty one! Don't let Orin – ! [20]

Pity for Christine is aroused, and fear that what she fears will happen. We feel that payment must be made somehow, and see the possibility of the introduction of social justice, which, with all its flaws, would certainly be kinder than the dreadful suffering both Lavinia and Orin cause in Christine. Horror at Lavinia's manipulation of Orin, and his subsequent jealous rage and what it might produce is also aroused. These emotions are qualified by the extenuating circumstances. Orin is ill from his head wound, and our anger at him is partially mitigated by this. Also, we are aware that Lavinia is entirely correct in desiring punishment for the two murderers (Christine and Brant), but this seems offset by the heartless manner in which she accomplishes that punishment.

The scene on the wharf is a break in tension as it begins. The comic figure of the chantyman relieves the tensions aroused, which are then brought to a greater pitch as the children overhear the confession of the lovers. The tension of the play is at its

[20]   Random House, II, 101.

greatest height in this scene, and it is quickly released by Brant's swift murder.

The final act inspires a deeper, broader pity in us as we witness Christine's suffering at the news of Brant's death. Suspense is heightened for a moment, and terror aroused at the prospect of what Christine will do. Fear and terror are released at her death, but pity for her is magnified; fear and pity are aroused for Orin and Lavinia as we wonder what their punishment will be, what horrible Nemesis will trap them in its nets, as it has inevitably trapped the guilty in *Homecoming* and *The Hunted*.

The description of this play that accounts for the greatest number of factors is the one involving passion. If the play is described as a play of passion stemming from a group of insubordinate loves (Orin, jealousy; Lavinia, hatred; Christine, fear), involving a complete change in the passions of the main characters, remorse, satisfaction, and despair, respectively, brought on by action and controlled by character and thought, the type of experience the play imitates is adequately described. O'Neill chose in this play to imitate defective passions that stem from the insubordination of the will of family members to a just pattern of familial behavior; that is, a pattern of behavior that will best supply the needs of the family as a whole unit, and make of it a unit that will successfully propagate itself. This is accomplished in a naturalistic mode, utilizing a complex but single plot with a triple issue in terms of passion, and a plaintive dialogue (extended in depth of emotion); all of which create this naturalistic milieu composed of casual realistic surfaces, a highly selective technique, and a super-subtle selection of detail for special effects, fused into a balanced whole that unifies interior motivations, exterior action, and the imitated environment in which the characters exist. Classical suspense is aroused through the audience's foreknowledge of the general pattern of events (though not their particular qualities); fear and pity are aroused for Christine and Brant, fear and suspense for them being released at their subsequent deaths – though pity is magnified. Fear and pity are aroused for Lavinia and Orin, and suspense at what their punishment will be in the subsequent play. The general emotional purpose of this play seems to be to demonstrate that punishment in itself is a terrible business, as criminal against humanity, in universal terms, as crimes themselves. The death agony of the officially just seems no more pitiable, no less moving, than the death agonies of the condemned.

Divine justice and social justice are effectively by-passed in this play as having any final role in the Nemesis that catches Brant and then Christine. References to the Divine are infrequent. The Congregational minister appears in the first scene, but plays a comparatively insignificant role. Ideas of divine justice simply play no significant part in *The Hunted.*

The threat of social justice, retribution according to society's laws, does provide a good deal of motivation in the play for its dramatic action. Much of that action is devoted to avoiding the possibility of social justice even entering the picture. This fear of social exposure provides supense. The threat of public exposure is often referred to by the characters. In a sense, fear of social justice controls the shape of the actual events. Never, however, does it enter into actual operation in the play. It appears as a catalyst for the action.

The effective circumvention of social justice, and the efficient absence of divine justice leave only one kind of Nemesis operative in the play, the Nemesis that stems from the *lex talionis.* But this undergoes tremendous modification as it did in the other plays with which this study deals.

The system of order central to this play is not divine or societal, it is familial. Nothing else counts directly. Fergusson comes very close to describing it when he writes:

O'Neill's fate is inside his characters; it is, I am afraid, nothing more cosmic than a complex – artistically a poor bodiless substitute for the Eumenides, 'like Gorgons, stoled in sable garb, entwined with swarming snakes'; and ethically, of course, quite without significance.'Psychological fate' is nothing but the crudest determinism: to accept it on Mr. O'Neill's terms is to confuse Evil with pathology, and so destroy all the meaning (except for the psychotherapist) of his characters' actions.[21]

[21]   Fergusson, p. 442.

What could be more "universal" than a play that imitates an action which establishes the familial unit as the final and absolute source of its system of order and value, I am at a loss to imagine. These imitated norms of behavior are, as pointed out in the above quotation, "ethically, of course, quite without significance", only if, of course, one considers the ethic of the Western familial unit "quite without significance". Valente, criticizing Engel's calling the play doctrinaire in Freudian terms, writes:

Gli eroi del Lutto s'addice ad Elettra non sono tipi astratti, non sono gli esemplificatori di una Dottrina. Sono esseri di carne e sangue, che vivono e Soffrono, non in nome di una qualsiasi filosofia, ma bensi' dei loro instinti e delle loro passioni, talvolta anche ferini. Ma questa massa, caotica e fluida, mai si sarebbe plasmata nel di un' opera, che non è retorica, appunto perché sentita, non morbosa, nell 'effeto complessivo, non truculenta, ma semplicemente umana, senza l'ispirazione dei due massimi tragici greci; Eschilo e Sofocle.[22]

Valente wisely goes on to say that O'Neill also rejects following Euripides in his notes for the play when he (O'Neill) indicates that Electra's marriage in Euripides' play is to him simply not a satisfactory end for her. Engel is aware of this change but does not give it the importance Valente ascribed to it.

Unless O'Neill is allowed the premise on which the play is based, the absolute autonomy of the familial unit in shaping human destiny, reflected in the absolute autonomy of the individual's either choosing to subordinate his will to the good of the family, or choosing to ignore that subordination of his will, the play can have no satisfactory "meaning". In attempting to induct the role of Nemesis from this action, having discovered the closed system of order on which the play is based – the order of the family – this study will induct its conclusions concerning Nemesis from that system of order.

Brant, providing the adulterous, exterior contact for Christine

[22] Pier Luigi Valente, "Il lutto s'addice ad Elettra di E. G. O'Neill e la tragedia greca", *Convivium*, XXVIII (Maggio-Giugno, 1960), 329. Valente refers to Edwin A. Engel's *The Haunted Heroes of Eugene O'Neill* (Cambridge, Massachusetts, Harvard University Press, 1953), pp. 239-259.

in the first play, repeats the insubordination Abe indulged in when he interfered in another potential family unit, that of David Mannon and Marie Brantôme. Christine actually repeats, not Marie Brantôme's actions (she was guiltless), but the other side of Abe's double insubordination or defection from familial harmony, that of seeking illicit release of passion outside the closed limits of O'Neill's ultra conservative system of family order. The adulterous passion on Brant's part is motivated purely by revenge. Christine's adulterous passion results from two motivations: dissatisfaction with Ezra's capabilities as a husband, and revenge for Orin. The problem is, of course, complicated by the fact that Brant is a carrier of Ezra's blood, and therefore blood relative of Orin and Lavinia. Brant, for his part in the killing of Ezra, is guilty of shedding kindred blood, while Christine is not. Brant is guilty of destroying a familial order as an intruder, and of having kindred blood on his hands, whereas Christine is guilty of the crime of going against the order of the family from the inside, but not guilty of shedding kindred blood.

Brant's punishment, or Nemesis, in this second play, stems from both blood guilt and from an adulterous – though not incestuous – intrusion of his passion from the outside, disturbing a family unit. His Nemesis stems from the murder of his own blood, and from an intruding passion, but ironically, his Nemesis is wreaked on him by a representative of his own bloodline, a man who resembles him, an image of himself directly related to him through blood. With a terrible irony, then, Brant's crime against his own substance is punished by that substance in another, though similar, body. To harm the familial substance is tantamount to committing suicide. The self committing a crime against the self is swiftly punished by self destruction. It is the crime against familial substance, and the crime against a partially independent familial unit that form the two sources of Brant's Nemesis.

Christine's crime is purely a single one of breaking familial order, not a crime of blood, and she is not destroyed by Lavinia and Orin directly; which, had they done so, would have been a continuation of the blood crime in her case. But they, in their turn for killing Brant, have to answer for the crime of blood in their attempt to maintain familial order. Christine's punishment for breaking the familial order with an adulterous passion, and for murdering her spouse, seems to be an intense despair, a horrible *malaise* of spirit, a cruelty inflicted by her children, that results directly in the loss of her will to live, and which drives her to immediate self destruction. Her Nemesis (resulting from internal defection from the family order) seems the most cruel, the most agonizing, as her children (immediate extensions of herself in blood and spirit) torture her with the news of Brant's death. Brant's Nemesis, by comparison, a swift and merciful death, seems a less horrible type of Nemesis than that wreaked on the familial member who defects from familial order from within.

The play leaves the children, then, guilty of these two supreme crimes: direct blood guilt (in Brant's case), and insubordination to the primary will of the mother from inside the familial structure (in Christine's case), no matter how right in an objective sense we feel the children to be.

Which of these survivors, then, will receive the most rigid punishment in the next play? Orin is directly guilty of the crime of shedding kindred blood, since he actually shoots Brant. But Orin is not as culpable as Lavinia in terms of the insubordination of the child's will to the will of the mother. Suffering seems the severest kind of Nemesis visited on the characters thus far in the two plays of the trilogy, a kind of mental anguish.

However complicated the foregoing peregrinations may seem it is clear that the source of Nemesis in this play, and the dramatic principle that shapes it into its particular manifestations, is the consequence of any departure from the imitated familial order the play makes dramatically explicit.

PART THREE: *THE HAUNTED*

Homecoming is divided into four acts. *The Hunted*, the second play of the trilogy, is composed of five acts, the fourth act of

which being the only act in the trilogy set away from the exterior
or the interior of the Mannon house. In this third play we find
a further departure in form from the original four-act structure
of *Homecoming*, for *The Haunted*, though it has only four acts
proper, is divided into two scenes in the first act. It also stands
apart structurally because there is a time lapse of one year between the end of *The Hunted* and the beginning of *The Haunted*.
The two previous plays together covered the comparatively short
time of thirteen days. Twelve months elapse before the third and
final play opens, and it covers in itself approximately one month
and three days, a longer period than the total time covered by
the first two plays of this trilogy. *Homecoming* covers one week
of time; two days elapse between the first and second play which
consumes four days.

Act One of *The Haunted* opens as have both the other plays
with a chorus of townspeople. They are approximately the same
types who had opened the first play, ordinary folk, rather than
as in the second play, town functionaries. Seth and some of his
cronies are drinking and indulging in a prank concerning ghosts,
betting that Abner Small will not be able to stay in the "haunted"
house until the rise of the moon at ten o'clock. Abner goes in,
and the foolishness is under way.

Hazel and Peter enter and begin to tell Seth that Lavinia and
Orin will be home soon, when Small rushes out of the front door
claiming he has seen the ghost of Ezra. Seth tells Abner it was
Ezra's portrait he has seen. Seth explains to Peter that he arranged this affair to "lay" the ghosts in the house; but at the same
time he urges Peter to convince Orin and Lavinia not to live in
the house when they return, for, as Seth explains, there may not
be individual ghosts roaming around the house, but it is inhabited
by a cold and generalized spirit of evil. Peter ridicules Seth's
notions, telling him they must ready the house that very night as
Lavinia and Orin are expected to arrive the following day. They
go into the house to make it ready.

Orin and Lavinia enter from the drive. Lavinia is remarkably
changed, looking as fresh and vital as her mother, rather than
stiff and shriveled as she had in the previous plays. Orin has

gone in the opposite direction, and is more deranged than ever, and is childlike, and threatening in the same breath. He points to the place where he last saw his mother alive. Lavinia orders him to be quiet and ushers him into the house.

Scene two takes place in the sitting-room of the Mannon house with no lapse of time. Lavinia enters, starts, as she realizes Orin has lagged behind and nervously summons him into the room. A long discussion of their trip ensues. Orin is shaky, maudlin, and seems about to reveal their secrets at every other word. Lavinia tells him they need not feel guilty, and that Christine had shot herself of her own free will, that her death was an act of justice inflicted on herself. Orin appears steadied by her persuasions, but they take much out of her.

Peter enters, and immediately he is struck with the change in Lavinia. They talk of this and of the trip. Orin, who has remained silent, comes sullenly away from the shutters from which he has been peering and nastily begins embarrassing Lavinia with details of their trip in the tropical islands, insinuating sexual lapses on Lavinia's part. She anxiously gains control of him, fussing over him like a mother, telling him to go see Hazel, all the while making apologies to Peter. Orin leaves.

An intense love scene takes place between Peter and Lavinia, after Lavinia explains that Orin's odd behavior is due to his increasing illness. Lavinia tells Peter that the islands made her think of love and of marrying him. They embrace passionately but are interrupted by Hazel and Orin. Orin is angry to discover them so; Lavinia and Peter hastily part in confusion. Orin congratulates Peter, but it is obvious that he is attempting to hide his jealousy of his sister.

Act Two takes place in the same room as act three of *The Hunted*. Orin is busily engaged in writing something. Lavinia knocks on the door which is locked. Orin starts guiltily, puts away his writing in the desk drawer, tries to disguise what he has been doing, and lets Lavinia in. She is suspicious and frightened. He tells her he has been writing the history of their family, and that he finds her the most interesting criminal of all. She is aghast. He accuses her of a series of lustful acts: with Wilkins, the first mate on their voyage to San Francisco, because he resembled Brant; with numerous flirtations in the islands, and especially with the native Avahanni. Lavinia lashes back at him, tells him she is not his property and goads him about her sexuel relations much as her mother had goaded her father in the first play. He calls her a whore and threatens to reveal his writings if she leaves him for Peter, telling her that he is the Mannon she is chained to. Finally, he completely distracts her, whereupon she almost threatens him with violence. He taunts her and enlarges his threats, telling her that he is on his guard. Lavinia breaks down sobbing, remonstrating that she is his sister who loves him. He tells her to stop crying for "The damned don't cry".[23] He slumps into his chair at the desk and wearily tells her to leave. She goes out, and Orin begins writing again.

Act Three begins in the sitting-room a few moments later. Lavinia rushes in from the study and her encounter with Orin. She wrings her hands as had her mother in the last act of *The Hunted*. She talks to herself, tortured by Orin's constantly suggesting that she kill him. Frustrated, she bitterly wonders aloud why he hasn't the courage to kill himself. She is shaken with remorse at this outburst.

(*Then in a frenzy of remorseful anguish, her eyes unconsciously seeking the Mannon portraits on the right wall, as if they were the visible symbol of her God*) Oh, God, don't let me have such thoughts! You know I love Orin! Show me the way to save him! Don't let me think of death! I couldn't bear another death! Please! Please! [24]

Seth interrupts, calling Lavinia to quiet the colored maid who swears she has seen ghosts. Lavinia leaves to tend to this.

Hazel and Peter enter. Seth explains where Lavinia is and then leaves them to reflect on the strange behavior of their two friends. Hazel asks Peter if he really intends to marry Lavinia. He insists emphatically that he does. Hazel quiets him as Orin enters. Peter leaves for a town council meeting.

Orin rushes back into the study and returns with the "history",

[23]   Random House, II, 156.
[24]   *Ibid.*, p. 157.

gives it to Hazel and tells her never to open it until his death, or until the wedding day of Lavinia and Peter. She does not comprehend and tries to get Orin to tell her what is the matter, but Orin cannot bring himself to confess. Then she reveals that Lavinia has told her that he, Orin, feels responsible for Christine's death (thus, Lavinia repeats Christine's tactic in *The Hunted*). Hazel tries to persuade Orin to come to their house and stay. They hear Lavinia returning from her errand. Orin hastily moves away from Hazel who hides the envelope which he has given her behind her back. Orin sits casually on the sofa, but his casualness does not conceal his guilt.

Lavinia enters and suspects something is amiss. She attempts to get out of them what is going on and discovers Hazel has an envelope. Lavinia orders Hazel to give her the envelope, which Lavinia now realizes is the record of the Mannon crimes that Orin has written. This effort fails, so she throws her arms around Orin pleading for him to get the envelope back from Hazel, telling him she will do anything, anything. Mysteriously, he echoes her words, reassuring himself that she will do "anything". Lavinia agrees. Orin gets the envelope from Hazel and tells her to forget him and asks her to leave. She does leave, and Orin hands the envelope to Lavinia telling her that this means that she will never be able to see Peter again. He tries to persuade her to form an incestuous and complete physical love relationship with him, tellling her that she will then be as guilty as he, and that she and he can then find peace. Lavinia is horrified at this. Orin then urges that they go to the law and confess and find peace. She is nearly persuaded by this, but, drawing herself up and summoning all her courage, she shouts, "No! You coward! There is nothing to confess! There was only justice!" [25]

Orin speaks to the portraits, arguing that they will find Lavinia Mannon harder to break than he. Lavinia, her control gone, turns on her brother in hatred and rage and tells him he would kill himself if he were not a coward, and that he is too vile to live. Orin is shocked and broken by this, but recovers and tells her

[25] *Ibid.*, p. 165.

she wants an eye for an eye and a tooth for a tooth, that his mother is speaking through her, that she is his mother. He addresses his dead mother saying, as though he were retching poison with the effort, that he will forgive Christine when he reaches the isle of death, and tells her he is glad that she found love with Adam, the intruder. He is about to leave for the study as Peter enters. He says crazily to Peter that he is going to the study to clean his pistol and leaves. Lavinia clings to Peter, forcing herself not to stop Orin from finding the peace of death. A shot sounds, and as Peter hurries out, she shouts at the portraits that now she is free. She hides the "history" Orin has written in the desk.

The fourth act opens on the day of Orin's funeral three days later. Seth is gardening in front of the house as Lavinia enters. She is completely transformed into what she was at the beginning of the trilogy: a wooden, sullen, military figure with a flat, sexless body. She tells Seth that she is going to marry Peter and leave the house.

Seth leaves as Hazel enters. She tries to pry out of Lavinia what caused Orin to shoot himself. She fails, then begs Lavinia not to marry her brother, Peter, if she has any sense of Mannon justice left in her. Hazel tells Lavinia that Peter has become sullen and unhappy since his engagement to her. Hazel reveals that she has told Peter of the envelope "history". Lavinia is enraged and threatens to kill her. They hear Peter coming, and Hazel says she knows Lavinia will do the right thing and not marry Peter, and that then God will forgive her. As she leaves Lavinia calls after her: "I'm not asking God or anybody for forgiveness. I forgive myself!" [26]

Peter enters, and though Lavinia tells him that Hazel does not want him to marry her, he insists, venting his spleen on his family and the town. She asks him to marry her immediately. He appears suspicious of her haste and mentions Orin's writings. She asks him to take her into the house and make love to her at once before they are married. She becomes so carried away with her

---

[26] *Ibid.*, p. 174.

passion that she says, "Want me! Take me, Adam!" [27] And this is the end of her trying. She knows that the dead will always come between. She tries to send Peter away, but he becomes curious to know what happened on the islands with the native, Avahanni. Lavinia is hurt momentarily, for obviously nothing had happened, but she suddenly sees this as a way to avoid hurting him and send him away angry and believing he has lost nothing. He leaves in fury. She begins to shout after him and tell him that the tale of the affair with Avanhanni is a lie, but she controls herself, resigning herself to the years of self-punishment and says, "It takes the Mannons to punish themselves for being born!" [28] She orders Seth to nail the shutters closed and to have Hannah throw out all the flowers. She marches woodenly into the house and closes the door behind her to begin paying out the Nemesis of the long years of self-punishment of her own free will and choosing.

Here, indeed, is an experience such as set Mrs. Alving thinking of the relations between the present and the past. *Ghosts* and *Mourning Becomes Electra* have not only a subject in common, but a vocabulary which permits of some intertranslation. In both plays 'ghosts' means a subtle combination of heredity and environment.[29]

Mrs. Alving, in the famous scene to which Lecky refers, sees the "character" of her husband being repeated in her son. We see in this trilogy the "characters" of Ezra and Christine being repeated in Orin and Lavinia. But only to a certain point, for Lavinia actually plays the role of her father in the final analysis, while Orin plays the role of his mother.

The first play of the trilogy was an imitation of the experience of action. The second play was an imitation of the experience of passion. A year passes, a year in which the consequences of the first two experiences have been allowed to run their course.

This, the third play, appears to be a play of character, involving a complete and slow change in the moral character of the two main characters, brought on by thought and controlled

---

[27]   *Ibid.*, p. 177.
[28]   Lecky, p. 323.
[29]   *Ibid.*, p. 178.

by passion and action. As the play begins, Orin's character seems quite similar to his father's character, and Lavinia's seems similar to her mother's. During the month they have to adjust and think about the significance of their past and their present state, their characters undergo a complete alteration. The change is so complete that Orin indulges in the characteristic behavior of his mother, seeking release for his natural instincts in any way available, and in his case not adultery, but in an incestuous relationship with his sister. Lavinia changes radically from the libidinous creature she is at the beginning of the play, and pointedly rejects the possibility of sexual release with Peter as soon as she realizes finally that she has desired Brant all along. Orin seeks peace from suffering in suicide as did Christine. Lavinia does not try to escape, but attempts to face her difficulties and her guilt as Ezra had (the shock of war having made him finally realize what he really was) in the first play of the trilogy. This is simply fine dramatic logic, for we cannot see, throughout the entire trilogy, Lavinia as anything but her father's daughter in flesh and spirit (not her mother's); as we cannot see Orin as anything but his mother's son (not his father's).

The tragedy of Orin and Christine lies in the possibility of fulfillment that comes too late, though they have desired it all along. The tragedy of Ezra and Lavinia lies in the realization of the need for fulfillment when it has become too late for such fulfillment to help them at all.

Doris Falk tells us, "The *ethos* or moral purpose of an O'Neill character is to perpetuate or strenghten an illusion about himself." [30] This is certainly not true of the major characters of this trilogy. All four of them are engaged in a merciless unmasking of their illusory selves, and we feel, as always in tragedy, that the price they pay for their efforts is not justly what they deserve, as would be the case were O'Neill's justice "poetic justice". The price they pay is beyond what is just, beyond fate; it is tragic justice in which the punishment always seems in quality, significance, and severity to exceed what is ordained, their moral

[30]   Doris V. Falk, *Eugene O'Neill and the Tragic Tension* (New Brunswick, New Jersey, Rutgers University Press, 1958), p. 139.

lapses recoiling upon them to their destruction in more than a physical sense alone, which is in fact Nemesis.

This study disagrees with Myers, also, who writes, "and as his tragedy ends, we know nothing more than that the orderly sequence will be carried out to the bitter end, that, as Lavinia turns back into the house, we have come to the last link in the chain of necessary events".[31] This could not be true even if we see the play strictly as a play of action. Seeing it as a play of character considerably alters its significance. The result of the orderly sequence in this play is a complete alteration in the moral character of Lavinia and of Orin. Ezra tries to give to Christine but is murdered before he can break the chain of the Mannons, which is a steady sequence of the insubordination of the will of the individual to the greater needs of the family, and, indeed, of all mankind. Lavinia breaks this chain (though in doing so she destroys the line and herself) by *giving* Peter his freedom as she "loves him too much" to hurt him. She literally denies herself that one moment of release, for she realizes that at this point such release can only be selfish.

In developing the possibilities of the poetic medium of character (character meaning moral agent), O'Neill has chosen characters from the upper strata of the society he imitates. They are elevated above the rest of the community as it is imitated. Here O'Neill, depending on the two plays that have gone before, has the advantage of not having to establish in this particular play a wealth of information about the characters that is established in the previous two plays. In the *Oresteia* we learn very little about Orestes and Electra in the first play. In O'Neill's first play we learn a great deal about Lavinia, and something of Orin's character. O'Neill can thus depend on greater continuity in development. We know from the start that Lavinia is in competition with her mother, that she vaguely resembles her mother. We know that Orin is ill from a head wound, that he resembles his father, and that he is attached to his mother. Battenhouse mentions Clark's comment that O'Neill shows a deeper understanding of

31   Myers, p. 23.

his characters as they act in the human situation than did Aeschylus:

> Mr. Clark says nothing in explanation of this deeper understanding which he credits to O'Neill. It is, in fact, not easy to explain. But, if attempted, explanation must begin, I think, by recognizing that O'Neill has made a more critical appraisal of the human background within which the crime of murder arises. The whole texture of the modern human situation, as he construes it, is criminally disposed. Even the prospective avengers are characterized by warped loves long before they face the challenge to deal out retribution. Orin and Lavinia exhibit from the beginning of the drama a bias, an illness of spirit, a 'complex' of nature, which is the direct or indirect reflection and continuation of the split home from which they have come.[32]

The possibilities O'Neill employs in this play, in terms of character, do not necessarily reflect a "deeper" understanding of the human situation. That O'Neill's concept of the human situation is far different from that of Aeschylus is quite readily apparent. Whereas Aeschylus' play in part imitates the relation of human character to itself, to the divine, and to society, O'Neill excludes in his third play (and for that matter in all three plays) any direct imitation of the force of society or the divine in shaping human destiny. Further, the *Eumenides* is primarily a play of thought, not a play of character. Aeschylus' pattern of plays is essentially *action, action, thought.* O'Neill's pattern is *action, passion, character.* The writer suggests that O'Neill merely took greater advantage of more complete presentation of his characters in his first two plays in order to present a greater depth of character in the final play. Aeschylus did not do this with his first two plays, for the reason that they do not intend to present the poetic object that O'Neill intended to present.

The object Aeschylus presents (the kind of experience he imitates) has its roots in the individual characters (their family relationships), in the societal order in which they function, and in the divine order of the universe as a whole. O'Neill, in presenting his object, excludes two of the possibilities employed in Aeschylus' imitation: society and the divine. It is true that society

---

[32] Battenhouse, p. 340. Battenhouse refers to Barrett H. Clark's article, "Aeschylus and O'Neill", *English Journal*, XXI (November, 1932), 707.

and the divine form a small operative element in the object of O'Neill's imitation, but they are vastly less important than they are to the nature of the object Aeschylus imitates. Ultimate order in O'Neill's imitation resides, not in society, not in divinity, but strictly in the relationships within the family and within the individuals who make up the family. In this final play he concentrates on the imitation of character, the moral agents who have functioned in a preëstablished way in a familial order; he imitates, within previously established patterns of action and passion, the final consequences of these patterns in their shaping force on these characters. Through the force of thought (reflection on the past in both characters – Orin's writing, Lavinia's rationalization) the characters develop. Lavinia moves from an escapism almost identical to her mother's which she has assumed due to the shock of the previous events and trials to the understanding, desire to atone, and assumption of responsibility for her crimes against the familial order that her father came to in the first play of the trilogy. Orin moves from the narrow puritanism of his father (which does not recognize the healthy, fleshly needs of the family members) into the escapism of allowing the driving sensual instincts the opportunity of fully expressing themselves for the first time, regardless of the disruption they may cause in the familial order, a pattern thoroughly acted out by his mother in the first play. The quality of the events that lead to this double surrender of the will to the needs inherent in the familial order (qualities for which both Lavinia and Orin are partially responsible) precludes a productive result from the final surrender to that order. For Orin, this final recognition leads to incest, and eventual suicide. For Lavinia it leads to self-sacrificing denial of fulfillment (out of responsible consideration for the potential husband, Peter), and hopeless sterility and barrenness. Certain possibilities of development having been allowed to develop within the characters by themselves (and partially forced on them by circumstance), it is absolutely impossible for the characters to reintegrate themselves into the familial order which they have both transgressed. In short, what they have become recoils upon them, destroying them, which is their Nemesis.

Much as we may approve or disapprove of the aesthetic framework O'Neill establishes here, in terms of the possibilities of the poetic medium of character he develops, we ought properly to evaluate what he has done in terms of how successfully he brings his intended effects to aesthetic fruition. It seems inaccurate to make the kind of statement about these three plays that is made by John Howard Lawson:

> *Mourning Becomes Electra* is a much more realistic play than *Strange Interlude*. The action is less diffuse and better integrated. But the movement of events, in spite of its violence, evades progression. The characters have no goal toward which they are moving. Having no attainable social aims, it is impossible for them to have attainable dramatic aims.[33]

Within the strict order of the family, O'Neill imitates in this final play the development of two characters attempting through thought to make some atonement for their willful insubordination of familial order. That such insubordination has made of them creatures who can no longer attain a proper realignment with the dictates of familial order is clearly made an ineluctable fact. They, as moral agents, are partially responsible for the inertia of the circumstances of character with which they find themselves ridden; but they are also partially victims of formative circumstances inflicted on them by their parents before them, as were their parents victims of circumstances inflicted on them by their own parents, circumstances over which they in fact had no control. O'Neill does not present the one-sided deterministic view that is usually ascribed to him. His view of human character is, in this respect, very similar to the balanced view Aeschylus presents in the *Oresteia*: the struggle of character to make the best of factors beyond its control, and factors for which it is partially responsible.

O'Neill is interested, too, in the individual character strictly as individual, in showing what his autonomous character becomes, a thing in himself, the result of insubordination of his will to familial order, and, also, as a result of attempting to reintegrate

---

[33]   John Howard Lawson, *Theory and Technique of Playwriting* (New York, G. P. Putnam, 1936), p. 140.

himself into that order. The characters ultimately find unity within themselves rather than in the external tenets of family order.

Of all the possible patterns of character imitation O'Neill might have chosen, he has limited himself in this play strictly to what Hegel has called the "romantic" pattern.

So, too, the unity of the human and divine nature is a conscious unity, only to be realized by *spiritual* knowledge and in *spirit*. Thus the new content, won by this unity, is not inseparable from sensuous representation, as if that were adequate to it, but is freed from this immediate existence, which has to be posited as negative, absorbed, and reflected into the spiritual unity. In this way, romantic art must be considered as art transcending itself, while remaining within the artistic sphere and in artistic form.

Therefore, in short, we may abide by the statement that in this third stage the object (of art) is *free,* concrete intellectual being, which has the function of revealing itself as spiritual existence for the inward world of spirit. In conformity with such an object-matter, art cannot work for sensuous perception. It must address itself to the inward mind, which coalesces with its object simply and as though this were itself, to the subjective inwardness, to the heart, the feeling, which, being spiritual, aspires to freedom within itself, and seeks and finds its reconciliation only in the spirit within. It is this *inner* world that forms the content of the romantic, and must therefore find its representation as such inward feeling, and in the show or presentation of such feeling. The world of inwardness celebrates its triumph over the outer world, and actually in the sphere of the outer and in its medium manifests this its victory, owing to which the sensuous appearance sinks into worthlessness.

But, on the other hand, this [romantic] type of Art, like every other, needs an external vehicle of expression. Now the spiritual has withdrawn into itself out of the external and its immediate oneness therewith. For this reason, the sensuous externality of concrete form is accepted and represented, as in Symbolic art, as something transient and fugitive. And the same measure is dealt to the subjective finite mind and will, even including the peculiarity or caprice of the individual, of character, action, etc., or of incident and plot. The aspect of external existence is committed to contigency, and left at the mercy of freaks of imagination, whose caprice is no more likely to mirror what is given *as* it is given, than to throw the shapes of the outer world into chance medley, or distort them into grotesqueness. For this external element no longer has its notion and significance, as in classical art, in its own sphere, and in its own medium. It has come to find them in the feelings, the display of which is *in themselves* instead of being in the external and *its* form of reality, and which have the power to preserve or to regain their state of reconciliation with themselves, in every accident, in every unessential circumstance that takes independent shape, in all misfortune and grief, and even in crime.

Owing to this, the characteristics of symbolic art, in difference, discrepancy, and severence of Idea and plastic shape, are here reproduced, but with an essential difference. In the sphere of the romantic, the Idea, whose defectiveness in the case of the symbol produced the defect of external shape, has to reveal itself in the medium of spirit and feelings as perfected in itself. And it is because of this higher perfection that it withdraws from any adequate union with the external element, inasmuch as it can seek and achieve its true reality and revelation nowhere but in itself.[34]

In character as O'Neill imitates it in this play, *all* significance finally resides in the individual. Schopenhauer, after Hegel, says much the same thing specifically in regard to tragic form and tragic character:

It is the strife of the will itself, which here, completely unfolded at the highest grade of its objectivity, comes into fearful prominence. It becomes visible in the suffering of men, which is now introduced, partly through chance and error, which appear as the rulers of the world, personified as fate, on account of their insidiousness, which even reaches the appearance of design; partly it proceeds from man himself, through the self-mortifying efforts of a few, through the wickedness and perversity of most. . . . the veil of Mâyâ, no longer deceives it. It sees through the form of the phenomenon, the *principium individuationis*. The egoism which rests on this perishes with it, so that now the *motives* that were so powerful before have lost their might, and instead of them the complete knowledge of the nature of the world, which has a *quieting* effect on the will, produces resignation, the surrender not merely of life, but of the very will to live.[35]

[34]   G. W. F. Hegel, "Part III: Of the Romantic Form of Art", *Lectures on Aesthetics*, trans. Bernard Bosanquet and W. M. Bryant; in *The Philosophy of Hegel*, ed. Carl J. Friedrich (New York, The Modern Library, Random House, 1954), pp. 381-383.
[35]   Schopenhauer, "The Idea, Independent of the Principle of Sufficient Reason: The Platonic Idea: The Object of Art", "Third Book, The World as Idea: Second Aspect", *The World As Will and Idea*; in *The Philosophy of Schopenhauer*, ed. Irwin Edman (New York, Random House, The Modern Library, 1956), p. 197.

Schopenhauer, "the great pessimist", actually writes a paean to the absoluteness of the individual who climbs to the summit of self-knowledge, perceives that the world is but the ugly and hopelessly confused battleground of the Will, and through this ultimate knowledge gains peace; for though there is no meaning in the world, there must be meaning in the individual who at the moment of tragic insight perceives meaninglessness, the truth of existence. But to perceive the truth! That is knowledge, that is the way to peace – inner peace – when the spirit, in Hegel's sense, discovers through the act of perceiving no meaning in the outward world, all meaning in the self.

For Lavinia, this exact moment of illumination, this romantic fulfillment of tragic character comes when she recognizes, after the *lapsus linguae*, that it is not Peter she loves, but Brant, who is dead, killed by her brother she goaded to the deed.

LAVINIA. (*in a dead voice*) I can't marry you, Peter. You mustn't ever see me again. (*He stares at her, stunned and stupid*) Go home. Make it up with your mother and Hazel. Marry someone else. Love isn't permitted to me. The dead are too strong! [36]

Nietzsche, following Schopenhauer (whose ideas he came finally to repudiate entirely), gives voice to similar sentiments concerning the audience's perception of tragic character, rather than the nature of tragic character itself. In *The Birth of Tragedy* he makes the following statement:

Dionysiac art, too, wishes to convince us of the eternal delight of existence, but it insists that we look for this delight not in the phenomena but behind them. It makes us realize that everything that is generated must be prepared to face its painful dissolution. It forces us to gaze into the horror of individual existence, yet without being turned to stone by the vision: a metaphysical solace momentarily lifts us above the whirl of shifting phenomena. For a brief moment we become, ourselves, the primal Being, and we experience its insatiable hunger for existence. Now we see the struggle, the pain, the destruction of appearances, as necessary, because of the constant proliferation of forms pushing into life, because of the extravagant fecundity of the world will. We feel the furious prodding of this travail in the very moment in which we become one with the im-

[36] Random House, II, 177.

mense lust for life and we are made aware of the eternity and indestructibility of that lust. Pity and terror notwithstanding, we realize our great good fortune in having life – not as individuals, but as a part of the life force with whose procreative lust we have become one.[37]

Even here, we see how Nietzsche is beginning to pull away from Schopenhauer, for he takes a more positive view of that vast and ugly panorama of the will. In doing so, he will approach finally his concept of *amor fati*, the love of necessity. O'Neill, however, creates in this third play of *Mourning Becomes Electra* a character that is truly "romantic" much more in Hegel's sense, than in Schopenhauer's or Nietzsche's sense.

The purpose in presenting the statements above was not to illustrate that O'Neill used Hegel's model of "romantic" art to create his "romantic" character Lavinia Mannon, nor to discredit the influence of Schopenhauer and Nietzsche on O'Neill's art. It would be difficult to *prove* such points in any case, either positively or negatively. The real purpose was to present, in the words of Hegel playing the role of aesthetician, a nearly perfect exposition of the aesthetic formula O'Neill utilized in creating the character of Lavinia Mannon as she appears in this final play of the trilogy.

Erich Heller, writing of the activity of poets, phrases the case in more compact terms: "For the 'real order' has to be 'created' where there is no intuitive conviction that it exists." [38] That is exactly what O'Neill makes his character do in this play. She punishes herself, and in so doing demonstrates explicitly the form of Nemesis which Myers says is the heart of tragic justice: "The equality of good and evil which constitutes justice can be found only in the individual, whose capacity for experiencing good is exactly equal to his capacity for experiencing evil." [39]

The Haunted is written, as were *Homecoming* and *The Hunted*, in a naturalistic dramatic mode. But it does not use a single plot.

---

[37]   Friedrich Nietzsche, *The Birth of Tragedy*, trans. Francis Golffing (Garden City, New York, Doubleday [Anchor Books], 1956), pp. 102-103.
[38]   Erich Heller, *The Disinherited Mind* (New York, Meridian Books, Inc., 1959), p. 170.
[39]   Myers, p. 27.

The plot is multiple and complex. The multiplicity of action consists in the different objects toward which the two characters strive: Orin toward incest with Lavinia, and Lavinia toward an exogamous relation with Peter. The issue is double: solitary confinement for Lavinia; suicide for Orin.

As in the two previous plays the dialogue is in prose, not verse. Such an obviously Freudian technique as Lavinia's *lapsus linguae* serves not so much to illustrate a doctrinaire concept of the playwright as it does to imitate poetically the "romantic" nature of the character's inner subjectivity, an explanation of which Hegel's aesthetic formula adequately provides for when he states: "And the same measure is dealt to the subjective finite mind and will, even including the peculiarity or caprice of the individual, of character, action, etc., or of incident and plot." O'Neill was aware of the departure of his dialogue from traditional standards of clarity. "There was a realistic New England insistence in my mind, too, which would have barred great language even in a dramatist capable of writing it, an insistence on the clotted and clogged and inarticulate." [40] But this shattering of the external niceties of diction represents a great virtue in the play, not a fault. It represents skill, not lack of it. The fractures in diction, as they operate collectively, constantly remind us of the inhibitions, the internal turmoil of these characters. Were the exact terms of these inhibitions to remain perpetually inaccessible to us, then the technique represented in the dialogue would be serving no purpose. But, finally, every scene in the play is made overwhelming clear in terms of character, passion, and thought, all of which represent the imperfect relationship that exists between the external world and the needs of the intense inner subjectivity of the characters in this play. With this cumulative driving inward of the dialogue, it comes as no surprise that the characters finally reject all outward forms of order, including the familial order, and find the sources for just action within themselves. That they wield the inescapable instruments of Nemesis themselves, affecting total responsibility for the inequities of

[40] Eugene O'Neill, "Second Thoughts", *The American Spectator* (December, 1932), p. 2.

existence in the external world is no surprise. It is an inescapable
premise of their aesthetic nature.

ORIN. And I find artificial light more appropriate for my work –
man's light, not God's – man's feeble striving to understand himself,
to exist for himself in the darkness! It's a symbol of his life – a lamp
burning out in a room of waiting shadows! [41]

The milieu of the play is naturalistic in Battenhouse's sense, and
is composed of casual realistic surfaces, a highly selective technique, and the super-subtle selection of detail for special effects;
all of which are fused into a balanced whole, unifying the interior
motivations of the characters, their external actions, and the
imitated environment in which they exist.

The purpose of this play is far different from either of the
other two plays, specifically in relation to the sequence of emotions and expectations it evokes and resolves. In *Homecoming*
it was the outcome of the events that held us and that evoked
and resolved our expectations. In *The Hunted* is was the depth
and intensity of the passions the characters displayed that held
us. Here, in *The Haunted*, it is the marvelous transformation of
the characters that is apparent at the beginning, and the subsequent and gradual alteration of their characters until they are
completely different.

We are surprised and amazed, as the play opens, to find that
the year has made of the characters what appears to be a complete reversal of their natures: Orin seems much like his father
before his father changed as a result of the war; Lavinia seems
like her mother in beauty and in her animal sensuality. As we
observe them reflect upon their past in an attempt to find some
way to cope with what the past has made of them, they gradually
change, Lavinia growing more like her father, and Orin more like
his mother. These expectations of change evoked in us by the
characters are finally resolved: Orin gives in fully to his sexual
desire for Lavinia, and then shoots himself to relieve his own
suffering as Christine had done; Lavinia faces her own guilt,
avoids the possibility of causing the potential husband, Peter,

<hr />

[41]   Random House, II, 150.

further suffering, and assumes the role of self-punisher, after realizing that love for her is an impossibility. General Mannon was, of course, murdered before he could develop this far; but at least Lavinia recognizes her errors and attempts some reconciliation with the familial pattern by attempting an exogamous relation with Peter.

We fear for the safety of these two characters as the play opens, for it becomes immediately apparent that the present state of their characters is not stable. Orin is still wandering mentally as a result of his head wound, and wavers between strength and weakness in concealing the family secrets. Lavinia is progressively drained of vitality in having to be with him every minute for fear he will disclose their secrets at any moment. When Orin resorts to secreting himself in the study and actually recording the proceding events, fear and suspense are brought to a pitch. The scene in which he gives the actual facts in an envelope to Hazel is the high point of this suspense. This is quickly resolved as Lavinia desperately promises she will do "anything" if Orin will get the envelope from Hazel. As Orin dismisses Hazel, it is apparent that he will turn to something even more dreadful for the two characters than his confessions would have been. Though fear is released when he retrieves the envelope, it is replaced with a sudden horror, which reaches its peak upon Orin's asking Lavinia to commit incest with him. When she refuses, we are relieved; but pity is aroused by Orin's plea that they go and confess to find peace. Pity for Orin is increased as Lavinia turns on him, practically telling him to kill himself. Pity for Orin is further magnified as he shoots himself, while terror for the situation is eased, for Lavinia hides the dark "history" which Orin has composed.

When the final act opens, and we see Lavinia altered physically to resemble her father, suspense is aroused as to what will be her end. Hope is inspired as she attempts to form an exogamous relation with Peter. We are shocked by the slip of her tongue, and pity is aroused as we realize that she is doomed. Her sacrifice intensifies this pity, as she actually relinquishes her one chance for happiness in giving up Peter. Admiration is evoked, also, and pity and fear for her are again magnified as we know she will not find any peace, but will force herself to suffer many years isolated and alone. Suspense and terror are released as we perceive her end, but pity and regret are magnified, for we realize that a character capable of such sacrifice and courage and strength could have found much happiness in marriage, had her past not been so horrendous. Yet the paradox is this: the grim experiences of her past bring her gradually to know courage and selflessness, but on the point of achieving sufficient courage and virtue to sustain the role of wife to Peter, those very earned abilities demand irrevocably that she give up even the opportunity to do so. She achieves virtue, but the very *process* of achieving the knowledge she needs to attain this virtue has deprived her of the right to exercise it.

Asselineau accurately describes the quality of Lavinia's sacrifice when he writes:

> ... she will be dead to the world, a lovely recluse shut up in the cursed house which witnessed her crimes and sufferings, a prey to remorse, torn by the ruthless Erinyes of her soul. Hers is a bloodless death, a death in life more cruel than real death – a moral suicide full of austere grandeur and no less tragic than the ostentatious death of a Greek or Elizabethan hero.[42]

Bringing together the four hypotheses which resulted from formulating answers to the four separate questions of fact, the form of this play may now be described. This play, *The Haunted*, is primarily a play of character, involving a complete and slow change in the moral character of the two central characters, brought on mainly by thought, but controlled by passion and action. Of all possible patterns of character development, O'Neill employs a double reversal of character: Orin changing from patriarchal behavior to matriarchal, and Lavinia from matriarchal to patriarchal; he also employs, as a final change, a pattern similar to Hegel's description of "romantic" character wherein the characters finally find unity within themselves rather than in the external tenets of family order.

[42] Roger Assilineau, "*Mourning Becomes Electra* as a Tragedy", *Modern Drama*, I, No. 3 (December, 1958), 144.

This is all accomplished in a naturalistic dramatic mode, employing a complex and multiple plot with a double issue in terms of character, and a dramatic prose that mirrors the imperfect relationship existing between the external world and the needs of the inner subjectivity of the characters. A highly selective technique, the super-subtle selection of detail for special effects (e.g., Lavinia's Freudian slip), and casual realistic surfaces are employed to create this naturalistic milieu in which the interior motivations of the characters, their external actions, and the imitated environment in which they exists are all fused into an aesthetically balanced whole.

Classical Suspense is aroused, alternating through successive states of pity and fear for the characters as the gradual changes in their moral characters unfold, with fear – not pity – being purged for Orin at his death, while fear and suspense are purged as Lavinia's doom is made clear, though pity is magnified and somewhat mitigated by amazement and admiration for her character when she renounces the world and enters the house, assuming years of self-punishment as payment for her crimes.

An induction from the above presented particulars of the role of Nemesis in the structure of this play produces results which are startlingly different from any so far formulated in this study. O'Neill efficiently excludes from this play Nemesis stemming from the demands of social justice, or from divine justice. The single act of grace in the entire trilogy is performed by a human character, Lavinia Mannon, when she frees Peter. The deterministic aspects of her Freudian slip are directly countered by her autonomous exercise of will, her free choice, in other words, to sacrifice her own selfish proclivities for the sake of her potential spouse, Peter Niles. Ultimate justice, tempered with mercy, is no longer (as it was in Aeschylus) the gift of divine agencies; ultimate justice becomes the autonomous province of a human agent in this play.

The material idea of social Nemesis in this play is shaped into a dramatic obstacle, the supervention of which drives the characters finally to the discovery of bases for just behavior within the familial order, and, ultimately, within themselves. That this can be accomplished in the play makes it essentially a very optimistic drama indeed. For it imitates human character as absolutely emancipated from any need to depend on the social or divine in discovering just and ordered bases for action.

The material idea of divine Nemesis is simply and effectively translated into the terms of the external demands on the individual of familial order, requiring the subordination of the will of each family member to the good of the whole family. As the play imitates the situation, the characters do not primarily transgress divine law, nor social law, but the law of the family which requires: (1) that the husband and father fulfill not only his own sexual needs, but those of his wife, also; (2) that the wife and mother reciprocate in this; (3) that neither husband nor wife seek external satisfaction of their needs, and that neither of them break the familial hierarchy of command within the family by alienating the affections of their offspring from either husband or wife; (4) finally, that the offspring recognize the relative authority (father primary, mother secondary) in the joint family rule, wherein the father is controller of the family in all external matters, food getting, provision for domicile, et cetera, while the mother is controller of the distribution within the family of the life sustaining commodities the father acquires.

Every one of the above laws is broken in one way or another by each character in the trilogy. Each transgression of these laws in the case of each character is punished, not by social agencies, but by the members of the family. The only *actual* homicide perpetrated *within* the family is Christine's murder of Ezra. Her children rise up to punish her by murdering her lover. She commits suicide. In effect, the Nemesis that awaits the breaker of the family law from within is self-destruction. Destroy the familial order from within, and one destroys oneself, for one has thereby destroyed that order which provides the basis for the existence of the self.

Lavinia is the chief offender against the internal order of the family. Her Nemesis is more hideous, in terms of anguish, than Brant's Nemesis. Lavinia's crime is greater than Christine's, for Christine turns against the husband-father (whose authority she shares), whereas Lavinia, the daughter, turns agains the wife-mother (whose authority is much greater than her own); conse-quently, the Nemesis visited on Lavinia is the most painful of all. Hers is the greater crime, and is served with the greater Nemesis.

Clark was well aware of the nature and source of order and Nemesis in this play, though he uses the term "fate".

Modern audiences, says O'Neill, have no general religious basis, no common fund of tradition to which they may refer the greatest prob-lems with which we are all concerned. The closest equivalent is our yet-infant science of psychology; fate, says O'Neill, is what happens to human beings because of what they are, not what some god tells them to be, and it is the business of the tragic dramatist to show how human destiny resides in the individual, the family, the race.[43]

CONCLUSION

Looking at this trilogy as a whole, now that its three component parts have been described, it is possible to synthesize a description of its overall form. It has a tripartite structure unified into one form. This consists of consecutive imitations of action, passion, and character. These involve, progressively, external actions symbolic of the internal action of the characters; defective pas-sions stemming from the insubordination of the will of the family members to a just pattern of familial behavior; and, finally, a double reversal of character: Orin, from fatherly inhibition to motherly indulgence; Lavinia, from motherly indulgence to fatherly attempt to balance indulgence and inhibition by exer-cising control.

All of this is accomplished in a naturalistic dramatic mode utilizing a series of plots; complex-multiple with triple issue; complex-single with triple issue; and, complex-multiple with double issue; written in a dramatic prose which mirrors the im-perfect relationship existing between the external world and the needs of the inner subjectivity of the characters, who ultimately reject all systems of external moral bases for action in favor of

[43] Barrett H. Clark, "Aeschylus and Eugene O'Neill", *English Journal*, XXI (November, 1932), 709.

the moral bases for action they discover within themselves.

A highly selective technique is used in the creation of this mode, utilizing the presentation of casual realistic surfaces and a super-subtle selection of detail for special effects (e.g., the chanty "Shenandoah", the clipper ship, Lavinia's *lapsus linguae*), which fuse interior motivations, external actions, and imitated environment into a balanced aesthetic whole.

Classical suspense is aroused and progressively purged throughout all three plays. action, passion, character. In the first play pity is not purged, but magnified, for Ezra and Lavinia, while moral censure is aroused for Christine, though terror is magnified for both Lavinia and Christine, but purged for Ezra at his death. In the second play moral censure is aroused against Orin and Lavinia (mitigated by the fact of Christine's guilt), while terror for Christine and Brant is purged by their death, though pity for them is magnified. Pity is magnified for Orin's remorse, while moral censure is aroused for Lavinia's vindictiveness, and fear and terror are aroused by the threat of exposure and suffering that hangs over the two children. In the third play terror for Orin is purged at his death, though pity for him is magnified; terror for Lavinia is purged as we perceive her end, though pity for her is magnified, and is mixed with admiration and amazement by her act of self-sacrifice and moral courage when she assumes the Nemesis of years of loneliness and self-punishment as payment for her crimes.

The total effect of the above structure is summed up cogently in Roger Asselineau's quotation from Pascal, which he applies to this trilogy:

The reader – or spectator – inevitably thinks of Pascal's famous definition of man as a 'thinking reed': 'L'homme n'est qu'un roseau, le plus faible de la nature, mais c'est un roseau pensent. Il ne faut pas que l'universe s'arme pour l'écraser: un vapeur, une goutte d'eau suffit pour le tuer. Mais, quand l'univers l'ecraserait, l'homme serait encore plus noble que ce qui le tue, parce qu'il sait qu'il meurt, et l'avantage que l'univers a sur lui, l'univers n'en sait rien.' [44]

The role of Nemesis in *Mourning Becomes Electra* is greater,

[44]   Asselineau, p. 148.

perhaps, than it has been in any of the other plays studied thus far, for a great deal of the substance of this trilogy consists of crime and punishment.

The Nemesis that overtakes Ezra stems from a two-fold source in relation to time and circumstance. But the system, the source of order, which is transgressed, thus setting off the punishment, is unilateral: the familial order. Ezra cannot avoid the personal vengeance Brant wreaks on him, for Brant essentially desires to punish Ezra for crimes against the familial order committed by Ezra's father, Abe Mannon (though Ezra is partially implicated through his refusal to aid Brant's ailing mother, Marie Brantôme). However, Ezra could avoid his own crimes against the familial order – the brutality he inflicts on his wife, and his sending Orin off to war at too young an age. He could also have chosen to aid Marie Brantôme, and thus have avoided the censure of Brant.

The main system of justice from which Nemesis stems is a just familial order. Christine's personal hatred, engendered by Ezra's abuse (the *lex talionis*), is the source of Nemesis that overtakes Ezra (for Brant's desire for vengeance could not have been operative if Ezra had not estranged his wife through brutality). Ezra is responsible for selfishly using his wife for lust alone. She seeks release outside the familial order, and, also, murders him. Ezra's Nemesis seems much greater than his crime. But now the chain is set again, for Christine's crime from within the familial order, and her adultery outside the familial order repeats precisely Abe Mannon's crime. Now it is a question of murder, and adultery, whereas in Abe's case it was *probably* cruelty to his wife and adulterous *designs* on Marie Brantôme. The problem is, then, how shall the crimes of adultery and homicide be justly punished? What Nemesis will entrap Christine?

In the second play, a play of passion, it is the defective passions of the children that operate from within the familial order to function as Christine's Nemesis. She is not quickly murdered as were Ezra and Brant. Since she defects from within the familial order, as well as outside it, her prolonged and frightful suffering during the play and up until the time of her suicide seems a more rigid kind of Nemesis than either Ezra's or Brant's. Her Nemesis stems not mainly from personal vengeance (the *lex talionis*), but from the collective forces within the family (a kind of *lex familias*). But the perpetrators of this Nemesis repeat both her crime and her husband's crime in administering their Nemesis. For, in order to punish Christine, the children must break the hierarchy of authority in the family, as Christine has broken it by killing her husband. The crime of the children is lesser in degree in one sense than is Christine's, even though they seem to wreak a more horrifying Nemesis on her. The problem then is, if the familial order is broken, to inflict punishment on a defecting familial member, how can the chain of crime and punishment be broken within the family? Where will the salvation of the individuals caught in this hideous cycle of Nemesis come from?

Whereas Aeschylus had solved his much different problem of Nemesis with a nice point of social law and with the aid of divine wisdom, O'Neill set out to solve his problem in an essentially different manner. Since the individuals have been so altered by the quality of the actions and events in which they have participated willfully that they cannot reintegrate themselves into the familial order, and since direct operation of divine order and of social order are essentially excluded from the order central to O'Neill's imitation of the human condition, there is only one sphere of order left: the autonomous order of the individual human character.

O'Neill breaks the chain by having Lavinia Mannon, his main character in the trilogy, discover a just basis for action inherent in her own individual moral nature. Through an autonomous act of grace, she relinquishes her potential spouse, Peter Niles, so that the proclivities of what she has become – partially through inherited characteristics, and partially through her own willful action – will not be further implemented by their marriage. Grace, as O'Neill imitates its atoning power in human affairs, is not the gift of the gods, nor of society. Justice with mercy is the absolute prerogative of each individual member of the human race. Man is totally responsible for justice. Each man provides his own Nemesis.

VI

THE ICEMAN COMETH

The Iceman Cometh is a very long play. About four and one-half hours are required for its production. It is, to say the least, an experimental play, daring in its selection of milieu, imitation of character, treatment of diction, and magnitude. Generally, it is taken to be either a boring stunt, or a truly original masterpiece. The great critical problem with this work lies in classifying it precisely. It has been called everything from "slice of life naturalism", to "highly symbolic". Clearly, the parts of the play cannot be described accurately until its identity as poetic object has been established with some degree of precision. For instance, what are we to make of the following speech of Harry Hope in the third act unless we can identify the poetic context in which it is uttered?

HOPE. (*beginning to collapse within himself – dully*) Yes, what's the use – now? All a lie? No automobile. But, bejees, something ran over me! Must have been myself, I guess.[1]

If we assume that this is a slice of life bit of naturalism, such a fanciful speech strikes us as wrong. If we assume that the play is a highly symbolic allegory of man's destiny, we have less trouble with the above speech; but it will be obvious to even the casual reader that nothing is hidden here, nothing is pointed to outside the piece (as in allegory which attempts to make a doctrine or thesis persuasive by casting it into a pseudo-poetic form). Everthing is explicit within that speech of Hope's. Again, what are we to make of his name? And so the problems multiply.

[1]   Random House, III, 691.

Following is a brief of this play from which we shall attempt to induct a working description of what the play is.

Act One takes place in the back room and a section of the bar at Harry Hope's Raines-Law hotel, a cheap dive, in the early morning of a summer's day in 1912. The place is occupied by an add assortment of derelicts. In the back room (actually part of the larger room that may be converted into a "back room" when a thin black curtain is drawn), sit Hugo Kalmar, a one-time editor of anarchist periodicals, and Larry Slade, a one-time syndicalist-anarchist. At the middle table in the front area sit Joe Mott, a former Negro gambling czar; Piet Wetjoen, a former Boer War general; James Cameron (Jimmy Tomorrow), one-time Boer War correspondent; and Cecil Lewis, who was once a British captain in the Boer War. At the right front table sit Harry Hope, proprietor of the dive and former Tammanyite ward-heeler; Pat McGloin, a decayed police lieutenant; and Ed Mosher, Hope's brother-in-law and a former circus man. In the second line of tables, front, sits Willie Oban, a Harvard Law School alumnus. As the act begins, Rocky Pioggi, the night bartender, walks from the bar, front, between the curtains, into the "back room" and furtively offers Larry Slade a free drink.

During the conversation thus precipitated between Rocky and Larry, Rocky speaks of the most ordinary, everyday concerns, typical of an uneducated person from the lower ranks, and is invariably answered in the highly rhetorical and philosophic discourse of Larry. When Rocky mentions Hope's threat to throw these derelicts out on their ear if they do not pay their bills, Larry jokes about their ships coming in; when Rocky answers that the ships will be loaded with dope, Larry's highly figurative reply runs in part:

To hell with the truth! As the history of the world proves, the truth has no bearing on anything. It's irrelevant and immaterial, as the lawyers say. The lie of a pipe dream is what gives life to the whole misbegotten mad lot of us, drunk or sober. And that's enough philosophic wisdom to give you for one drink of rot-gut.[2]

Larry's rhetoric increases in tempo and wakes up Hugo, who

[2] *Ibid.*, p. 578.

promptly falls asleep again after mumbling some ritualistic, anarchist jargon. Rocky complains that Hugo is constantly intimating that he, Rocky, is a pimp, and explains in typically ignorant speech why he is not a pimp. The expected arrival of Theodore Hickman, a traveling hardware salesman, is the next topic of conversation. This is interrupted by the drunken twitching and mumbling of Willie in his sleep, who has gone on the skids partly because of his father's being caught up in a public scandal resulting from his illicit "bucket-shop" operations. Willie's gyrations wake Hope, who promptly tells Rocky to give Willie a stiff drink to quiet him so he, Hope, can get some sleep in his own bar. Hope rants for some time, in his usual fashion, about how everybody including his bartenders Rocky and Chuck (the day bartender) is robbing him blind, and falls asleep again. Willie hungrily consumes the liquor offered him and fades into quiescence. Joe Mott wakes up and asks for a drink at this point. Joe, refused by Rocky, indicates he will wait till Hickey comes for Harry Hope's birthday party (which Hickey does yearly), then they will all be treated to free whiskey. Joe thinks of a new arrival at the hotel, Don Parritt, from whom he might get a free drink. But Rocky tells Joe that Parritt is broke. Larry denies being a friend of Parritt, and tells them Rosa Parritt, the recently arrested I. W. W. leader in California, is Don's mother.

Parritt enters, shiftily greets everyone, especially Larry, and continues to talk in a suspiciously explanatory manner. Rocky leaves to take a nap behind the bar. Joe falls asleep, asking to be wakened if Hickey comes. A long conversation ensues between Larry and Parritt, touching on Parritt's leaving the "movement", Larry's previous relations with Rosa Parritt (a free love advocate), the nature of the derelicts in the saloon, and Larry's general disinterestedness in life and all humanity. We gather there is something suspicious about Parritt's flight from California and that he has sought out Larry, who Parritt thinks can help him in some strange fashion. Near the end of this long exposition, Larry tells Parritt, "I was born condemned to be one of those who has to see all sides of a question. When you're damned like that, the questions multiply for you until in the end it is all question and no answer".[3] Larry continues, telling Parritt it is a mistake to suppose he, Larry, can, or will, be of help to anyone. And that the only answer he has is Heine's:

'Lo, sleep is good; better is death; in sooth,
The best of all were never to be born.[4]

Parritt tells Larry that his mother's betrayal from within the movement has destroyed his belief in everything.

Hugo wakes, makes his habitual anarchist statements and drunkenly calls Parritt a stool pigeon. Parritt reacts strongly and suspiciously to this innocuous accusation, and seems to take Hugo too seriously for one who claims he is not guilty. Hugo falls asleep again. Parritt quickly changes the subject and asks about the other people in the room, who they are, what they are doing there, and what Larry thinks of their lot. Larry launches into a speech of complete explanation.

As he finishes, Willie Oban wakes, volunteers his own life history, then begs Parritt for a drink. When he finds out who and what Parritt is, he advises him to leave, for Hugo, according to Willie, is enough of Parritt's type for one place. Willie then goes into a Tom Lehrer satire in the sophisticated intellectual tradition on everything and everybody, which includes a noisy, bawdy ballad. This wakes Harry, who orders Rocky to lock Willie in his room. Rocky actually starts to manhandle Willie, who crumbles at this, while Hope scolds Rocky for taking his orders too seriously, and tells Rocky to give Willie a drink. Willie downs his drink and fades again into oblivion.

This commotion wakes Captain Lewis, Wetjoen, Joe, and Jimmy Tomorrow. There follows a long exchange among these newly awakened personages and Hope, Larry, Parritt, and later McGloin and Mosher. This consists of each of them, in turn, arguing how he will buck up "tomorrow", and regain his former status; all except Larry, who says he only waits for welcomed death, and Parritt, who sits amazed at this seemingly mad and pointless activity.

[3] *Ibid.*, p. 590.
[4] *Ibid.*, p. 591.

As McGloin excuses his removal from the police force for graft, Willie Oban rouses from his sleep and commences a mock, but skillful cross-examination of McGloin, breaks madly into the bawdy ballad again and is silenced by Rocky at Hope's command. So the rationalizing and cataloguing of ways to get back on one's feet continues, but not without some very lively burlesque of humorous scenes from the past.

Rocky enters from the bar again, telling Harry it is time to open; simultaneously, Rocky's two tarts, Pearl and Margie, are heard coming up the street. Rocky goes to usher them in, shushing them lest they wake up the gang, all of whom, except Larry and Parritt, have drifted off again. A humorous accounting of funds and exploits takes place between Rocky and his tarts.

Chuck (the day bartender) and his tart, Cora, enter. Their pipedream, we have been told, consists of impossible dreams of getting married. A long comic scene ensues between the two pimps and their tarts. Cora reveals that she has seen Hickey down the street.

Hope wakens at this and the whole place becomes wide-eyed with anticipation, for it seems Hickey has made some joke about bringing them all, all the old gang, salvation and peace and freedom from their nagging pipe dreams.

Hickey enters shortly. But he is a changed Hickey, and they are all suspicious and disappointed at his abstinence from drink, although he says he does not object to others who drink. Then, with frenetic good humor, Hickey vaguely challenges each of their pipe dreams in turn, and falls asleep exhausted.

The act closes with everyone worried about the exact intentions of one Theodore Hickman in relation to themselves, and with Mosher quelling their fears with a story about an old doctor he once knew who advised him to do nothing, since he was incapable of doing anything. Hickey wakes at this, telling them all that Mosher's optimism is the proper attitude, and that he does not want to be a wet blanket, and that he also wants to see them "happy", and with this word he falls asleep again as the act ends.

Act Two takes place in the back room about midnight of the same day. The back room has been prepared for Harry Hope's birthday party. Cora, Chuck, Margie, Pearl, and Rocky are putting final touches on the coming party. Hugo sleeps as usual, and Larry stares straight ahead in troubled reverie. The two pimps and their tarts discuss their respective pipe dreams rather comically for some time, but presently fall to fighting. The party air is strained for some reason. Everyone blames this on Hickey.

Larry wakes Hugo, tellling him to witness the new revolution. Hugo wakes, but his anarchist cant has turned to ashes in his mouth. He now sneers, despite himself, at the lower classes, and gives voice to autocratic sentiments. He curses, saying Hickey has done this to him, and falls intro troubled sleep. The discussion of Hickey continues, but is interrupted by Joe Mott, who has become surly and resentful of his white companions. All agree that Hickey has soured the derelicts. Larry suggests that whatever it is that has happened to Hickey, despite his suavity and his frenetic kidding of everyone's pipe dream, he (Hickey) wants desperately to tell them something that has happened to him.

Hickey enters, his cheer and bravado even more forced, but in spite of themselves, all cannot help liking him. His arms are loaded with packages. Hickey good naturedly kids Larry about Larry's professed wish to die, intimating that this is just Larry's odd pipe dream, the oddest of all. Larry reacts to this angrily. Hickey has a surprise for them, a huge basket filled with quarts of champagne for Hope's party. All are delighted. Hickey continues to challenge their pipe dreams insinuatingly each time he speaks to one of them. Finally, after Hugo has made a rare and happy remark, Hickey insinuates that Hugo really wants to be a slave master. Hugo appears mortally wounded by this. Larry attacks Hickey telling him to leave Hugo alone, and that Hugo has earned his pipe dream having rotted ten years in prison for his anarchist beliefs. Hickey counters quickly with a long speech in which he defines "the right kind of pity":

No, sir. The kind of pity I feel now is after final results that will really save the poor guy, and make him contented with what he is, and quit battling himself, and find peace for the rest of his life. Oh, I know how you resent the way I have to show you up to yourself.

I don't blame you. I know from my own experience it's bitter medicine, facing yourself in the mirror with the old false whiskers off. But you forget that, once you're cured. You'll be grateful to me . . .[5]

Larry snarls at this, but Hickey continues, telling him among other things that he will have to show the right kind of pity for Don Parritt, and help Parritt punish himself, for, Hickey says, he knows that Parritt suffers from a crushing guilt. Larry insists that he, Larry, is in the grandstand and is not going to help anyone. Hickey drops the subject, turning again in bustling good cheer to the party preparations, and finally leaves to attend to some detail.

Willie Oban enters, a changed man, and reveals that Hickey has persuaded him to stop drinking and apply for a job in the District Attorney's office, as he has been threatening to do for some years.

Parritt enters furtively, having been driven from his room by Hickey. Parritt engages Larry again (much against Larry's will) in conversation about Rosa Parritt. Parritt finally reveals that *he* has betrayed the movement and his mother for "patriotic reasons". Larry refuses to listen to Parritt's point of view, and Parritt attacks him, calling him a faker. Larry springs to the attack momentarily, stung as he is by Parritt's mockery, and warns Parritt: "Look out how you try to taunt me back into life, I warn you! I might remember the thing they call justice there, and the punishment for –." [6] He stops short, refusing to go further.

A fight occurs in the hall between the two friends, Lewis and Wetjoen. Rocky and Chuck break it up and bring the two old soldiers in, both soldiers accusing Hickey of having set them against one another. Mosher and McGloin enter, fearfully discussing the possible outcome for them if Hickey convinces Hope to take his walk around the ward the following day, a walk which Hope has delayed for twenty years. Their discussion ends in a near fight, which is avoided by the interference of Rocky and Chuck.

Hickey comes in telling everyone to get set, for Hope is on

---

[5] *Ibid.*, p. 641.
[6] *Ibid.*, p. 649.

his way down from his room with Jimmy Tomorrow. Hope enters to a spiritless singing of "Happy Birthday". Hope launches into a tirade against everyone in the room, finally causing the girls to break down and cry. He is in earnest, but when Hickey tells him not to take his own self-hatred out on the others Hope insists he is only kidding, and gets support for this obvious falsehood from everyone except Hickey. Hickey, in the following exchange of memories about Hope's and Jimmy Tomorrow's wives, brings out the fact that they both actually hated their wives, and then in an unguarded moment says, "I know how it is, Jimmy, I —".[7] But he stops abruptly, appearing confused and uncertain. Larry rushes into the breach and says:

LARRY. (*seizing on this with vindictive relish*) Ha! So that's what happened to you, is it? Your iceman joke finally came home to roost, did it? (*He grins tauntingly*) You should have remembered there's truth in the old superstition that you'd better look out what you call because in the end it comes to you! [8]

(On previous visits Hickey used to joke that he left his wife in the hay with the iceman.) Hickey recovers his stability, cutting Larry off with a taunt about Larry's pretended interest in death. But the attack on Hickey continues from all sides. He attempts to explain that all he wants is that they find peace and happiness through facing the lie of their pipe dreams. They eventually drive him into a corner and force his hand with their lewd jokes about his wife's unfaithfulness; he tells them quietly that Evelyn, his wife, is dead. They are stunned, remorseful, but Hickey reassures them, saying that all Evelyn wanted in life was to make him happy. He looks at them with simple and gentle frankness as the act ends.

Act Three is set in the bar and a section of the back room; it is mid-morning the following day. Rocky, Parritt, Hugo, and Larry are present. A discussion takes place between Rocky and Larry concerning Hickey. Then Parritt reveals that the real reason for his betrayal of the movement was simply for money, not for patriotism. There is speculation over what happened to

---

[7]   *Ibid.*, p. 657.
[8]   *Ibid.*

Hickey's wife, Larry suggesting that perhaps she committed
suicide.

A long sequence follows in which each of the derelicts in turn
braces himself to go out into the world and accomplish in reality
what his particular pipe dream consists of, the dream in each case
being that of regaining the former occupation and status in
society. All this is, of course, initiated and controlled by Hickey.

Finally, Hope, the weakest of them all, faces his trial by fire.
Hickey persuades him to take his threatened walk around the
ward. Hope manages to get out the door, but returns in a few
minutes a completely shattered man, telling a lie about how he
came back because an automobile nearly ran him down. Hickey
divests him of this illusion, and everyone remarks the fact that
Harry Hope now looks quite dead.

Larry springs to the attack again, for Hope's unfavorable reaction has unsettled Hickey. Hickey discloses that his wife died
from a bullet through her head. Larry accuses Hickey of having
driven his wife to suicide, but Hickey counters that his Evelyn
would never have done that, and that she had been murdered.

Hickey becomes very concerned about Hope, for the effect of
Hope's facing his pipe dream and realizing its impossibility has
given Harry Hope no relief. The act ends with Hickey saying to
Hope, "That's what worries me about you, Governor. It's time
you began to feel happy –." [9]

The fourth act takes place in the back room and a section of
the bar about one-thirty the following morning. All of the derelicts have returned in defeat, having faced their pipe dreams and
failed. The whole scene is enveloped in an even heavier miasma
of despair than it was as the play opened. The derelicts are not
able even to get drunk, for Hickey has removed the effectiveness
of their drinking with his truth crusade. Hickey has gone to make
a mysterious phone call. All discuss their present state of unbearable misery and hope that Hickey will not return. Larry
assures them that he will.

Hickey returns and gives vent to his feeling that they have

cheated him by not being happy with what he has done for them. He begins to explain what he has done to kill his own pipe dream. It becomes apparent that he has killed his wife, as he says, to give her peace from the hell he has made of her life with the years of his periodical drinking binges, and his affairs with cheap women. He has killed Evelyn because he loved her. Larry interrupts to tell him to be quiet, for they all remember the good old days with him, and love him very much. They do not, says Larry, want to know things about him that might send him to the electric chair. But Hickey is determined to explain the whole thing to them, so that they will see the value of what he has tried to do for them.

Hickey plunges into an extremely long confession (nearly eight pages) which is interrupted from time to time by brief exchanges with the derelicts. His narrative begins from the time he and Evelyn were childhood sweethearts and ends with his killing her some twenty years later. The sum of the story is that Evelyn's continual and protracted forgiveness of him over the years has caused him to hate himself, and that the reason he has killed Evelyn instead of himself is because that would have hurt her too much. Parritt breaks in to tell Larry that the real reason he betrayed the movement is because he hated his mother, Rosa Parritt. Shortly after this, Hickey comes to the shocking revelation that he himself has killed Evelyn because he hated her. Now all the truth is out about everyone. All are like living dead men.

Two police officers, whom Hickey himself has phoned, are now present. But Hickey tells himself and the others that he must have been insane to have killed Evelyn and to have called her a damned bitch when she was dead. The derelicts fasten on this; it restores their hope, for if Hickey has been insane all this time, what he has done to them all should have no effect on them. Hickey resists their point of view, but as he sees the newborn joy in their faces begin to die, he purposely helps them convince themselves that he is insane. Then he himself battens onto the pipe dream of his own insanity, for he sees this saves him from the unbearable torture of believing that he has killed Evelyn in rank hatred. He tells the officers that he wants the

chair, for he does not have a single lying hope or pipe dream
left; in the same breath he turns to the crowd and tells them that
if he had not been insane, he would have killed himself before
he killed Evelyn. It is clear at this point that Hickey knows the
truth about himself, that he has killed Evelyn in hatred; but it is
also clear that he wants the derelicts to think he has been insane,
so that they may go on living. The officers take him away, while
all the derelicts resume their pipe dreams.

Parritt at last persuades Larry to pass judgment on him. Larry
tells Parritt to go and kill himself by leaping from the fire escape.
Parritt thanks Larry and leaves to do just that. Larry waits in
agonized terror for the sound of Parritt's falling body, as the
other derelicts begin afresh to enjoy their new found lease on
life. Larry hears Parritt hurtle from the fire escape and winces
in terror. He then says that he, Larry, is the only real convert to
death that Hickey has made, and that he means it now.

Larry sits in stupified silence, staring straight ahead. The gang,
after Hugo declaims "The days grow hot, O Babylon!" take up
the next line, shouting in a loud jeering chorus, "Tis cool beneath
thy willow tree!" [10] They pound their glasses on the table, but
Larry is oblivious to their racket, as the play ends.

The experience this play imitates does not seem to be primarily the experience of action. The action of the play appears to
turn around a dead center. At that center seems to be an odd
notion of truth. Vivian Hopkins tells us, in her comparison of
The Iceman Cometh to Gorky's *The Lower Depths*, that:

O'Neill's analysis of social reform, of course, goes deeper than
Gorky's. Through Larry he presents the concept that a rearrangement
of material goods cannot alter men's spirit.[11]

But O'Neill does not present an "analysis of social reform". The
intent of this play is not didactic, for it implies no workable
program to deal with the issues it raises.

Neither does it seem to be a play of character, involving as a
synthesizing principle complete alteration in moral character,

10   *Ibid.*, pp. 727-728.
11   Vivian C. Hopkins, " '*The Iceman*' Seen through '*The Lower Depths*' ",
College English (November, 1949), p. 87.

brought on or controlled by action, and made apparent in itself
in thought and feeling. The experience in which all of these
characters most frequently participate, just in terms of sheer
quantity, is thought. Hickman presents them with the grim challenge of objectively thinking about what they really are. This
starts in the first act, and on whatever level of thought they are
capable of functioning, they proceed for three acts to *think* about
themselves and what they really are, divesting themselves of
every one of their illusions in the process. Though Larry and
Hickey are the two major characters, all the others indulge in
the same activity – driven on by Hickey, and comforted by
Larry.

Comparisons of *The Iceman Comith* to Ibsen's *The Wild Duck*
are numerous. Sverre Arestad's is especially illuminating:

> It is a curious fact that O'Neill, after a lapse of more than sixty
> years, should take up again the subject that Ibsen discussed in *The
> Wild Duck,* but it is not strange that the idea should be rejected with
> even greater finality by O'Neill than it was by his predecessor. The
> reason is that O'Neill approaches the problem of humanity's ability
> or willingness to accept truth as the basis of life from the viewpoint
> of a pessimist, His conclusion, therefore, leads inevitably to death
> upon the acceptance of truth.[12]

It is Arestad's use of the word "discussed" that is so significant.
For the play is not primarily "dynamic" in structure. It is a
"discussion" play in Shaw's sense of that word. Most of the
issues are settled, in terms of any possible salvaging action on
the part of the characters, when the play begins. And the play
turns into one long, grand discussion, only occasionally relieved
by some startling revelation, or by humor of an obtuse nature
from the lower types in the play, and the jaded and refined
humor of the developed character types such as Larry and Willie
Oban.

What we have before us, then, is a play of "thought" in Crane's
sense of that word. The type of experience most often imitated
in the play is the experience of thought. The play may be de-

---

[12]   Sverre Arestad, "*The Iceman Cometh* and *The Wild Duck*", *Scandinavian Studies*, XX (1948), 9.

scribed as a play primarily involving a change in thought of the main characters (and in their feelings, subsequently), controlled and formed by character and action.

But it is important to remember that this is not a thesis play in the ordinary meaning of that word. The significance of the play is not primarily extensive. It does not attempt overtly to manipulate the sensibilities of its auditors to initiate a program of action, nor to convince them of a thesis, nor to create a change in their feelings. It imitates the experience of thought in a strange medley of characters under peculiar circumstances; and the beautiful and just rendering of that experience into words seems to be the sufficient end of the play. It remains an object for contemplation, an aesthetic object.

The possibilities of the poetic medium of thought employed by O'Neill in this play are numerous. The most striking possibility he has used resides in the manifold types of thought he imitates. They range from the thoughts of the low and uneducated to the most elevated and protracted realm of speculation witnessed in the subtly balanced perception of a true thinker, Larry Slade. But these various kinds of thought become centered on one problem in the play: the relative value of truth versus illusion. This is the dead center around which the thought of all the characters revolves.

Most of the characters do not think efficiently about the problem. The two who do are Larry Slade and Theodore Hickman. Hickey's mode of thought is primarily intuitive. He progresses by trial and error. Larry Slade's mode of thought, however, is analytic, depending strictly on evidence, and especially on immediately observed fact. Larry is the scientist; Hickey, the poet-priest. Both men arrive at the truth about *themselves*, however; Hickey by intuitive progression, and Larry by analysis.

Hickey kills his wife under the guise of love. It is his intuition that this has given him a sense of peace and release he has never been able to experience, and assumes that if everyone will face up to himself as he has done (by destroying his pipe dream, which, in his case, was the dream of some day living up to Evelyn's expectations of him), he will find the same peace and freedom. However, he discovers intuitively, through an act of protracted faith in his original intuition, during his long confession to the gang, that his killing his wife was not motivated by love, but by hate. He tells them that he had decided to kill himself so that Evelyn might be spared the continuous pain of his moral defections, but realized instead that if she loved him as much as she seemed to, his suicide would only increase her pain. There was only one course open to him if he were to put an end to her pain, he says, and that was to kill Evelyn. But at the moment he is describing his "mercy" killing, he remembers that he said, "Well, you know what you can do with your pipe dream now, you damned bitch!" [13] His intuitive knowledge is double edged; he has found peace, release, a new lease on life, but it comes from the satisfaction of his hatred, rather than from a fulfillment of his love. And in the end he knows intuitively that other men cannot live with this truth any more than he can; thus, he allows them their pipe dreams, convincing them that he must have been insane.

Larry's case is different. He has spent years in the observation of men, and has inducted the truth from the collective facts of his observations to be that they cannot live without their illusions. He has not known the truth about himself, however. Whereas he had always thought that he loved death, and that he was happily awaiting death, free of all illusions, Hickey, the intuitive thinker, perceives immediately that Larry desperately clings to life, and in reality does not want death. Larry's love of death is also a pipe dream that sustains life, that sets him apart in his own mind, that gives him a false sense of dignity. When Hickey tells him this, Larry is shaken, for the possible power and accuracy of Hickey's intuitive thought has been concretely demonstrated for Larry by Hickey's knowing there is something wrong with Parritt after having seen Parritt for the first time:

LARRY. For the love of God, mind your own business! (*With forced scorn*) A lot you know about him! He's hardly spoken to you!
HICKEY. No, that's right. But I do know a lot about him just the same. I've had hell inside me. I can spot it in others. (*Frowning*) Maybe

[13]   Random House, III, 716.

that's what gives me the feeling there's something familiar about him, something between us.[14]

At the end of the play Larry realizes that he is truly afraid of death. Proceeding by analysis, he reasons that if his supposed love of death has been the pipe dream that has sustained his life, and that according to the observed facts men cannot live deprived of their illusions, and that he finally has been irrevocably deprived of his illusion, the facts of the case plainly illustrate that he is the only convert to death that Hickey has made; for the others easily take up their pipe dreams again, whereas he cannot, for the power of his thought is too penetrating.

The many less important characters, without Larry's and Hickey's power of thought, are guided into the more mundane course of *action* by Hickey. He sets up an illustrative exercise for each of them to pace through, and the result of the action proves to them that which they cannot arrive at clearly through thought. Larry, the man who has learned by the analysis of the facts that such a course means destruction for them, attempts to protect them and to defend them from Hickey's undermining advice and teaching.

We may say, then, that the playwright has limited the possibilities of the poetic medium of thought in that he has created a long discussion drama that imitates thought on many levels, which has as its center thought that evaluates truth in relation to illusion. In this discussion he has pitted the analytic thinker against the intuitive thinker, giving the analytic thinker the role of defending the less skillful thinkers against the intuitive thinker. The analytic thinker wins out in the end, for the intuitive thinker surrenders his truth in order that the other thinkers in the play may sustain life through illusion – the only possible way for all men to sustain life. So, though the intuitive thinker is defeated in the argument, so also is the analytic thinker; for in analyzing the intuition of the intuitive thinker, the analytic thinker recognizes the truth that even he cannot live without an illusion. The power of Larry's analysis makes it impossible for him to regain his

[14]   *Ibid.*, p. 642.

illusion of being in love with death. In these terms, the play ends
in a dead heat, for in their struggle the two most powerful
thinkers have destroyed their desire to live, while the other, less
powerful thinkers are able to regain their illusions and continue
living. Truth, therefore, whether arrived at analytically or intuitively, kills.

Rudolf Stamm supports this aesthetic view of the play by saying:

Were Evelyn's faith and love, the cause of so much acute distress for
Hickey in his depraved condition, fundamentally different from the
'pipe dreams' and alcoholic illusions, making the shadowy existences
of Harry's drunkards bearable and sometimes even comfortable?
O'Neill does not ask such questions, nor does he answer them. But
they will trouble many students of his work, which at first sight, appears to be wholly devoted to the explanation of a human condition
where life is only to be had at the price of illusions, and where self-
knowledge kills.[15]

Quite clearly Evelyn's faith in Hickey was a pipe dream, an
illusion. As to whether or not it was "fundamentally different
from the pipe dreams and alcoholic illusions" of Hope's drunkards, we may answer that it definitely was, an inference we may
draw from the action of the play. It differs in that it was simply
more selfish, for its fulfillment (as Hickey proves) demanded no
effort from Evelyn, but placed *all* responsibility for its fulfillment on another person, Hickey himself. In contrast, all of the
other pipe dreams imitated in the play place the responsibility
for their fulfillment squarely on the shoulders of the individual.
It should also be remembered that Stamm's above inference that
the mode of life imitated here is somehow inferior only gets at
one-half the truth, for as Sophus Keith Winther says of most of
the derelicts:

But the paradox is that they are also symbols of the ideals by which
men live. They have fought in the Cause. They have been leaders of
the Great Movement. They were heroes in wars, national and social.
Hugo served ten years in prison for the Cause. Each in his own way
has been apprenticed to the Ideal, and when the Ideal failed he

---

[15] Rudolf Stamm, "A New Play by Eugene O'Neill", *English Studies*,
XXIX (1948), 143.

drifted to this Last Resort Saloon where he nourishes his pipe dream and drinks rotgut whiskey, waiting for the Big Day.[16]

Stamm's real contribution to the study of this play consists in his statement that "O'Neill does not ask such questions, nor does he answer them". For it was this seemingly odd statement of his, the consequences of which are woven throughout his article, that first brought this writer to the realization that the intent of the play is not didactic, but imitative. Such questions are not overtly asked or answered by the play itself, which is devoted to the imitation, but can be asked and answered by the auditor of the play within the terms of the closed aesthetic entity which the play vividly presents.

The mode of imitation of this play is purely dramatic, with all of the speakers speaking in scene. The distinctive coloring of the dialogue, the fanciful flights of speech, even of the lowest characters at times, are easily justifiable if the play is accepted as a play of thought. The pressure of thought, omnipresent as it is, seems an adequate motivation for some of the more fanciful flights of dialogue on the part of the less educated characters. The speech of Hope quoted above is a good example. We expect the speech of Hickey and Larry to be capable of great depths of insight; for sizing up all classes of people has been Hickey's stock in trade, and thought has been the main activity of Larry for years. The strange, seemingly symbolic utterance with which the play abounds is actually the result of characters in a "supernaturalistic" milieu engaged in exasperated thought about the problem of the relative value of truth as opposed to illusion. The problem they confront must inevitably produce a rich and highly colored dialogue. Concerning the veracity of the character Hugo, Doris Alexander says:

Bentley seems to make a quantitative distinction between realism and naturalism, with naturalism simply including more details in its photograph. Whatever he holds realism to be, Bentley thinks it is endangered by philosophy, by selection on the basis of ideas. So it seems to be a fairly literal kind of reproduction of life. Gibbs'

[16] Sophus Keith Winther, "*The Iceman Cometh:* A Study in Technique", *Arizona Quarterly*, III (Winter, 1947), 295.

[Wolcott Gibbs] concept of realism seems very similar, since he defines the non-realism of O'Neill's dialogue as a failure to hear 'the accent of the voice or the structure of the sentence' of the people he is reproducing in literature. So both critics base their idea of realism on a close reproduction of life, and then proceed to damn as unrealistic a character who has been modeled with utmost exactitude on a living person [Hippolyte Havel].[17]

As Alexander convincingly points out, Hugo's speech corresponds exactly with other recorders of Havel's speech, appearance, and mannerisms. She further suggests that the colorful nature of the model, Havel, explains the seemingly overly fanciful quality of the imitation, Hugo. If Bentley's criterion for naturalism is applied here ("naturalism simply including more details in its photograph" than does realism), we may call Hugo a naturalistic character. And since Alexander proves beyond doubt that O'Neill has actually presented a fuller imitation of Havel (and a more accurate one) than any of the other reporters of Havel, we may safely add the word "super" to our description of the mode of the play. But we must remember, too, that O'Neill makes all this "supernaturalism" quite plausible by setting it in the context of a casual selection of realistic detail, including such mundane considerations as the time of day, and in one scene a perfectly plausible explanation of why the bar is empty of its usual customers long after opening time, which is early morning. Rocky says:

Nuttin' now till de noon rush from de Market. I'm goin' to rest my fanny.[18]

The plot of this play, in the sense of the arrangement of the incidents, is complex, all reversal and discovery arising naturally from the incidents themselves. But it is not a single plot, it is multiple, containing four interwoven lines of action: the bulk of the derelicts facing up to their pipe dreams, the gradual discovery of Parritt's hatred for his mother, the progressive analysis of Larry, and the progression of the intuitive thought of Hickey.

---

[17] Doris Alexander, "Hugo of *The Iceman Cometh:* Realism and O'Neill", *American Quarterly*, V (1953), 363-364.
[18] Random House, III, 665.

There are also four separate issues: the bulk of the derelicts recapture their illusions, Parritt commits suicide to punish himself for his betrayal of his mother, Larry loses and is unable to regain his illusion, and Hickey finally intuits the truth of his hatred for Evelyn.

The mode of the play may be described as a supernaturalistic dramatic mode that involves the use of casual realistic surfaces blended with a highly selective technique which involves the super-subtle selection of detail (e.g., Hickey's recalling the exact words he had uttered upon killing Evelyn), which are fused into a balanced whole. The characters, their prose dialogue, and the setting all contribute to this unity which expresses ultimately their preference for illusion over reality through their thought, made explicit in their dialogue and action. The arrangement of the incidents is complex, multiple, and involves a quadruple issue.

The sequence of emotions and expectations this play intends to evoke and resolve as it unfolds seems much different from the other plays with which this study deals. The overall intent is clearly tragic, but the emphasis on thought seems to trenchantly mitigate the emotional impact. Helen Muchnic is aware of this "cooling off", as it has been called, when she says:

If the tone of the plays is on the whole tragic, the tragedy inheres not in the doom of the central characters but in the pathos of various episodes, and even more in implications, in what is not, rather than in what is, done or said.[19]

In many respects this is one of O'Neill's most humorous plays, and though the barroom burlesque often has a grim and devilish bite to it, the dialogue is unparalleled for its graveyard wit.

Curiosity is perhaps a better word than suspense to describe the central effect this play is intended to evoke in terms of expectation. Since the outcome of Hickey's advice, regarding the effect it will have on each of the lesser derelicts, is clearly not going to result in disaster, we are curious to see how each one in

[19]   Helen Muchnic, "Circe's Swine: Plays by Gorky and O'Neill", *Comparative Literature*, III (Spring, 1951), 124.

turn reacts to the truth object lesson Hickey sets up for him. Suspense is aroused, however, in regard to Hickey, Larry, and Parritt, for it grows more and more clear that the issue of their separate struggles is going to result in three painful catastrophes. Pity of a minor sort is evoked for the bulk of the derelicts, and is removed altogether as we see Hickey give back their lease on life by at last relinquishing his truth for their sake. Pity is magnified for Larry, for we realize that he cannot regain life. Pity is greatly magnified for Hickey, for the truth has utterly annihilated him, as it has Parritt. The nadir of despair may be seen in Larry at the end of the play, and we gently pity him for this, as he has, after all, attempted to protect everyone (including Hickey) from destruction by resisting Hickey's well intended truth crusade. But the Bridegroom, life, is irrevocably pre-empted by the adulterous and evil Iceman, death. Man's marriage to life must end in his divorce from life caused by death. One of the surest truths of man's existence is death, the end, for which, it seems, he is born.

Having answered the four questions, and having arrived through those four answers at the statement of the four multiple working hypotheses, we can now synthesize the hypotheses into a description of the play's form, or mode of existence. The play may be described as a play essentially involving a change of thought in the main characters (and their feelings, subsequently), controlled and formed by character and action. In this imitation of thought the analytic thinker is pitted against the intuitive thinker. But both the analytic thinker and the intuitive thinker are destroyed in the end, as the power of both methods of thought is so great in them as to make it impossible for them to regain their illusions. This is all accomplished in a supernaturalistic dramatic mode that involves the use of casual realistic surfaces blended with a highly selective technique, which involves the super-subtle selection of detail, all of which are fused into a balanced whole. The characters, their prose dialogue, and the setting all contribute to this unity which expresses finally their preference for illusion over reality through their thought, made explicit in their dialogue and action. The arrangement of the incidents is complex, multiple, and involves a quadruple issue. Pity of a minor sort is evoked for the bulk of the derelicts, but is finally removed altogether as we see Hickey, the intuitive thinker, give back their lease on life by at last relinquishing his truth for them. Pity is magnified for Larry, the analytic thinker, for we realize he cannot regain life; pity is greatly magnified for Hickey, because truth has utterly annihilated him, as it has Parritt. The nadir of despair may be seen in Larry at the end of the play, and we gently pity him for this, as he has, after all, attempted to protect everyone (including Hickey) from destruction by resisting Hickey's well intended truth crusade. Thus, in a sense, our pity is greater for the intuitive thinker, as he is defeated by the analytic thinker in the end.

Nemesis stemming from the breaking of the *lex talionis* in this play seems at first unimportant, perhaps because of the emphasis on thought in the play. However, Hickey and Parritt become victims of the *lex talionis*; Hickey goes to the electric chair for having killed his wife, and Parritt kills himself for the betrayal of his comrades and his mother, with Larry acting as his judge and prosecutor, though Parritt carries out the sentence on himself. Too, we find that hatred is the motivation for Hickey's crime, as it is for Parritt's. Though we find that it is hatred that hides beneath the actions of the bulk of the derelicts, they are spared from destruction, through Hickey's act of love (allowing them to regain their illusions through his own claim of insanity). Larry appears to avoid hatred, or tries to avoid it, by assuming a detached air. This is essentially an expression of hatred also, and he pays for this by being deprived of any illusions at all. Ironically, what Hickey calls "the right kind of pity" turns out to be motivated actually by hatred, rather than love, which is the giving of comfort. He reverts to the "wrong kind of pity" at the end of the play, relenting in his merciless crusade for truth, and allows the gang to keep their illusions. Hatred, the *lex talionis,* is shown in the play to be the central driving force in human character, until the very end.

Nemesis stemming from social justice is brought into the play late. Hickey's phone call is the first inkling we have of it, and it is ironic that Hickey himself calls it in, not for the purpose of paying his penalty before society, but for the strictly personal desire to find peace in death. Social justice is shown, as the play imitates it in general terms, to be ineffective. Hugo's suffering for his beliefs, the failure of the movement, and other episodes of the miscarriage of social justice are frequently referred to in the play. It becomes apparent that justice must reside in another place than the forms of society.

The idea of Nemesis stemming from the divine is never broached in any significant manner in the play. Man is imitated as isolated in a disinterested universe as Larry says:

Honor or dishonor, faith or treachery are nothing to me but the opposites of the same stupidity which is ruler and king of life, and in the end they rot into dust in the same grave. All things are the same meaningless joke to me, for they grin at me from the one skull of death.[20]

The ultimate justice of grace in this play resides in the individual himself, as does tragic justice. And it must reside in love, not in hatred; in "the wrong kind of pity", not in the cruel, illusion depriving "right kind of pity" that Hickey promotes until the very end. It must reside in *understanding* pity, for this is what Larry so helplessly tries to do; "Larry, whose cynical philosophy is coupled with an instinctive sympathy of which he is ashamed, and whose sense of justice is based on a hopeless understanding of human beings".[21] Hickey punishes himself, when through the power of his intuitive thought he is able to recognize what he has actually done. Parritt punishes himself, when, with Larry's help, he recognizes that no one else can punish him as much as he needs to be punished. Larry analyses himself into a living death through reflecting on the truth of Hickey's intuitive thrust of thought, a thrust that completely shatters Larry's intellectual pride in his own disinterested pretense. John Mason Brown sums it up neatly when he says:

In *The Iceman Cometh* Mr. O'Neill may continue to work as a symbolist. But instead of seeking to relate men to the unseen agents of

20   Random House, III, 649.
21   Muchnic, p. 128.

their destiny, he occupies himself with what they must live by within themselves.[22]

Thought, naked thought, the power of which gives man his identity, is the instrument of Nemesis in this play, as Hickey, Larry, and Parritt discover. Thought generated by hatred destroys; thought generated by love *can* effect salvation. Each man may control his thought as he wills, and is, therefore, responsible for his own destiny. Hickey's refusal to temper his truth with mercy in his Nemesis, for though man lives through illusion, and illusions are not "true" in the absolute sense, it is just as great a truth that he must die without his illusions.

[22] John Mason Brown, "All O'Neilling", *Saturday Review of Literature*, XXIX (October 19, 1946), 27.

VII

LONG DAY'S JOURNEY INTO NIGHT

In this chapter we are to deal with O'Neill's first posthumously published play. Another posthumous play, *More Stately Mansions*,[1] was recently published.

The focus of this study requires that the obvious autobiographical elements in *Long Day's Journey into Night* be kept peripheral, and that they be drawn upon only when they appear critical to the discussion of the play's aesthetic identity. In other words, this play will not be considered primarily as a document that furthers the study of the poet's life. Considering this play primarily from the standpoint of its autobiographical significance, or the significance of autobiography in its artistic production, is another whole study and cannot be dealt with adequately here. As Arthur and Barbara Gelb constantly point out, O'Neill frequently distorted the actual relations between himself and members of his family, both in conversation and in his letters, and often in his works, for purely personal reasons, but primarily for aesthetic ends. A trenchant example of this is the picture O'Neill presents of his father. Whereas in this play James Tyrone, Sr., is the worst sort of miser, in actual life James O'Neill was one of the greatest financial contributors to his son's writing career. James O'Neill bought the beautiful studio, Peaked Hill Bar, and presented it to O'Neill and his second wife, Agnes Boulton, as a gift in anticipation of their coming child. It was

---

[1] Eugene O'Neill, *More Stately Mansions* (New Haven, Yale University Press, 1964), pp. vii-x.

in this magnificent studio, a gift from his father, that O'Neill was enabled to write his early masterpieces.[2]

Following is a brief of the play from which will be inducted the formal description of the play, and, subsequently, the role of Nemesis in that structure.

Act One takes place in the living room of the Tyrones' summer home on a day in August, 1912, beginning at eight-thirty in the morning. Mary and James Tyrone enter from the back parlor, having just finished breakfast. A casual morning conversation between husband and wife takes place, which is, however, undercut by suggestions of James' foolish speculation in real estate, concern over Mary's recent illness and the possibility of its recurrence, the illness of Edmund (the younger son), and the profligacy of James (the older son), while Edmund and James are still at the breakfast table noisily enjoying some joke between them.

Edmund and James enter, and the conversation continues pleasantly enough, touching upon Mary's present good health and Tyrone's snoring, but is interrupted by Tyrone's sudden attack on the worthlessness of James, Jr. This last is uneasily smoothed over, and the boys tell the story they had been laughing over at breakfast, which Tyrone suspected was at his expense. Tyrone quells his obvious enjoyment of the story, and once again begins to attack his sons: Edmund for his anarchist views, and James for his lack of ambition. Edmund leaves in a huff, while James stoically attempts to ignore his father's senseless ill humor. Edmund's illness is brought up again, with Tyrone obviously trying to prevent James from revealing the possible seriousness of it to Mary. The subject changes to Mary's surviving beauty. Mary leaves, and Tyrone begins scolding James for having risked revealing the seriousness of Edmund's illness to Mary.

Edmund's illness, which we learn is probably tuberculosis, and Tyrone's miserliness in his plans for having it treated, now form the center of a bitter argument which develops again into an attack by Tyrone on James' profligacy. But James turns the

[2] Arthur and Barbara Gelb, *O'Neill* (New York, Harper & Brothers, 1962), p. 392.

argument back into an attack on his father's miserly intentions to treat Edmund's consumption. Tyrone then tells James that he is to blame for Edmund's condition by having led him to liquor and women, intimating that James may unknowingly have tried to harm his brother. James denies this, but suggests that Edmund is no more successful than himself. Tyrone defends Edmund's recent work on the local paper, the writing of parodies, and general repertorial writing, whereas he had made complete light of James' acting career. They turn to discussing Mary's recent return from the sanatorium, and James' suspicion that Mary may have begun taking dope again the previous night, but decide that James has been mistaken. We learn that the cause of her habit had been large doses administered by a cheap hotel doctor that Tyrone had hired to treat her just prior to her confinement with Edmund. Mary interrupts James' bitter accusation of Tyrone, and they pretend they are discussing the day of yard work ahead of them. They leave to work, cautioning Mary to "take care of herself", but she resents their accusing concern.

Edmund enters and a long discussion of Mary's constant unhappiness ensues. She indicates that though Tyrone is extremely wealthy, he has never given her a home in a community she liked, where she might have friends and not feel isolated. All he has ever given her is this tawdry summer home, and a continual round of cheap hotels in the winter. But Edmund counters that the real reason she cannot have friends is because of her illness, though it may have been Tyrone's fault in the beginning. Mary complains that her husband and sons leave her alone all the time, preferring barroom company to her own. Edmund then gets Mary to promise that she will not revert to her habit, if his illness turns out to be more serious than it now appears to be. As the act ends, Edmund leaves to join Tyrone and James, with his mother accusing him of not trusting her when she is alone.

Act Two is divided into two scenes, both of which are set in the living room. Scene One begins about twelve forty-five p.m.; Scene Two, a half-our later. As Scene One opens Edmund and Cathleen, the second girl servant, are discussing the problem of getting Tyrone and James to come in for lunch. Cathleen goes to get them. James comes in, leaving his father engrossed in conversation with a neighbor. The boys filch a whiskey before lunch from their father's jealously watched supply in the decanter on the table. They discuss Edmund's illness, and finally James asks where Mary is. Edmund says she has gone to the spare room to take a nap, and James berates his brother for leaving her alone.

Mary enters, peculiarly detached. James perceives immediately that she has begun taking morphine again, and he is angered by Edmund's lack of awareness of this. His consequent cynicism in addressing his mother is sharply countered by her resentful attack on him. When Edmund leaps to his defense, Mary gives in, saying:

But I suppose life has made him like that, and he can't help it. None of us can help the things that life has done to us. They're done before you realize it, and once they're done they make you do other things until at last everything comes between you and what you'd like to be, and you've lost your true self forever.[3]

Mary leaves shortly.

Tyrone finally comes in, indulges the boys in a huge drink (their second, unbeknownst to him), and their minor bickering and quarreling continues, Jamie hinting that Tyrone will soon discover something that will make him unhappy.

Mary returns through the parlor and guiltily begins a long monologue. It is obvious to everyone, including Tyrone, that she has begun taking morphine again. The two boys go to lunch, while Mary and Tyrone stay, Tyrone expressing his disappointment in Mary. As the scene ends they go to lunch.

As Scene Two begins the family is returning from lunch steeped in gloom, which Mary ineffectually tries to dispel with nervous talk. Dr. Hardy, the family physician, whom both the boys insist is unskilled, telephones. It is plain from the tone of Tyrone's talk on the phone that he has bad news about Edmund, though Tyrone tries to disguise his alarm and tells the doctor that he will see that Edmund goes to his office at four that afternoon. Mary goes upstairs, and the three men engage in exasperated

---

[3]   Yale, p. 61.

conversation concerning Mary's relapse, and their own failures. Tyrone blames his sons' lack of success on their turning from the Catholic church, which, he says, results in self-destruction. Edmund gives his explanation with a quotation from Nietzsche's *Thus Spake Zarathustra*: "God is dead: of His pity for man hath God died." [4] Edmund leaves to dress; Tyrone and James extend the quarrel they had begun after breakfast, touching on the same matters. Mary comes in as James leaves to dress for town. Tyrone and Mary indulge in a long series of mutual recriminations, including the *used* car that Tyrone has bought her. Mary begins to drift backward into reveries of her life before she met Tyrone. When Tyrone asks her to forget the past she counters:

Why? How can I? The past is the present, isn't it? It's the future, too. We all try to lie out of that but life won't let us. [5]

Mary eventually blames her misfortune on God's punishment for having another baby, Edmund, since she had proved she wasn't able to take care of their dead son, Eugene.

Edmund enters, dressed; as Tyrone is leaving to dress, Edmund asks him for some carfare. Tyrone gives him ten dollars, and before he can go up to dress Mary pointlessly attacks Edmund, accusing him of malingering. Tyrone leaves asking Edmund to talk with Mary about being strong, as they had agreed previously he should do. Edmund does this, but it ends in a quarrel with Mary. The others call to him to come on or they will be late. He leaves, and Mary is alone, saying to herself she is glad they are gone for their contempt and disgust are not pleasant company, and the second act ends.

Act Three begins around half past six the same evening. Mary is alone with Cathleen in the living room. She has been fraternizing with Cathleen and giving her whiskey to keep her there to talk. They are waiting for the men to return for dinner. She reminisces for Cathleen about her early courtship and marriage to Tyrone, lost in the past. Finally Cathleen escapes into the kitchen, and Mary continues to reminisce.

4   *Ibid.*, p. 78.
5   *Ibid.*, p. 87.

Edmund and Tyrone come in from the street. The family quarrels continue until Edmund leaves to walk in the fog without his supper. Tyrone is too drunk to eat, though he carries it well, and Mary does not want to eat either. After Tyrone has revealed to Mary that Edmund has tuberculosis and must go to a sanatorium to be cured, she excuses herself to go upstairs and take some more "poison", as Tyrone guesses. Tyrone exits sadly to the dining room as the act ends.

Act Four begins around midnight of the same day in the Tyrone living room. Tyrone sits alone at the table playing solitaire. He is very drunk. Edmund comes home and a long argument follows concerning whether or not Edmund is going to turn off the hall light, the miserly concern of Tyrone. Edmund tells him that Jamie is probably drunk in some brothel (Edmund had split the ten dollars that Tyrone had given him with James). A drunken philosophical discussion begins; Tyrone defending "sense", and Edmund defending "lack of sense". Edmund says:

Don't look at me as if I'd gone nutty. I'm talking sense. Who wants to see life as it is, if they can help it? It's the three Gorgons in one. You look in their faces and turn to stone. Or it's Pan. You see him and you die – that is, inside you – and have to go on living as a ghost.[6]

A discussion of James follows this, Edmund quoting from Baudelaire and others to characterize his brother. Tyrone attacks Edmund's taste in literature, defending the worth of Shakespeare against the whole lot.

The discussion turns to Mary as they hear her moving around upstairs. Tyrone hopes she goes to sleep soon, saying that if she comes down she will be lost in a dream of the past, which Tyrone insists she glorifies. All this while the two have been playing casino, but paying little attention to their game of cards. Tyrone tells Edmund the worst part of it all is that Mary seems lost in a bank of fog, fog like that which was present the previous night and also tonight, through which Edmund has walked most of the night, enjoying, as he has reported, the sensation of being lost in

6   *Ibid.*, p. 131.

it. Edmund then accuses Tyrone of sending him to the state in-
stitution, Hilltown Sanatorium, for his tuberculosis cure because
it is cheap. Tyrone denies any miserly motivation for this. Tyrone
launches into a long personal history about his poverty as a boy,
revealing that he had to work in a machine shop when he was
only ten, and that knowing the press of poverty has not made
him a miser, but has given him a healthy respect for the dollar.
He compares Edmund's wanderings to foreign countries and
making his own way to a game he has played. Edmund answers
sarcastically that it certainly was, that's why he had tried to
commit suicide at Jimmy the Priest's bar in New York. Tyrone
tells Edmund he can go to any sanatorium he chooses, but still
there is unintentional comedy in the way he makes this generous
offer, for Tyrone qualifies his offer so much that it is plain to
see he has said this against his helplessly miserly will. Edmund
agrees with amusement that he will go to Hilltown.

They resume playing casino, but Tyrone forgets the cards and
plunges into a confession of how he ruined his artistic career,
how he gave up becoming a great Shakesperian actor (which
even so great a Shakesperian actor as Edwin Booth said he could
become), to sell his artistic soul for fifty thousand dollars net
profit a year in a popular but shoddy play about the French
Revolution, in which he played a nobleman. Edmund is moved
by the sanity and honesty of this confession.

Tyrone, concerned again about the cost of electricity, gets up
shakily to turn off the chandelier he had previously turned on.
Edmund laughs, and when Tyrone asks why he laughs, Edmund
tells him that he laughs at life, because it is so funny. Tyrone
counters immediately that nothing is wrong with life and quotes
from Shakespeare, Cassius' line:

The fault, dear Brutus, is not in our stars, but in ourselves that we
are underlings.[7]

They notice again that Mary is moving around upstairs. Then
Edmund breaks into a long reminiscence in which he describes
for his father rare moments of beatitude:

[7] *Ibid.*, p. 152.

And several other times in my life, when I was swimming far out, or
lying alone on a beach, I have had the same experience. Became the
sun, the hot sand, green seaweed anchored to a rock, swaying in the
tide. Like a saint's vision of beatitude. Like the veil of things as
they seem drawn back by an unseen hand. For a second you see –
and seeing the secret, are the secret. For a second there is meaning!
Then the hand lets the veil fall and you are alone, lost in the fog
again, and you stumble on toward nowhere, for no good reason! [8]

James returns, stumbles in comically, and Tyrone leaves to avoid
him, going out onto the back porch. A humorous account of
James' adventures ensues, in which he tries mawkishly to defend
the mystique of his profligacy. James asks where the "hophead",
meaning Mary, has gone. Edmund strikes him in the face. James
apologizes, but admits his envy and hatred of Edmund, which
he declares to be against his will. He says at least he is being
honest with Edmund; that he loves him and hates him all at the
same time. But, he says, he must take revenge on everyone else
for what has happened to him. He then adds strangely:

Remember I warned you – for your sake. Give me credit. Greater
love hath no man than this, that he saveth his brother from himself.[9]

Shortly after this he loses consciousness from having consumed
too much liquor, and Tyrone returns from the porch, where he
has been waiting for James to fall asleep. He tells Edmund that
he should realize now that he, Tyrone, has told Edmund the
truth about James' hatred. Edmund will not listen to this. James
wakes and viciously attacks his father for his miserliness. However, soon Tyrone and James fall asleep.

Suddenly Edmund hears Mary coming downstairs. He is dis-
tracted, starts to leave the room to escape, but then sits down,
waiting, his hands gripping the arms of his chair. Mary goes first
into the front parlor and tries to play Chopin with her hands
which are crippled by rheumatism. Her two dreams before her
marriage to Tyrone had been to become a concert pianist or a
nun. Presently she appears in the doorway, completely immersed
in her morphine dream. James wakes up and says, "The Mad

8   *Ibid.*, p. 153.
9   *Ibid.*, p. 167.

Scene. Enter Ophelia!" [10] Edmund slaps James across the mouth, which Tyrone approves. Mary is carrying her wedding dress. They try to get her attention, but she is lost in the past. She is looking for something, something she cannot define but which she knows she has lost. It becomes apparent that she searches for her lost innocence. Finally she launches into a long speech, searching in the past for what she cannot find in the present. The narrative begins when she was a young girl in a convent and had direct communion in her prayer with the Blessed Virgin. It continues with her Mother Superior's sending her out to live a secular live for a few years to determine if convent life were truly what she wanted. The play ends as Mary's speech ends:

She pauses and a look of growing uneasiness comes over her face. She passes a hand over her forehead as if brushing cobwebs from her brain – vaguely.

That was in the winter of senior year. Then in the spring something happened to me. Yes, I remember. I fell in love with James Tyrone and was so happy for a time.

She stares before her in a sad dream. Tyrone stirs in his chair. Edmund and Jamie remain motionless.[11]

The synthesizing, or formal controlling principle, certainly is not action in this play. For, as the brief demonstrates, the thought of the main characters circles in endless repetition around four facts: Mary's illness, Edmund's illness, the profligacy of James, and the miserliness of Tyrone. These four characteristics are subtly hinted at in the first dialogue of the play between Mary and Tyrone. The thought expended on the characteristics, however, does not get very far in terms of progression. The passions of the characters are so varied, so subject to the moment, that they do not form a cohesive center about which the drama revolves either.

Clearly, the synthesizing principle of this play is the progressive revelation and analysis of character. From the first beat of the play the characters undergo a progressive revelation ending

10   *Ibid.*, p. 170.
11   *Ibid.*, p. 176.

in the nadir of despair. The play may safely be described as a play of character, involving complete alteration in moral character, brought on and controlled by action, and made apparent in itself and in thought and feeling. As Stephen Whicher says:

The most poignant effect of the play is the counter-movement by which the mother retreats into illusion while the others move to a clear sight of truth.[12]

The possibilities of the poetic medium of character that O'Neill employs in this play again reside in the family relationships expressed in the play, as they did in *The Haunted*, the third play of his trilogy, *Mourning Becomes Electra*. But this play differs in three respects. The family is a contemporary family, and the members are not of so high a station in the town as were the Mannons; nor does the transgression of the family order, in the form of the insubordination of the will of the individual to that order, progress so far as to *completely* break with the hierarchy of command within the family. The result is that physical violence is completely replaced with psychological violence in this play. The Nemesis, then, visited on these characters is that of prolonged suffering, the most severe type of Nemesis that O'Neill has employed in any of the plays dealt with in this study.

O'Neill uses the possibility contained primarily in the defection of the father from a just pattern of familial order. Tyrone's greed causes him to usurp the mother's role of distribution of goods within the family. His role should be that of acquiring necessary family commodities, but he attempts both roles: acquisition and distribution; this leaves the mother, Mary, deprived of one of her most necessary functions. This, in turn, affects the two children, Edmund and James. Because of the frustration imposed on her by Tyrone, Mary is unable to provide the proper sort of matrix in which to train her sons. They in turn, lacking a stable environment in which to develop, are not able to make productive contacts with the world at large, which they both obviously fear and mistrust, as a result of the fear and mistrust they have

[12] Stephen Whicher, "O'Neill's Long Journey", *Commonweal*, XLIII (March 16, 1956), 615.

learned to have for their familial situation. Tyrone's greed indirectly causes, or extends, the psychological wound already inflicted
on Mary, when in his penuriousness he actually has her attended
by an inferior physician, who gives her large doses of morphine
which develop into a drug habit. Tyrone's greed, then, is the key
to the disintegration apparent in himself, and in each member
of his family.

Mary, as a character, lacks sufficient moral fiber to regain the
role of distributor in the family. Her very infatuation with Tyrone,
whom she had loved romantically and unquestioningly in the
beginning, does not allow her to exert sufficient force against
Tyrone to correct his usurpation of her role of distributor of
goods. It is her very innocence, her sweetness of temper, her
long suffering qualities, that further contribute to the gradual
disintegration of the proper hierarchy of authority within the
family. Mary's very gentleness of character, as O'Neill imitates
her, is her greatest liability. Not having the force of character
to assert her just authority, she retreats progressively from the
present into the past. Her escape into morphine is not the primary causal factor of her retreat as the play imitates her character. The escape into the drug is merely an extension of her
prior retreat from the responsibility of maintaining her role of
establishing the proper sort of matrix for the rearing of her
children. This is not supposition, for Mary *knows quite consciously* what her defects of character are when she says:

I blame only myself. I swore after Eugene died I would never have
another baby. I was to blame for his death. If I hadn't left him with
my mother to join you on the road, because you wrote telling me
you missed me and were so lonely, Jamie would never have been
allowed, when he still had measles, to go in the baby's room.[13]   . .

James, having constantly lacked the reference to a point of
authority in the family, either patriarchal or matriarchal, seeks
only disorganized relationships in the world at large. Mary knows
what is wrong with James (as well as knowing what is wrong
with herself, Tyrone, and Edmund), when she says further along
in the above quoted speech:

[13]   Yale, p. 87.

I've always believed Jamie did it on purpose. He was jealous of the baby. He hated him.

As Tyrone starts to protest.

Oh, I know Jamie was only seven, but he was never stupid. He'd been warned it might kill the baby. He knew. I've never been able to forgive him for that.[14]

We find later that James hates and loves Edmund; hates him against his own will, for never having been *sure* of love and direction from his parents, he hates anything that threatens what little attention he does get from them. Paradoxically, it is his very need for love, and the control that goes with it, that drives him to take revenge on the world for what his parents have not given him. James knows this, and states it clearly:

Never wanted you to succeed and make me look even worse by comparison. Wanted you to fail. Always jealous of you. Mama's baby, Papa's pet! [15]

But all this does not excuse these characters for their defective behavior, because O'Neill has chosen to include in this imitated group of characters the character of Edmund. Edmund, despite the damage done to his character, has succeeded in partially breaking from the family, and has at least attempted positive and independent action, after a period of aimless wandering and an attempted suicide. He is now seriously ill, but his restraint, his desire to understand himself and the other characters, is a continuing and positive force within the play.

The possibilities of the poetic medium of character O'Neill chose to imitate in this play may be summarized in the following manner. O'Neill imitates a family of characters in which the father has usurped, through greed, the distributive function of the mother, who is herself too weak to reëstablish her proper authority; the father's usurpation and the mother's weakness produce two sons, one of them, James, completely unable to relate to the larger world in any truly productive way, and the other, Edmund, only partially able to relate to the larger world

---

[14] *Ibid.*
[15] *Ibid.*, p. 165.

in a productive way. Further, all the characters are essentially aware of what their individual character flaws happen to be; but only two of them, Mary and Edmund, have significant knowledge of what is wrong with the others. Tyrone knows that he is greedy, but will not accept the fact that this has ruined the family. James knows that he hates, but will not accept total responsibility for his hatred.

The mode of this play is slightly different from that of *Desire under the Elms*, or O'Neills' other naturalistic plays. Up to a certain point, the dialogue in prose depends primarily on the evocation of casual realistic surfaces, but in the final act a heavily textured prose, interspersed with long quotations from verse, is employed. The dialogue at this point becomes more lyrical than it has in any of O'Neill's other plays considered in this study, with the exception perhaps of *The Hairy Ape*. The plot, in the sense of the structure of incidents in this play, is clearly a simple plot according to Aristotle's definition. There appears to be no super-subtle selection of detail for special effects.

When we come to look at the question of the purpose of the play in regard to the sequence of emotions and expectations it intends to evoke, we find that suspense has been almost entirely replaced by another effect, cumulative revelation. It is the gradual filling in of the details of character pretty well established from the beginning that holds our attention here. This is similar to the effect of suspense, but is, at the same time, significantly different. It is the cumulative knowledge about the characters revealed to us through their analysis of themselves, and one another, that fairly rivets out attention in this play. We know approximately what they are from the outset. As the play progresses their characters are progressively revealed in greater detail. And the more we come to know about the characters, the more we pity them, with the pity of *understanding* that gradually increases our knowledge of why they are what they have become. The thing that makes the pity increasingly painful for us to bear is the fact that the potential in the characters for becoming something other than what they are is made clear at every step of the progressive character revelation. It is the appalling waste of human capabilities that so moves us here. But this progressive state of knowledge is also an intrinsic part of the development and exposition of each character. The overwhelming effect in the play exists in the significant lack of dramatic irony, wherein the audience knows more than the characters speaking. As the characters learn more about themselves, the audience, moving exactly parallel with their increase in knowledge, learns more, too. This has the effect of erasing the distance between the audience and the characters, as the characters discover that it is not fate in the external sense that has so affected them, but their own actions, for which they are directly responsible. This forms their Nemesis. The universality of Mary's discovery of why she has lost her innocence is the final climactic effect in this regard. We learn that she has lost her innocence through the experience of love for the first time, an experience so close to the universal experience of man, that finally we are drawn into a complete identification with her and the other characters. But oddly enough, it is Mary, at this point, through the aid of the drug, who has something comparable to an aesthetic distance in relation to the discovery about herself. We, the audience, are the ones who have little or no protection from the poignancy of the discovery, and it is just this that makes Mary's final speech so overwhelmingly powerful. We have become identified with her, but she is safe from the awful force of this knowledge, the effect of the drug having given her sufficient insulation from the tragic fact of existence. In this sense, the play leads us to the discovery of ourselves.

As Richard Hayes says:

The movement of *Long Day's Journey* spirals inward to the tragic fact: within that adamantine chamber its four major personages weave a seamless pattern of time, suffering and nobility, those constants of tragic experience which, ever since Oedipus, have brought the hero to transcendence.[16]

If we combine the essentials of the answers to our four questions of fact, we arrive at the following formal description of this play. This play is a play of character, involving *a progressive and*

[16] Richard Hayes, "A Requiem for Mortality", *Commonweal*, LXV (February 1, 1957), p. 467.

thorough revelation of moral character (not, as originally hypo-
thesized, *a complete alteration*), brought on and controlled by
thought, and made apparent in itself and in feeling and action.
The character of a father who has usurped the distributive functions of the mother, through his own greed, is revealed through
the imitation, along with a mother too weak to regain her lost
authority and unable to provide a stable background for the two
sons, whose characters are also revealed. The elder son is revealed as completely unable to establish productive relationships
in society, while the younger son is revealed as a character who,
though damaged by the family situation, is able to relate to the
larger world of society productively, though in a limited way.
The dramatic mode consists primarily of an imitation of casual
realistic surfaces in ordinary prose dialogue, until the fourth act
in which the dialogue becomes heavily lyrical, and the speeches
of the characters become steeped in an introspective subjectivity.
All of this is accomplished with a simple plot. With the gradual
revelation of character two effects are achieved: the effect of
suspense is replaced by the parallel acquisition of character
knowledge on the part of the characters and the audience; this,
in turn, erases the distance between the audience and the characters, allowing thorough identification of the audience with the
characters. When the final tragic fact (that *unqualified* love destroys innocence, the moral integrity of each of us as autonomous
beings) is revealed, the roles of the audience and of the characters have essentially been reversed; for the characters, through
the aid of alcohol and morphine, have established an even greater
distance from the poignancy of the tragic fact than that distance
which is usually the sole prerogative of the audience.

If we return to the Introduction of this study, we find a perfect
description of the Nemesis that is operative in this play. As in
the quotation from Smyth,[17] this play seems to say relentlessly:
"character is destiny."

The *lex talionis* operates primarily through the characters of
James and Tyrone. James constantly speaks of revenging himself

[17]   This study, p. 17.

on the world for what it has done to him. He personally hates his brother, Edmund, and has actually tried to lead him into the unproductive paths he himself has taken. This is also a kind of indirect attack, a vengeful reaction against his father's miserliness. An eye for an eye and a tooth for a tooth, is also illustrated in Tyrone's behavior; for all his fastening on the goods of this world, his maniacal possessiveness is, as he clearly shows through actions and words, a reaction against the deprivations he suffered as a child. So the father's vindictive and overly possessive behavior is mirrored in the behavior of his son, James. However, James implements the code of the *lex talionis* in terms entirely different from those of the distributive code of material goods. James, in his vindictive behavior, trades directly and purposefully on the value of human relationships. In the end, it is just these two things that cause James and his father so much pain. They get what they give, only in greater measure. Tyrone indirectly destroys his family and himself with his grasping nature; and James has only injured himself through his hateful manipulation of human behavior.

The resultant social Nemesis that has visited itself on the family is the Nemesis of almost total isolation from any real intercourse with society. The vengeful behavior of Tyrone and James has also injured the innocents, Edmund and Mary. Mary is unable to cope with the injury done to her by husband and son, and so pays the penalty of her weakness by retreat into a drug habit, which has the effect of even further isolating her from her family and from society. Edmund, however, has partially overcome the ill effects of the anti-social behavior of his family as a whole.

Divine Nemesis enters succinctly into the fabric of this drama in a much more vital way than it has in all the other plays studied here. Tyrone has told his sons that their turning from the Catholic faith leads to self-destruction, thus seeming to exonerate himself from the responsibilty which is primarily his own for having usurped the familial role of distributor within the family structure. And certainly James' behavior appears to bear this out, for he seems to be the personification of evil, many references being made by Edmund to James in terms of Baudelaire, Swineburne, and other professors and practicers of the black arts of personal dissolution. But Tyrone is obviously incorrect in terms of two of the characters, the only two who demonstrate knowledge of truly religious experience. Mary has had visions and personal communion with the Blessed Virgin as a young girl, and somehow her gentleness and direct insight into the truth of what is wrong with the family seem vitally connected with this genuine religious experience. Edmund, too, tells his father of impressive (though not necessarily Catholic) mystical experiences of a kind of absolute unity with the cosmos. And it is these experiences, he tells his father, that have made it possible for him to even entertain the thought of continuing life. Certainly Edmund's role of peace-maker and truth-finder is directly associated with his superior religious experience within the play. The reward (Divine Nemesis) of seeking and finding religious experience above the ordinary, seems to be the gift of being able to express love in *some* way, no matter how limited it may seem. For both Mary and Edmund are capable of love in the play, while Tyrone and James may be said to be capable of loving none but themselves. They must be aided to a knowledge of the truth of themselves by the divinely inspired Mary and Edmund. For truth and religious experience are inextricably bound together in the character revelation which is the center, or *dynamis* of the whole play. To know truth – through religious experience, whether orthodox or strictly mystical and personal – is to learn compassion, the only vital force that can mitigate the horrors of existence in this world. This is what the play seems to come to in the end. Justice is compassion. And compassion can only be had through understanding, which stems primarily from religious experience. And the grace of such understanding, as the play imitates the experience, seems to be the prerogative of those who have had a truly vital religious experience.[18]

[18] Grant Redford, "Dramatic Art vs. Autobiography: A Look at *Long Day's Journey into Night*", *College English*, XXV (April, 1964), pp. 527-535. Mr. Redford's article is an excellent exposition of the atonement through compassion produced as a result of understanding, as it occurs in *Long Day's Journey into Night*.

Tragic justice, in the case of this play, as in the case of the other plays considered in this study, seems, therefore, to be based on a purely individual scheme. But here, as in *Mourning Becomes Electra*, it stems from participation in the order of the family. That order, the familial, has been shattered by a series of insubordinations on the part of the individuals who make up the family; until finally two individuals in the family, Mary and Edmund, find within themselves a force (vital religious experience) that will lead them and the other family members to the necessary comprehension of the truth of themselves, a form of knowledge that stimulates compassion, the only grace that makes life possible, and a grace that is strictly the province of the individual. The Nemesis that has plagued these collective breakers of familial order is continual pain, and the dissolution of the healthy family situation. Three of them are effectively destroyed, Tyrone, Mary, and James, while some hope remains for Edmund. They find, at the apogee of their dissolution, the grace of individual compassion, as Mary acts out before them the tragic impasse of all human existence.

VIII

CONCLUSION

As pointed out in Chapter One, Nemesis is the personification of an idea: the idea of justice-in-action. When we speak of the Nemesis of a character in drama, we are speaking essentially of his final position with regard to certain definite aspects of his relation to particular parts of his experience as they are imitated in the closed aesthetic form which is the play. These aspects are three in number: parts of the character's experience over which he has no control, choices among courses of action which he may pursue, and the resultant circumstances that develop in action as consequences of his previous choices. This is far different from speaking of the fatalistic aspects of the character's experience. For fate, as defined by Smyth, consists entirely of those "externals" of experience over which the character has no control. If these "externals" are thought to be the sum of a character's experience, then the idea of justice is untenable, for justice involves weighing and considering, the idea of responsibility. However, it would be an error to attempt to exclude altogether the idea of "externals", ineluctable factors of experience, factors which are beyond the character's control, for such factors are immediately recognizable as part of the actual experience of men. And if art is an imitation of life, in the fullest sense, then it is very likely that the virtual experience present in the artist's imitation could include these "externals" in its form.

Tragic Nemesis, however, as stated in Chapter One, seems to stem from the aesthetic nature generated in imitating the above mentioned actual aspects of man's experience. Thus, it seems purely virtual in nature, for it appears, as Myers insists, that presented as creatures having the power to choose, and their choices are shown to be important in shaping the Nemesis that overtakes them.

Abortion utilized the *lex talionis* as personified by Joe Murray's desire to kill Jack Townsend, whom Murray felt responsible for Nellie Murray's death. Murray's desire for personal vengeance drives the play forward and creates suspense. But in the final analysis, Murray's desire to fulfill his personal vengeance is translated into an improper perversion of social justice to serve the ends of the *lex talionis*. Ultimate Nemesis, in relation to Divine justice, never enters the fabric of *Aborton* in any significant fashion. The agent of tragic Nemesis in the play is Jack, the protagonist himself, who, upon finding no just basis for supporting existence within himself, destroys the distorted thing he has become by his own hand as the *action* of the play engulfs him.

In *Thirst*, the *lex talionis* is reduced, through the dramatic manipulation of the characters in an extremely limited situation, to its most cruel and elemental form: the survival of the fittest at almost an animal level in the characters' struggle over the basic nutrients of life, food and water. Social justice is effectively excluded when the emergency extension of the equitable distribution of life substances is ignored by the Sailor. Tragic justice, then, stems primarily from what the characters are. The Dancer destroys herself dancing. The Gentleman is destroyed in his attempt to uphold social justice in a context of action where it can no longer be productively applied. And the Sailor is destroyed inadvertently as he attempts to kill the Gentleman for breaking the law of survival of the fittest. In a sense each character is destroyed by what he is or has become. Ultimate justice seems to reside in a condition that exists before the play begins, the *phthonos* of a jealous God, who is personified in the active cruelty of the environment of the characters.

The function of Nemesis in *Moon of the Caribbees* seems exactly parallel, in respect to its relative lack of severity, with the delicate sustaining of a specially qualified passion of melancholy. The *lex talionis* adhered to by the women and Cocky

tragedy moves through factors beyond man's control, l
and the results of his choices. These three aspects of a
experience, which tragedy rejects in turn, finally are
in an imitation of the source of justice as though it
clusively to be found in the perfect self-equality of the
tragic character, whose capacity for experiencing evil is
equal to his capacity for experiencing good. It is the pe
of this balance, of course, that makes tragic justice virtual
than actual; for we will be at a loss to think of actual indi
who achieve this balance. Poetry, as Aristotle says, does no
with things as they are, the verifiable historicity of part
experience; it deals with things as they might be, or thin
they ought to be, and therefore transcends history, which ca
rise above the given facts.

It should be pointed out here that the three aspects of m
experience mentioned above, things over which man has
control, man's choices, and the circumstances that follow up
those choices, are in perfect parallel with the imitated sources
Nemesis mentioned in this study: respectively, the *lex talion*
(determined factors), social justice (factors stemming from choice)
and ultimate justice (factors stemming from the results of choice);
excluding, of course, tragic justice, which appears to be directly
dependent on the activity of the imitation itself.

Nemesis then, as used in this study, has four aspects and may
appear in any intercombination, excluding or including any
particular aspects, depending upon the special manipulation of
them in any given form. Therefore, it must be concluded that
Nemesis is not always the same in every instance. The description
of Nemesis and how it functions in any given play has varied in
this study from play to play strictly in relation to the structure of
the play under consideration. Even tragic Nemesis has varied
from play to play, as the characters who encounter it are themselves varied.

One of the important conclusions this study has led to is that
O'Neill characters, generally speaking, are not victims of a single
and determined sequence of factors in their experience, mere
playthings of a blindly deterministic universe. His characters are

clashes directly with the idea of social justice represented by the
Captain, who invokes distributive maxims against the women and
against the crew, depriving them of tangible and intangible commodities. Tragic Nemesis is again provided by the individuals
themselves, which is especially apparent in the case of Smitty,
who really punishes himself by continually treating other human
beings in a petty and unfair manner (though Smitty's lack of
insight into the problem tends to make this action not properly
tragic, but somewhere between the tragic and the comic). Ultimate Nemesis stems from the cosmos, which remains intensely
beautiful and grand, while the characters in the drama remain
insignificant, and actively contribute to their continual insignificance, despite the inviting beauty that surrounds them.

The character of Yank Smith in *The Hairy Ape* strictly shapes
the function of Nemesis in that play. The *lex talionis* drives the
play forward as the tremendous and brutal energy of Yank is
directed toward his desire to "get even", first with Mildred, then
with her father, and finally with the whole of society. Yank's
brutality is partially the result of his own actions, and partially
the result of circumstances inflicted on him by his society. Social
justice is shown to be a sham in the play, for Yank discovers
that the society he comes to hate is not in much better control
of its future than he, Yank, is of his own destiny. Ultimate
Nemesis seems totally impossible in Yank's environment, for that
environment has no real relation to anything divine. Tragic
Nemesis is again specially qualified by the shaping form of the
play; for when Yank discovers that he not only looks like an ape
from the outside, but is like an ape on the inside (his interior
characteristics being fully imitated by the manipulation of his
reaction to, and projection of, images symbolic of his internal
nature), he seeks out that image (the gorilla) in the external world
and allows it to destroy him. Yank restores the balance for which
he hungers by killing himself *as he is*, in recognition of the previous destruction by himself and by society of the more delicate
aspects of human sensibility within him.

Again, in *Desire Under the Elms*, the *lex talionis* is utilized
to drive the play forward on its course, but the motive force

stems from passion rather than from action or character. Eben
does not simply desire *revenge* against his father, Ephraim. Eben's
desire for the land, the desire to possess it, is expressed through
his desire to deprive Ephraim of the land in order to make
Ephraim pay for having worked his, Eben's, mother to death.
This sets the play in motion at the beginning. Eben wants to
deprive Ephraim of the object of Ephraim's consuming passion.
This is altered in the course of the play as the desire to possess
is transformed into the passion of love in Abbie and Eben,
whereas Ephraim's passion remains bound to the distributive
code of the *lex talionis* evident in his perpetually unaltered desire
to materially possess the land. Ephraim's punishment consists in
his continual isolation, as the very *things* he cannot transcend
become his prison. Social Nemesis is enacted on Ephraim, also,
in his continual isolation from society. Social Nemesis demands
the death of Abbie for the slaying of her child, done with pre-
meditated intent; but tragic Nemesis enters the play when Eben,
too, submits, of his own free will, to the same social retribution
that punishes Abbie. Eben considers himself responsible for
Abbie's action, and will share death with her, if he cannot share
life, the demand of the law of love, which requires sharing (a
giving and taking), not simply selfish acquisition. Ultimate justice
comes partially into consideration here in that Abbie wants God
to forgive her for killing her child, but does not want forgiveness
for loving Eben. Grace, then, exists in this play, for her love for
Eben seems directly justified by Eben's demonstration of his
love in sharing her death. Murder, according to social and divine
law, must be punished with death; but love, in terms of ultimate
justice, must be rewarded with fulfillment. The *lex talionis* and
social justice in their concatenation in this dramatic action directly
precipitate the tragic and divine grace of love, the ultimate justice.

Mourning Becomes Electra effectively excludes the direct
operation of divine and social Nemesis, and introduces a highly
conservative familial order as a norm in the light of which all
behavior must be judged. With this shift of emphasis there is an
accompanying increase of importance of the individual character.
The pattern of order of this trilogy bears repeating here, as it is

one of the most significant discoveries of this study. It consists of four central maxims: (1) the husband and father shall fulfill not only his own sexual needs, but also those of his wife, (2) the wife and mother shall reciprocate in this, (3) neither husband nor wife shall seek external satisfaction of their needs nor break the familial hierarchy of command within the family by alienating the affections of their offspring from either husband or wife, (4) and finally, the offspring shall recognize the relative authority (father primary, mother secondary) in the joint family rule, wherein the father is controller of the family in all external matters (food getting, provisions for domicile, et cetera), while the mother is controller of the distribution within the family of the life sustaining commodities the father acquires. Everyone of these maxims is broken in this trilogy, as each of the characters in his familial role insubordinates his will to the collective purposes of the family. In so doing, he not only destroys the familial order, but also destroys himself, for the familial order forms that principle in the play which is necessary to the existence of the self.

In the first play, *Homecoming,* essentially a play of action, all the maxims are broken by all the characters; their Nemesis then becoming a violent change in their situations, depriving all of them of the fulfillment of their several needs for love. *The Hunted,* essentially a play of passion, imitates the punishment of the mother and her lover by the children, the lover being destroyed, but the mother being visited with the Nemesis of overwhelming anguish and despair as a result of which she takes her own life. But this has involved the children in further family crime, for they must, in punishing the mother, break the familial hierarchy of command. The son suffers despair; while the daughter, for the moment, seems unharmed by her insubordination of the familial order. *The Haunted,* essentially a play of character, illustrates the final working out of the problem in the Nemesis visited on the children, though the solution, as we discover, does not lack the element of grace. Orin destroys himself, for his original breaking of the familial hierarchy of command has made of him a person who cannot reintegrate himself into the order of the family. His basis for punishment comes then from himself, a kind of tragic justice. But the most cruel form of Nemesis is visited on Lavinia, perpetual suffering, anguish, sterility, and isolation, because her crime against the mother involved a direct superseding of the mother's superior position of authority; and especially is this so because the severest penalties are paid by characters in the trilogy who defect from the familial order from within the familial structure. The *lex talionis* becomes operative in the trilogy the moment a familial member defects from the familial order in any way. But tragic justice (the finding of bases for moral action within the imitated self of the character) is finally transcendent in the character of Lavinia, and, by association, in the whole trilogy. For the act of grace that unsnarls the progressive chain of crime and punishment within the trilogy does not come from a transcendent divine source, nor from society, nor from a modification of the *lex talionis*. Lavinia, in her love for Peter Niles (the prospective spouse), relinquishes him, sets him free, and thus ends the chain of twisted relationships of distorted order; and paradoxically, in doing so she destroys herself.

The *lex talionis* in *The Iceman Cometh* is strangely adumbrated by the sheer complexity of the controlling principle of the play which is thought. The thinkers conceal their desire for personal vengeance in past actions under the aegis of rationalization. Inadvertently, each thinker rips the mask of pretended love from his own face and from the faces of the other characters, revealing the primitive hatreds of the *lex talionis,* which demands an eye for an eye, and a tooth for a tooth. The *lex talionis*, then, indirectly provides the forward moving drive of the play in that the speakers attempt to avoid or escape from the truth of its existence within themselves, but, paradoxically, move directly toward that which they hope to escape. The three main characters, Larry, Hickey, and Parritt, pay for their hatreds in even greater measure, finally, than that required by the demands of the *lex talionis*. Social justice is called in by Hickey essentially after the issues are decided, and it may be said that social justice is constantly shown to be a sham in the play.

Ultimate justice, stemming from the divine, is repeatedly and summarily dismissed by the characters; directly by Hickey and Larry, and through inference by the lesser characters. Tragic justice, stemming from the internal resources of character, is the prime seat of Nemesis in *The Iceman Cometh*; but grace, directly supplied by human agents, is also shown to be operative in this play. And its substance is love, the love demonstrated by Hickey in relinquishing his "truth" and his "right kind of pity" for the sake of the majority of the derelicts in the play. This love is also demonstrated by Larry, when he finally relinquishes his sham disinterest and involves himself in Parritt's Nemesis, and helps Parritt to find the courage to kill himself.

This grace of love first appeared in this study in connection with *Desire under the Elms*, but was partially connected with the divine. In *Mourning Becomes Electra* it was stricly the province of human agents, as it is in *The Iceman Cometh*.

In *Long Day's Journey into Night*, a surprising synthesis is discovered between the norms of familial order (first clearly outlined in *Mourning Becomes Electra*), the bases for just action combined with individual grace within the self, and ultimate justice or grace, stemming directly from the divine (first suggested in *Desire under the Elms*). The *lex talionis* is mirrored primarily in Tyrone's usurpation of the role of distributor within the family, and his battening on material goods as a result of his miserly nature. This is also mirrored in James, who trades distributively, on the basis of an eye for an eye and a tooth for a tooth, not on material goods, but on the value of human relationships. Tyrone has destroyed his family, while James has destroyed himself, and has attempted to destroy his brother, Edmund. Compassion, love, and understanding, the mitigating factors in this tragedy of family and therefore personal disintegration, are the province of two of the family members who have found within themselves at the same time in their lives, a vital and moving religious experience. They are Edmund, the younger son, and Mary, the mother. Their personal insight cannot *save* the situation, but their understanding and their love seem to make the horror of the situation somewhat more bearable; though Mary is completely destroyed, and only a faint glimmer of hope remains for Edmund. The mitigating and ultimate justice of love through understanding, then, seems to make the unavoidable disintegration of the family (its Nemesis), and the almost complete disintegration of the individuals within the family, more than completely meaningless. And while these factors of ultimate justice seem to be, as in *Mourning Becomes Electra,* the strict province of the individual, the individual can only develop the ability to apply them through an intensely personal religious experience, which, as the play demonstrates, may be orthodox (Mary), or unorthodox (Edmund).

Oddly enough, the *lex talionis* functions in all the plays as a force that drives them forward, but its operation is not exactly the same in all the plays, and its nature seems to be significantly altered by the formal controlling principle of each play. Only in two of the plays studied does it seem allowed to run its course, so that the Nemesis of the characters seems in large measure based on its tenets. They are *Thirst* and *The Moon of the Caribbees.* It is significant to notice, too, that in these plays ultimate justice involving the ingredient of grace is entirely absent, though in *Thirst* the divine seems totally cruel, while in *The Moon of the Caribbees* the divine cosmos seems incredibly beautiful.

In *Abortion, The Moon of the Caribbees,* and *Desire under the Elms,* social Nemesis plays an important role, but only in *Desire under the Elms* does that role seem positive. In the other two plays social justice is shown to be perverted, or corrupt. In all the other plays studied, the role of social Nemesis is either very slight, or is shown to be corrupt.

In *The Moon of the Caribbees* and *Thirst,* ultimate Nemesis stemming from the divine is present, but not directly in the consciousness of the characters, and it does not involve grace. In *Desire under the Elms,* its role is direct, and essentially contributes to atonement. In *Long Day's Journey into Night,* the ultimate Nemesis of the characters seems directly mitigated by individual awareness of the divine. It plays no significant role in *Abortion, The Hairy Ape, Mourning Becomes Electra,* or *The Iceman Cometh.* Its ultimate functions are superseded in terms of grace by human agents in *Mourning Becomes Electra* and *The Iceman Cometh.*

Tragic Nemesis (the perfect self equality of the characters) plays its role directly and forcefully in all the plays considered in this study with the exception of *The Moon of the Caribbees.*

The two most outstanding effects O'Neill employs in his manipulation of the many sided concept of Nemesis are his superseding of ultimate Nemesis stemming from divine grace with human agents, and his forging of a moral system on the basis of the human family unit, as in *Mourning Becomes Electra.*

It is also interesting to note that in terms of sheer quantity the *lex talionis* and tragic Nemesis form the greatest elements of Nemesis employed by O'Neill in the ten plays studied.

Certainly this study leaves untouched over three-quarters of the published output of this playwright. Further investigation of O'Neill's form in relation to Nemesis should be undertaken. The study of *The Hairy Ape* and *Mourning Becomes Electra* in this present work indicates that the linguistic analysis of O'Neill's dialogue in relation to his structure would be a productive field of further study. This, in turn, immediately suggests a study of the O'Neill manuscripts, many of which are in existence in progressive revisions. Such study would, perhaps, give further insight into the finished plays in terms of their linguistic nature, and their formal identity.[1]

The Bibliography appended to this study is a selective one, and includes primarily the works quoted within the study. Certain standard reference sources which are consulted are, nevertheless, not included in the Bibliography of this study, since they are taken generally to be common knowledge among scholars interested in this field.

---

[1] The only study I have discovered which approaches these problems with depth and breadth is: Y. M. Biese, "Eugene O'Neill's *Strange Interlude* and the Linguistic Presentation of the Interior Monologue", *Suomalaisen Tiedeakatemian Toimituksia Annales Academiae Scientiarum Fennicae*, Sarja-Series B, Nide-Tom. 118, No. 3 (Helsinki, 1963), pp. 1-73.

BIBLIOGRAPHY

PRIMARY SOURCES

Plays

O'Neill, Eugene Gladstone, *Hughie* (New Haven, Connecticut, Yale University Press, 1959).
——, *More Stately Mansions* (New Haven, Connecticut, Yale University Press, 1964).
——, *Long Day's Journey into Night* (New Haven, Connecticut, Yale University Press, 1956).
——, *Lost Plays of Eugene O'Neill* (New York, The Citadel Press, 1958).
——, *The Plays of Eugene O'Neill*, 3 vols. (New York, Random House, 1955).
——, *Thirst and Other One Act Plays* (Boston, The Gorham Press, 1914).
——, *A Touch of the Poet* (New Haven, Connecticut, Yale University Press [A Yale Paperbound], 1957).

Miscellaneous

O'Neill, Eugene Gladstone, "Memoranda on Masks", *The American Spectator*, I (November, 1932), 3.
——, "Second Thoughts", *The American Spectator*, I (December, 1932), 2.
——, "Strindberg and Our Theatre", *Provincetown Playbill*, No. 1 (Season 1923-1924), pp. 1, 3.
——, "Working Notes and Extracts from a Fragmentary Work Diary", in *European Theories of the Drama*, edited by Barrett H. Clark (New York, Crown Publishers, Inc., 1959), pp. 530-536.
——, Letter from Eugene O'Neill to George Nathan, in Isaac Goldberg's *The Theatre of George Jean Nathan* (New York, Simon and Schuster, 1926), pp. 158-159.
——, Letter from Eugene O'Neill to Barrett H. Clark, in Barrett H. Clark's *Eugene O'Neill: The Man and His Plays* (New York, Robert M. McBride and Co., 1929), pp. 41-43.
——, An interview with Harold Stark, in Stark's *People You Know* (New York, Boni and Liveright, 1923), pp. 244-247.

SECONDARY SOURCES

Books

Aristotle, *Rhetoric and Poetics*, translated by W. Rhys Roberts and Ingram
Bywater, respectively, edited with an introduction and notes by Fre-
drich Solmsen (New York, Random House [The Modern Library],
1954).
Auerbach, Erich, *Mimesis*, translated by Willard Trask (Princeton, New
Jersey, Princeton University Press, 1953).
Bacon, Wallace A., and Breen, Robert S., *Literature As Experience* (New
York, McGraw-Hill Book Co., Inc., 1959).
Cargill, Oscar, *Intellectual America* (New York, The Macmillan Co., 1941).
Clark, Barrett H., *Eugene O'Neill: The Man and His Plays*, revised version
(New York, Dover Publications, Inc., 1947).
—— (ed.), *European Theories of the Drama* (New York, Crown Publishers,
Inc., 1959).
Clark, William S., II, *Chief Patterns of World Drama* (New York, Hough-
ton Mifflin, 1946).
Commager, Henry Steele, *The American Mind* (New Haven, Connecticut,
Yale University Press, 1950).
Crane, Ronald S. (ed.), *Critics and Criticism*, 2d abridged ed. (Chicago,
University of Chicago Press [Phoenix Books], 1957).
——, *The Languages of Criticism and the Structure of Poetry* (Toronto,
University of Toronto Press, 1957).
Dateller, Roger, *Drama and Life* (London, Rockliff, 1956).
Ellis-Fermor, Una, *The Frontiers of Drama* (London, Methuen, 1945).
Engel, Edwin A., *The Haunted Heroes of Eugene O'Neill* (Cambridge,
Massachusetts, Harvard University Press, 1953).
Falk, Doris V., *Eugene O'Neill and the Tragic Tension* (New Brunswick,
New Jersey, Rutgers University Press, 1958).
Fraigneau, André, *Cocteau on the Film*, translated by Vera Traill (New
York, Roy Publishers, 1954).
Gelb, Arthur and Barbara, *O'Neill* (New York, Harper and Brothers,
1962).
Greene, William Chase, *Moira: Fate, Good and Evil in Greek Thought*
(Cambridge, Massachusetts, Harvard University Press, 1944).
Harris, Mark, *The Case for Tragedy* (New York, G. P. Putnam's Sons,
1932).
Hegel, G. F. W., *The Philosophy of Hegel*, translated by Bernard Bosanquet
and W. M. Bryant, edited by Carl J. Friedrich (New York, Random
House [The Modern Library], 1954).
Heller, Erich, *The Disinherited Mind* (New York, Meridian Books, Inc.,
1959).
Lawson, J. H., *Theory and Technique of Playwriting* (New York, G. P.
Putnam, 1936).
Leech, Clifford, *O'Neill* (London, Oliver and Boyd, 1963).
Myers, Henry Alonzo, *Tragedy: A View of Life* (Ithaca, New York,
Cornell University Press, 1956).

Nicoll, Allardyce, *Theory of Drama* (London, George G. Harrap & Co., Ltd., 1937).

Nietzsche, Friedrich, *The Birth of Tragedy, and the Genealogy of Morals*, translated by Francis Golffing (Garden City, New York, Doubleday and Co. [Anchor Books], 1956).

Oates, Whitney J. and O'Neill, Eugene, Jr. (eds.), *The Complete Greek Drama*, 2 vols. (New York, Random House, 1938).

Oxford Classical Dictionary, edited by M. Cary, *et al.* (London, Oxford University Press, 1953).

Plato, *Five Great Dialogues*, translated by B. Jowett, edited by Louise Ropes Loomis (New York, Walter J. Black, 1942).

Raleigh, John H., *The Plays of Eugene O'Neill* (Carbondale, Illinois, Southern Illinois University Press, 1965).

Roethke, Theodore, *Words for the Wind* (Garden City, New York, Doubleday & Co., Inc., 1958).

Schopenhauer, *The Philosophy of Schopenhauer*, edited by Irwin Edman (New York, Random House [The Modern Library], 1956).

Smyth, H. W., *Aeschylean Tragedy* (Berkeley, California, University of California Press, 1924).

Wellek, René, and Warren, Austin, *Theory of Literature* (New York, Harcourt, Brace and Co. [Harvest Books], 1956).

Winther, Sophus Keith, *Eugene O'Neill: A Critical Study*, 2d revised ed. (Russell and Russell, 1961).

Articles and Periodicals

Alexander, Doris M., "Hugo of *The Iceman Cometh:* Realism and O'Neill", *American Quarterly*, V (Winter, 1953), 357-366.

Amico, S. d', "*I primi drammi di O'Neill*", *Nuova Antologia*, CCCLXV (January 16, 1933), 297-299.

Arestad, Sverre, "*The Iceman Cometh* and *The Wild Duck*", *Scandinavian Studies*, XX (February, 1948), 1-11.

Asselineau, Roger, "*Mourning Becomes Electra* as a Tragedy", *Modern Drama*, I (December, 1958), 143-150.

Baker, George Pierce, "O'Neill's First Decade", *Yale Review*, XV (July, 1926), 789-792.

Battenhouse, Roy, "*Mourning Becomes Electra*", *Christendom*, VII (Summer, 1942), 332-345.

Baum, B., "*Tempest and Hairy Ape:* The Literary Incarnation of Mythos", *Modern Language Quarterly*, XIV (September, 1953), 258-273.

Biese, Y. M., "Eugene O'Neill's *Strange Interlude*, and the Linguistic Presentation of the Interior Monologue", *Annales Academiae Scientiarum Fennicae*, Sarja-Ser. B, Nide-Tom. 118, No. 3 (1963), pp. 1-73.

Brown, John Mason, "All O'Neilling", *Saturday Review of Literature*, XXIX (October 19, 1946), 26-28, 30.

Catel, J., "*Critique*", *Mercure de France*, CLXXIX (May 1, 1925), 836-838.

Clark, Barrett H., "Aeschylus and Eugene O'Neill", *English Journal*, XXI (November, 1932), 699-710.

——, "Lost Plays of Eugene O'Neill", *Theatre Arts*, XXIV (July, 1950), 7.

Colin, Saul, "Without O'Neill's Imprimatur", *New York Times*, XCIX (June 18, 1950), sec. 7, p. 4.

Dobrée, Bonamy, "The Plays of Eugene O'Neill", *Southern Review*, II (Winter, 1937), 435-446.

Ellis-Fermor, Una, "The Nature of Character in Drama, with Special Reference to Tragedy", in *English Studies Today*, edited by C. L. Wrenn and G. Bullough (Oxford, University Press, 1951), pp. 11-21.

——, "The Nature of Plot in Drama", in *English Association Essays and Studies*, collected by M. St. Clare Byrne (London, John Murray, 1960), pp. 65-81.

Fergusson, Francis, "A Month of the Theatre", *Bookman*, LXXIV (December, 1931), 440-445.

Groff, Edward, "Point of View in Modern Drama", *Modern Drama*, II (December, 1959), 268-282.

Gump, Margaret, "From Ape to Man and from Man to Ape", *Kentucky Foreign Language Quarterly*, IV, No. 4 (1957), pp. 177-185.

Hamilton, Clayton, "A Shelf of Printed Plays", *Bookman*, XLI (April, 1915), 182.

Hayes, Richard, "A Requiem for Mortality", *Commonweal*, LXIV (February 1, 1957), 467-468.

Hayward, I. N., "Strindberg's Influence on Eugene O'Neill", *Poet Lore*, XXXIX (December, 1928), 596-604.

Hofmannsthal, Hugo von, "Eugene O'Neill", translated by Barrett H. Clark, *The Freeman*, VII (March 21, 1923), 39-41.

Hopkins, Vivian C., " 'The Iceman' Seen through 'The Lower Depths' ", *College English*, XI (November, 1949), 81-87.

Jones, C., "A Sailor's O'Neill", *Revue anglo-américaine*, XII (February, 1935), 226-229.

Kernodle, G. R., "Patterns of Belief in Contemporary Drama", in *Spiritual Problems in Contemporary Drama*, edited by S. Hopper (New York, Institute for Religious and Social Studies, distributed by Harper, 1952), pp. 187-206.

Kimmelman, George, "The Concept of Tragedy in Modern Criticism", *Journal of Aesthetics and Art Criticism*, IV (March, 1946), 141-160.

Krutch, Joseph Wood, "Drama", *The Nation*, CLXIII (October 26, 1946), 481-482.

——, "O'Neill's Tragic Sense", *American Scholar*, XVI (Summer, 1947), 283-290.

——, "Our Electra", *The Nation*, CXXXIII (November 18, 1931), 551-552.

Leach, A., "Fate and Free Will", in *The Greek Genius and Its Influence*, edited by Lane Cooper (New Haven, Connecticut, Yale University Press, 1917), pp. 144-155.

Lecky, Eleazer, "*Ghosts* and *Mourning Becomes Electra*: Two Versions of Fate", *Arizona Quarterly*, XXII (Winter, 1957), 320-338.

MacCarthy, Desmond, "Hairy Ape or Bronze Ajax?", *The New Statesman and Nation*, I (May 23, 1931), 461-462.

——, "A Tremendous Play and Great Acting", *The New Statesman and Nation*, XIV (November 27, 1937), 875-877.

"Moon of the Caribbees, The", *The Dial*, LXVI (May 17, 1919), 524.

Motherwell, Hiram, "*Mourning Becomes Electra*", *Theatre Guild Magazine*, IX (December, 1931), 14-20.

Muchnic, Helen, "Circe's Swine: Plays by Gorky and O'Neill", *Comparative Literature*, III (Spring, 1951), 119-128.

Nathan, George Jean, "The Theatre", *American Mercury*, IV (January, 1925), 119.

Perry, William, "Does the Buskin Fit O'Neill?", *University of Kansas City Review*, XV (Spring, 1949), 281-287.

Redford, Grant H., "Dramatic Art vs. Autobiography: A Look at *Long Day's Journey into Night*", *College English*, XXV (April, 1964), pp. 527-535.

Rosati, Salvatore, "Eugene O'Neill, *pessimista eroico*", *Nuova Antologia*, XLD (January, 1954), 61-66.

Stamm, Rudolf, "The Dramatic Experiments of Eugene O'Neill", *English Studies*, XXVIII (February, 1947), 1-15.

——, "A New Play by Eugene O'Neill", *English Studies*, XXIX (October, 1948), 138-145.

——, "The Orestes Theme in Three Plays by Eugene O'Neill, T. S. Eliot, and Jean Paul Sartre", *English Studies*, XXX (October, 1949), 244-255.

Straumann, Heinrich, "The Philosophical Background of the Modern American Drama", *English Studies*, XXVI (June, 1944), 65-78.

Tapper, B., "Eugene O'Neill's World View", *The Personalist*, XVIII (January, 1937), 40-48.

Valente, Pier Luigi, "Il lutto s'addice ad Elettra di E. G. O'Neill e la tragedia greca", *Convivium*, XXVIII (Maggio-Giugno, 1960), 318-329.

Whicher, Stephen, "O'Neill's Long Journey", *Commonweal*, LXIII (March 16, 1956), 614-615.

Winther, Sophus Keith, "*Desire under the Elms:* A Modern Tragedy", *Modern Drama*, III (December, 1960), 326-332.

——, "*The Iceman Cometh:* A Study in Technique", *Arizona Quarterly*, III (Winter, 1947), 293-300.

"World Premiere for O'Neill Play", *Chicago Sun Times*, XIV (December 12, 1961), sec. 2, p. 10.

Young, Stark, "Eugene O'Neill's New Play", *The New Republic*, LXVIII (November 11, 1931), 352-355.

BIBLIOGRAPHIES

Books

Sanborn, Ralph, and Clark, Barrett H., *A Bibliography of the Works of Eugene O'Neill* (New York, Random House, 1931).

Periodicals

Frenz, Horst, "A List of Foreign Editions and Translations of Eugene O'Neill's Drama", *Bulletin of Bibliography*, XVIII (September-December, 1943), 33-34.

——, "O'Neill Collections I Have Seen", *Indiana Quarterly for Bookmen*, I (January, 1945), 27-34.

Loveman, Amy, "Clearing House: Books about Eugene O'Neill", *The Saturday Review of Literature*, XV (February 20, 1937), 18.

Nicholls, N., "Check List of Eugene O'Neill", *Bookman* (London), LXXXIV (September, 1933), 300.

Stratman, Carl J., "O'Neill", unpublished Dissertations in the History and Theory of Tragedy, 1889-1957, *Bulletin of Bibliography*, XXXIII (January-April, 1960), 20.

Unpublished

Brown, Ann Duncan, "Eugene O'Neill: A List of Recent References", Washington, D. C., Division of Bibliography No. 1467, Library of Congress, 1940 (Typewritten).

"List of References on Eugene Gladstone O'Neill", Washington, D. C., Division of Bibliography No. [?], Library of Congress, 1922 (Typewritten).

Miller, Jordan Yale, "A Critical Bibliography of Eugene O'Neill", unpublised Ph.D. dissertation, Department of Philosophy, Columbia University, Ann Arbor, Michigan, University Microfilms, 1957.